Building the
Milwaukee Bucks

Building the Milwaukee Bucks

*Kareem Abdul-Jabbar, Oscar Robertson
and the Rapid Rise of an
NBA Franchise, 1968–1975*

JORDAN TRESKE

McFarland & Company, Inc., Publishers
Jefferson, North Carolina

ISBN (print) 978-1-4766-9775-8
ISBN (ebook) 978-1-4766-5574-1

LIBRARY OF CONGRESS CATALOGING DATA ARE AVAILABLE

Library of Congress Control Number 2025024126

© 2025 Jordan Treske. All rights reserved

No part of this book may be reproduced or transmitted in any form or by any means, electronic or mechanical, including photocopying or recording, or by any information storage and retrieval system, without permission in writing from the publisher.

Front cover images (left to right): Milwaukee Bucks center Kareem Abdul-Jabbar and point guard Oscar Robertson

Printed in the United States of America

*McFarland & Company, Inc., Publishers
Box 611, Jefferson, North Carolina 28640
www.mcfarlandpub.com*

To all fans of the Milwaukee Bucks everywhere.

Acknowledgments

Writing this book has been a three-year-long odyssey, and what started out as a trip down history lane turned out to be something much bigger than I could have imagined. Simply put, this would not have been possible without the help of many people all throughout the process. First off, a huge thank you to McFarland for taking this plunge and helping me publish my first book. They showed great interest from the beginning and I am indebted to them—specifically Gary Mitchem—for making this book go from a dream to a reality. The same easily applies to the people at the Milwaukee Public Library. The library's extensive archives of the *Milwaukee Journal* and *Milwaukee Sentinel* helped me find the basis of this book. The stories that were just sitting there in the excellent work of Milwaukee Bucks beat writers like Bob Wolf, Rel Bochat, Lou Chapman, Terry Bledsoe, Bill Dwyre, Bud Lea, Tracy Dodds and so many others from this era truly helped me uncover history that felt lost to time in many ways. Being able to access that archive in my many trips to the library over many years has been invaluable to this work and it's important that we never take our public libraries for granted. A huge thank-you goes to the people at the Milwaukee County Historical Society, who guided me through their own archives. Some of the historical society's Bucks photos are featured in this book.

I never in a million years would have expected to have interviewed legendary Bucks announcer Jim Paschke after all the time I spent working on this project. I sincerely can't thank Jim enough for our chat and especially for all of the memories he has narrated throughout my years as a Bucks fan. He voiced the rise of the Bucks to where the franchise stands today and I appreciate him taking the time to join me for a talk I'll never forget. Along those same lines, I wanted to do every Bucks player, owner and coach a service within the book and to honor the impact that they had on the franchise from the ground floor. Ultimately, I wanted to tell the story as accurately as possible and I hope to have done that in an entertaining way that leaves everyone knowing more about the Bucks than they already knew.

Acknowledgments

To my brothers at the Gyro Step Podcast Network, thank you for indulging me on this long journey down the rabbit hole through Bucks history. To Adam McGee, my original podcasting partner with *Win in 6*: Your handling and work at Behind the Buck Pass and FanSided was the impetus of all of this and my writing journey. Everything that has come from the moment I responded to your call wanting more writers to talk about the Bucks long before they became NBA champions is owed to your dedication to telling the story of this team that continues to endure. To Ti Windisch and Rohan Katti, who are the best Bucks podcasters in the game and break down every detail that relates to the team with great enthusiasm and joy. To Alex Nemec, my other podcasting partner for *Talk of the Tundra*, and whose commitment to helping shape this book was more than I could have imagined. Thank you for taking the time to edit and making it more polished. To Andrew Snyder, who has adopted Milwaukee sports through *Crewsing for a Brewsing* and whose support throughout this endeavor kept me going. I can't thank you enough for all you have done and for championing this pursuit of mine in the years before it became published. GSPN for life.

To my brother Eric, my mother Micky, and my father Dave. You have always instilled in me the importance of pursuing my dreams, no matter what that might look like. To my nephews Caiden and Jayden and sister-in-law Jasmin, for helping grow our family and always being there when we need each other. Lastly, to my lovely wife Amber. You had a first-row seat in seeing how much time, energy and effort went into this project. You picked me up when I was down or wasn't sure where to take the next step. You were so eager to read the manuscript well before it was something worth reading and kept encouraging me to take this farther than I could have thought when it all started. You are my everything and my biggest supporter in life. I couldn't ask for anyone better to have on my side and help keep my eye on the prize. I love you forever and always, sweetheart.

Table of Contents

Acknowledgments — vii
Preface — 1
Introduction — 3

1. Marvin Fishman Answers the Call — 7
2. Milwaukee's Turbulent 1960s — 14
3. Milwaukee's Second Chance — 17
4. They're Called the Bucks — 25
5. Here Comes the Captain — 30
6. Losing for Lew (The 1968–69 Season) — 35
7. With the Flip of a Coin — 45
8. Alcindor Arrives (The 1969–70 Season) — 51
9. Here Comes the Big O — 69
10. Marching Toward a Title (The 1970–71 Season) — 78
11. Dynasty in the Making? (The 1971–72 Season) — 101
12. The Captain Makes History — 109
13. Missed Opportunities (Dr. J and the 1972–73 Season) — 119
14. One Last Run (The 1973–74 Season) — 131
15. Exit Strategies — 142
16. You're Now Leaving Kareem City — 145

Epilogue: Larry's Last Stand	163
Chapter Notes	171
Bibliography	179
Index	181

Preface

The beginnings of this project date to the summer of 2021, just weeks after the Milwaukee Bucks won their first NBA championship in 50 years. Seeing them do something I never thought was possible, I began to reflect on the past and the Bucks' origins, after years of writing and podcasting about the Bucks' present. What started as a way to explore the Bucks' first championship team in 1971 quickly turned into something much bigger. There have been recent books covering the Bucks in light of their recent championship season. *Built for This: The Milwaukee Bucks' Historic Run to the 2021 NBA Title* by The Athletic or *Giannis: The Improbable Rise of an NBA Champion* by the wonderful Mirin Fader are just two. The otherworldly excellence of current Bucks superstar Giannis Antetokounmpo has brought the Bucks back into the spotlight, highlighted by the team's first championship in 50 years.

This story, however, centers on the Bucks' rapid rise to the top of professional basketball from their beginnings. In three years, the Bucks went from being an expansion team in 1968 to being champions of the National Basketball Association by 1971. Their original head coach, Larry Costello, was not their first choice when the franchise formed, but he proved to be the right man to head up a team that were largely castoffs from around the league. A year later in 1969, the Bucks landed the original face of their franchise in Kareem Abdul-Jabbar, then known as Lew Alcindor, with the flip of a coin and beat out the American Basketball Association with a blind bid at Abdul-Jabbar's behest. Abdul-Jabbar's arrival eventually spurred the arrival of Oscar Robertson by the end of the 1969–70 NBA season. Robertson stands as a trailblazer who came to Milwaukee looking to capture the elusive championship that was missing from his superstar career after a decade in the NBA and was in the midst of changing the league forever as the president of the National Basketball Players Association.

The Bucks didn't just enter the NBA. They made history with a duo that helped lead one of the greatest teams to ever be built—and at an unmatched pace. They were a dynasty in the making, or so it seemed at the time. That fell apart just as fast as they rose to the top of the NBA. The Bucks gave the city of Milwaukee more than a good story. They legitimized a city scarred by the departure of the Milwaukee Braves and Major League Baseball. The Bucks then filled a void, thanks to the efforts of Marvin Fishman and Wesley Pavalon. Founding the franchise on January 22, 1968, when they were in one of two expansion cities accepted into the NBA, Fishman and Pavalon helped give Milwaukee its second shot in the world of professional sports. At the core of this story and the Bucks' rise to the top of the sporting world is the frosty relationship between Abdul-Jabbar and the city of Milwaukee. Though he played six seasons with the Bucks, Abdul-Jabbar was never at home in the city and did not hide that fact. His discomfort living in Milwaukee and the personal transformation he underwent during those six years are big reasons why a Bucks dynasty never came to fruition. Last but certainly not least, this book examines the place of Wayne Embry, the Bucks' original captain. While initially reluctant to come to Milwaukee through the expansion draft, Embry played a vital role in the formation of the Bucks. He influenced Robertson's decision to join the Bucks, which led indirectly to Embry's becoming the first Black general manager in any professional sports league in North America back in 1972. Feeling the weight of being a pioneer, Embry oversaw Abdul-Jabbar's exit from Milwaukee and helped sustain the Bucks in the decade that followed as he built the team with the future in mind.

This book tells the story of those early Bucks years by focusing heavily on the individuals who were key in establishing one of the longest-running NBA franchises today. Rick Schabowski's book *From Coin Toss to Championship: 1971—The Year of the Milwaukee Bucks* captures every detail of the Bucks' 1970–71 season and highlights the key additions the Bucks made in going from entering the NBA to winning a championship in three years. The scope of *Building the Milwaukee Bucks* is broader. It not only tells the story of the Bucks, but it also covers the individuals whose jerseys have been memorialized since. It tells the story of Milwaukee and the Bucks' important role in restoring the city's sporting pride. More importantly, I hope this book shows why the Bucks' history is worth retelling in this kind of scope. It's worth re-examining how all of the pieces fell into place to make the Bucks a team unlike any other in professional sports and how it all just unraveled in an equal amount of time.

Introduction

Approaching the finish line of this project, I knew there was something missing. The story that you will read requires looking back and captures how events occurred in real time. How the Milwaukee Bucks came to be, how quickly they ascended to the top of the NBA and how they won a championship faster than any other NBA franchise has before and since. The presence of basketball legends like Kareem Abdul-Jabbar and Oscar Robertson—in particular—helped legitimize an upstart Bucks team that established championship success as the standard from the outset. Not only did the Bucks carve out their place in NBA history with an unparalleled entrance into the league, it was the manner in which they helped the city of Milwaukee find its place again that was as significant as anything else. The significance of those early years was not lost on longtime Bucks play-by-play announcer Jim Paschke, whom I had the pleasure of interviewing for this book. "The Bucks caught lightning in a bottle very quickly and I think that solidified the franchise in Milwaukee and in Wisconsin for all time, essentially. I think the Bucks re-energized this city and helped put Milwaukee back on the sports map," said Paschke, when reminiscing on the Bucks' early years.

For 35 seasons from 1986 to 2021, Paschke served as the Bucks' play-by-play announcer for television broadcasts. He had a front-row seat for all things Bucks before retiring right as the Bucks won their first NBA title on July 20, 2021—their first championship in 50 seasons. The Bucks' origins and rise to the top of the NBA may have come before his time with the organization, but Paschke's mark on the organization can still be felt even after his retirement. Not only does a banner hang in the rafters of Fiserv Forum—the Bucks' current home arena—that commemorates Paschke's 30-year run with Bucks legend Jon McGlocklin and their work on Bucks broadcasts together, but also the room where interviews with Bucks players and coaches are conducted before and after games is named the Jim Paschke Media Room. Factoring in his time working for WITI—Milwaukee's local FOX affiliate—and announcing Milwaukee Brewers games, Paschke is synonymous with these franchises that have become part of the bedrock of Milwaukee and Wisconsin as a whole. His perspective on the sports culture that has developed in Milwaukee with the Bucks and the Brewers and the long reach of the Green Bay Packers throughout the state of Wisconsin rings true to this day as all three franchises have remained established in their respective sports.

As the saying goes, lightning doesn't strike twice in the same place, and the odyssey the Bucks went on after winning that 1971 championship proved how hard it is to win in the NBA, even with some of the greatest players to have ever played the game. "It's surprising to me that it didn't happen more than once, but that's how elusive championships are in any sport and especially in the NBA. It's hard to win and it's certainly hard to win more than once in succession," Paschke said when discussing why that Bucks team captured just one title. The next 50 years before they won their second NBA title in 2021 proved to be one long, strange trip, and Paschke himself narrated many of the experiences. The Bucks' leanest years may have occurred while Paschke was broadcasting, but they did little to dampen his excitement and enthusiasm for presenting Bucks basketball for more than half of the team's lifetime. Yet Paschke credits that original championship and the collection of players who achieved that goal for the Bucks carrying on to this day. "Of course, there are other reasons for the fans' interest in the team, but I think winning that title in 1971 helped hold the interest in the Bucks for 50 years until they won another one," Paschke declared.

While Paschke himself is not from Milwaukee (or even Wisconsin; he is a Rochester, Minnesota, native), he's seen how the city has embraced its professional sports teams. He's witnessed the many benefactors that have continued to make Milwaukee a major league city for many years. For as long as professional sports has existed in this country, the city of Milwaukee has viewed entry into any pro league as a source of legitimacy. Milwaukee—the biggest city in the state of Wisconsin—only had to look to the north to cities that stand in its shadow but have housed successful franchises in different sports. The Packers in Green Bay—the smallest city in all of North America to have a professional sports team—helped establish the National Football League as the top-flight football league in the country. They have endured because of their championship excellence across decades and because being a community-owned, nonprofit team has ensured their existence for more than a century. Even smaller Wisconsin cities like Oshkosh and Sheboygan can boast a history of housing professional basketball teams before and during World War II, though the basketball world has left those cities behind. To the west, Madison—Wisconsin's capital city—is the home of the University of Wisconsin Badgers and has stood near the top of college athletics.

Milwaukee certainly had its fair share of pro teams over the years in various leagues, most of which struggled to achieve success and even survive. It was the American Association, with the minor league and the third iteration of the Milwaukee Brewers, that stood as the shining example Milwaukeeans could turn to in order to enjoy the national pastime within their own city. For more than 50 years, the Brewers made Borchert Field, on the north side of the city, their home. Over that span, they won five league championships, with the last of those titles coming in 1951. Those Brewers helped Milwaukee find their love for the game of baseball, and for a while, being considered the best in the minor leagues was more than enough for Milwaukee. But by the end of World War II, being a minor league city was no longer a title Milwaukee wanted to wear. The city was growing, and influential forces within Milwaukee had set their sights on being considered a big-league city and raising the city's prospects to something greater. It became clear early on that it would be done by any means possible.

Eventually, Milwaukee was a city that was burned by the professional sports world when the Milwaukee Braves left for Atlanta after the 1965 MLB season. After being on the outside for so long, being a major league city had suited Milwaukee well. The hurdles that Milwaukee had to overcome to distinguish itself as a city worthy of professional sports never truly went away. A city of Milwaukee's size—big enough to be considered, but too small to ever guarantee its inclusion without committed local ownership in place—required the dedication of natives willing to stand up for their city. The response to the Braves' ugly departure generated by a wide variety of civic leaders spread like wildfire throughout the Milwaukee community and showed that being cast out from the world of professional sports was not something they were going to stand for. "The people here are extremely prideful, in my opinion. They love their city, they love their state. It means a lot to them and don't forget: Milwaukee has Chicago to the south and Minneapolis to the north and west. Both are major league cities. Why should Milwaukee not be part of that?" asked Jim Paschke. "It certainly speaks to the advocacy I've seen throughout my entire time in Milwaukee from certain people who want to keep this a major league city, and the fans certainly support that notion."

Throughout their 56 seasons and counting, the Bucks have had a number of advocates preside over the franchise and their impact was there from the beginning. This is the story of how the Bucks were started long before that 1971 championship banner hung from the rafters, before basketball's biggest legends came to town, or even before January 22, 1968—the date that the Bucks were officially accepted in the NBA. It was the mission of one Milwaukee native, who simply wanted to put the city back on the sporting map.

1

Marvin Fishman Answers the Call

By 1965, the Milwaukee Braves were intent on leaving Milwaukee. The happy days seen on the popular sitcom by the same name were over. Eight years after the Braves won their World Series title, the team's ownership was now headed by chairman Bill Bartholomay of the Chicago-based LaSalle Corporation which wanted to move the Braves to Atlanta, giving MLB its first franchise rooted in the Deep South. The city of Atlanta offered Bartholomay and the Braves ownership things they felt Milwaukee no longer provided: a brand-new 60,000-seat stadium and a wide-open television market that would instantly boost the Braves' profitability.

It wasn't like this from the start. The Braves were not Milwaukee's first entry into pro sports, but they were the first professional franchise that the city truly embraced. In order for Milwaukee to put itself on the map and catch the attention of Major League Baseball specifically, it had to convince the powers that be to come to Milwaukee, to see the city for what it was and how it was growing after World War II. The city was in the midst of a transformation that would change Milwaukee forever. A new zoo, a new public museum, a new public library, a new war memorial and a new arena (with plans to build an expressway) would all dot Milwaukee's cityscape at the turn of the city's second century. As that plan went into motion, the civic-minded Milwaukee community helped lure the MLB and hatched the city's first true love with the Braves. When the Braves' relocation from Boston to Milwaukee was officially approved by National League baseball owners on March 18, 1953, it was dubbed "the Milwaukee Miracle." They were the first MLB team to move to another city in a half-century and it would not have been possible without the birth of Milwaukee County Stadium, the crown jewel of Milwaukee's physical transformation. County Stadium was the first publicly financed stadium to be built in the country at the time it opened in 1953 and it was originally going to be home to the minor-league Brewers, which were the top minor league affiliate of the Braves. Braves owner Lou Perini was a proud Boston native and didn't want to move his beloved franchise from his home state, but the Braves played second fiddle to the Red Sox in Boston. A slump in the standings and sagging attendance numbers—even after winning the NL pennant in 1948—forced Perini's hand to move the Braves to Milwaukee three weeks before the start of the 1953 MLB season. Whatever political warfare was waged to take on debt in order to publicly finance County Stadium had fallen by the wayside. Milwaukee had started a trend. If you build it, they will come.

The Braves quickly captured hearts and minds all over Milwaukee. Before they even played a game in their new digs, the Braves received a welcome parade that had 50,000 Milwaukee citizens packed down Wisconsin Avenue on April 8, 1953. Whereas the Braves took a back seat in their native Boston, Milwaukee restored their relevance. It certainly helped to field a team that quickly contended for pennants. The players and coaches were showered with free gifts by many Milwaukee establishments that always paid it forward for their Braves players. For 12 years, the Braves would put Milwaukee on the map as a great sports city and they never once had a losing season. Braves fans quickly responded to their arrival in the city by making the team the biggest draw in all of baseball throughout the rest of the 1950s. Winning the 1957 World Series over the larger-than-life New York Yankees led to 225,000 Milwaukeeans marching back down Wisconsin Avenue in a complete daze that October. In the end, they had won and gave Milwaukee their only World Series title to date. It seemed that nothing would break the bond between Milwaukee and their Braves.

Of course, it didn't stay that way forever. By the 1960s, the Braves were winning, but they were no longer in the thick of pennant races. They boasted good attendance numbers, but no longer had the drawing power that changed the face of baseball. Perini sold to Bartholomay and his partners who made up the LaSalle Corp. after the end of the 1962 MLB season, and it didn't take long for rumors of relocation to start spreading through the papers. Eventually, the cat was out of the bag and the Braves announced their intention to move to Atlanta after the 1964 MLB season. Milwaukee itself was blamed for why things had gone so south so quickly. In turn, Braves fans and Milwaukee natives referred to Braves management as carpetbaggers for leaving the city high and dry.

Whether they intended to or not, Milwaukeeans had created a blueprint for how to lure professional sports to a city. Atlanta took a page out of Milwaukee's playbook by building its own municipal stadium and, instead of Miller Brewing Co. offering to foot the bill to help lure the Braves to Milwaukee, Atlanta had the financial backing of the Coca-Cola Company.

As much as Milwaukee and the state of Wisconsin tried to keep their Braves by any legal challenge possible—which included the Braves playing a lame duck year for the 1965 MLB season in Milwaukee to fulfill their lease with County Stadium—it only delayed the inevitable. There was no miracle coming to save the Braves and keep them in Milwaukee. Not only did the Braves' Chicago–based ownership want to relocate, so too did National League owners.

Atlanta only did what Milwaukee had done to Boston. Battle lines had been drawn as cities were pitted against each other when the Braves moved to Milwaukee. The game of baseball welcomed it. In a span of 12 years, the Braves had given Milwaukeeans the greatest and worst experiences one can feel as a sports fan. For as fast as it all came together, it was all undone just as quickly. The fight to keep the Braves in Milwaukee only deepened the wounds and trauma the city felt when County Stadium lay vacant at the start of the 1966 MLB season, especially when there was no promise of an expansion franchise to take the Braves' place. Ripped away from Milwaukee were Braves superstars and fan favorites, the biggest being Henry "Hank" Aaron—who regarded Milwaukee as his adopted home and initially protested moving back down South with the franchise.[1] Meanwhile, Atlanta savored the moment it broke through into the big leagues. Georgia governor Carl Sanders said the Braves relocating to Atlanta meant "the most to us since we lost the Civil War."[2]

The Braves' departure left Milwaukee with a black eye and a massive void. It was a void Marvin Fishman was seeking to fill, though he was far from the only one doing so. Fishman had one simple mission and that was to form a sports team that sported a Milwaukee label, as he'd often put it. He was the son of Russian immigrants and he was a proud Milwaukeean all his life. He graduated from North Division High School before studying at Marquette University. His studies were disrupted by World War II when he was drafted into the army where he served as a radioman in various bases across the country. Upon returning home, Fishman studied at the University of Wisconsin where he earned his bachelor's degree in marketing and his master's in business administration. Fishman broke into the real estate business to develop homes under his businesses, the M.L. Fishman Building Corp. and the M.L. Fishman Realty Company. He later earned the nickname "The Cape Cod King," based on the homes he developed in and around Milwaukee.

Fishman was in the hospital suffering from a bout of pericarditis when he decided to pursue a future in professional sports. By 1965, the city of Milwaukee was the 11th-largest city in the United States, with a population of 741,324 people. Here they were, about to lose the Braves, which would leave them with nothing. No representation in any of the major sports leagues throughout North America, despite having a reputation of being a good sports town. It was something Fishman could not stand for. "For what good reason was Milwaukee not a big league city? It seemed that somebody ought to do something about that. I had to talk somebody into taking action, into seeing the obvious need. So I did. I talked myself into it, had myself convinced in a matter of days that I was as good a somebody as any for the job. It wasn't that I had the time or money to casually buy and sell sports franchises. Not at all. But I did have the means to execute business deals involving franchises. I had the ability, I thought, to conclude such a venture, and to sell the idea to others, too. My basic premise was that a city could not be considered a major league city unless it had all the sports that major leagues in this country have—pro football, basketball, baseball, and hockey."[3]

For months, while he recovered, Fishman stayed in multiple hospitals. He sought ways to break into the halls of power and make Milwaukee major league again. He started that odyssey by trying to bring an expansion team to the city through the American Football League. The AFL sought to expand their league during the mid–Sixties and continue their challenge against the more established National Football League. The upstart AFL had overcome numerous early problems—low attendance, teams relocating or folding altogether, and the escalating bidding war between it and the NFL. The game changer was when they secured a five-year, $36 million national television contract with NBC that went into effect for the 1965 AFL season.

By securing that massive TV deal, the AFL drew closer to equal footing with the NFL and it was clear why Fishman wanted in. The AFL kept turning the screws on the NFL by introducing expansion teams, and competition was high to gain entry into what was then an eight-team league. The *Milwaukee Journal* reported on January 15, 1965, that there were up to 38 prospective ownership groups that showed interest in an AFL franchise, including three groups from Milwaukee. The only interested party mentioned by name in the article? Marvin Fishman. Fishman canvassed the AFL ownership groups and found the league to be on solid footing. He eventually contacted AFL commissioner Joe Foss and found him to be very high on Milwaukee as an AFL market. If Fishman was going to get anywhere with bringing an AFL team to Milwaukee, he had to find a home for it. And there was one big problem with using County Stadium in any capacity.

By challenging the NFL, Fishman was challenging the Green Bay Packers. These were Vince Lombardi's Packers. They were in the middle of one of the greatest runs the world of pro football has ever seen. They had just won three NFL titles in five years and they would add two more titles before the decade was done. They were the NFL's flagship franchise at the time and were viewed as such inside and outside of little Green Bay. The Packers had played in Milwaukee since 1933, starting at State Fair Park and then at County Stadium since the 1953 season, when it opened. County Stadium's existence played an indirect role in how hallowed Lambeau Field was built. County Stadium was built twice the size of the Packers' original home in Green Bay, City Stadium. There was a growing desire among Packers rivals and opponents to play more games in Milwaukee, the simple reason being that more fans in attendance meant more money for everyone involved. Thus, Lambeau Field opened in 1957 after city voters approved bonds to build the stadium and give the NFL its first football-specific venue. The Packers viewed the Milwaukee area as vital to their success. Milwaukee had been within the Packers' territory since 1931. When Lombardi arrived in Green Bay, he reinforced how important Milwaukee was to the Packers. If Fishman wanted County Stadium, that meant dealing with Lombardi himself. Lombardi was perhaps the most famous man associated with professional sports. He restored glory to a franchise that had fallen on hard times. And he, in turn, was treated as a benevolent god. There's a reason he was called "The Pope" after the Packers finished with a winning season—their first in 12 years—in Lombardi's first year in Green Bay. It was never Fishman's intention to harm the Packers in any way. Far from it, in fact. But they were the *Green Bay* Packers and not the Milwaukee Packers. Fishman believed that a Milwaukee AFL franchise could co-exist with the Packers within the same stadium. He vowed to let the Packers have their first choice of playing dates, too.

It was simple and sound according to Fishman. The Braves were no longer going to call Milwaukee and County Stadium their home after the 1965 MLB season. With only three Packers home games on the calendar for County Stadium, you'd think Fishman's pursuits to bring an AFL franchise would be widely encouraged and supported throughout the Milwaukee community. That couldn't be further from the truth. Fishman's efforts were met with plenty of resistance by many who were opposed to seeing the Packers hurt in any way. Though it was not what he intended, Fishman couldn't believe what he was hearing and what he was reading in the Milwaukee papers. It prompted him to ask the all-important question, "Is there anything wrong in getting off our duff and giving Milwaukee a big league team with a Milwaukee label?"[4] Just a couple of weeks later, on a WTMJ news program, Lombardi addressed the prospect of the Packers sharing County Stadium with another football team in Milwaukee: "We have an exclusive contract there and we're not going to surrender our rights. I think Milwaukee is a one-team city."[5] Oh, the irony of Lombardi saying that Milwaukee was a one-team city. Just as what was once the pride of Milwaukee were about to call Atlanta their new home. And saying it about a team that played two hours north of the city's limits. Whether it was his intention or not, Lombardi's words cut to the core of a city's sports identity that was at a major crossroads. No matter what, though, the Packers' exclusive County Stadium contract, which ran to the 1968 season, was an unmistakable hurdle.

Undeterred, Fishman brought on more investors. He had a guaranteed base of $30,000 worth of season tickets by the end of 1965. He viewed the fall of 1968 as the earliest for when there could be a Milwaukee AFL franchise. He wanted to host an exhibition game between the Miami Dolphins and the New York Jets on August 20, 1966. Still, it was all no good to a County Stadium board that did not want the slightest risk of jeopardizing their relationship to Lombardi and the Packers. At least, according to Eugene Grobschmidt, the chairman of the Milwaukee County Stadium board: "I wouldn't do anything that would hurt the Packers here. Unless Vince Lombardi OKs it, I won't go along with it."[6] The powerful influence of Lombardi extended beyond the Packers and the city of Green Bay, and Fishman was learning that firsthand. His plan to have the Dolphins and Jets play at County Stadium came and went, and so did his grand plan to join the AFL. On June 9, 1966, the war that had been brewing within pro football was over. The AFL and the NFL announced their intention to merge the leagues and retain all 26 teams that were established up to that point. As Lombardi had hoped, Milwaukee was deemed a one-team city—just for a team that played 116 miles north. Fishman had anticipated a merger occurring between the two leagues, but it all happened sooner than he or anyone could have expected. He did not give up on his dream of bringing professional football to Milwaukee.

Fishman pivoted toward bringing a Milwaukee franchise to the Continental Football League, which had originated in 1965. The league had franchises across North America and saw Milwaukee as a viable market, as they were trying to expand into the Midwest. Initially, Fishman sought to find a home at a renovated stadium in State Fair Park, but there wasn't enough funds or time to finish that project by the start of the 1968 season, the proposed launch date for a Milwaukee franchise. Once again, Fishman reached out to the Milwaukee County board and a meeting was arranged for 4 p.m. on September 1, 1966. As Fishman made his pitch before the board at the Milwaukee County Courthouse, Lombardi boarded a private plane bound for Milwaukee. By 6 p.m., Lombardi had extended the Packers' exclusive lease of County Stadium through 1975.

While he entertained filing a lawsuit to challenge that, Fishman realized that would be foolhardy. "For one thing, a legal battle would take so long that it could outlive the Continental Football League. And for another, challenging Lombardi in Wisconsin was like challenging God."⁷ There was no resentment on Fishman's side, but the failed efforts to bring Milwaukee a pro football team left him wanting to rest and regroup.

2

Milwaukee's Turbulent 1960s

The Milwaukee that Fishman was fighting to win representation for in the world of professional sports could not have been more different from the Milwaukee that was over the moon when the Braves had come to town. The Braves being ripped away from Milwaukee was only the tip of the iceberg of social upheaval that went on to define the 1960s for the city. That decade saw Milwaukee's divisions—both literally and figuratively—come front and center as the struggle for civil rights and equality put a magnifying glass on the discrimination that hadn't been addressed as the city grew during and after World War II. Milwaukee's segregation could be felt where people lived, where children went to school and where people worked. It always affected people of color, who were trying to live within a predominantly white society that was resistant to change.

Milwaukee's Black population had boomed during World War II. The promise of a manufacturing job in a city that had loads of them, good pay and the hope for a better life away from the "Jim Crow" South made Milwaukee a destination in the latter stages of the Great Migration. But what African Americans found once they settled in Milwaukee was as insidious as the life they chose to leave behind. People of color were confined to certain neighborhoods throughout the city. African Americans were relegated to an area on the north side of Milwaukee that was known as the Inner Core. The Inner Core was a six-square-mile strip that predominantly housed the influx of Milwaukee's Black population as it ascended during the middle of the twentieth century. Its inhabitants lived in homes that were often neglected and in a state of disrepair. The jobs that they had were low-income and vulnerable to economic downturns. Inner city schools had enacted what was termed "intact busing," which was ostensibly designed to alleviate overcrowded schools. Ultimately, it fostered segregation for students of color, who were the ones most affected by the city's archaic busing system. All of this continued even after the landmark decision of *Brown v. Board of Education* in 1954.

The thought of living with better means was not impossible for Black

2. Milwaukee's Turbulent 1960s

Milwaukeeans, but it certainly was improbable for the vast majority. Neighboring communities around metro Milwaukee that grew as a result of the city's rising population had deeds that restricted people of color and minorities from buying houses. Redlining cast divisions throughout Milwaukee and white flight set in once the city's makeup started changing. These developments brought forth key civil rights icons within the city who marched, protested and shined a light on the issues that faced the people who were most disadvantaged by the city's many inequalities.

Memphis–born lawyer Lloyd Barbee challenged the segregation in the Milwaukee Public Schools district with his Milwaukee United School Integration Committee (MUSIC) boycotts. Protesters blocked schools and buses within the system. Vel Phillips was Milwaukee's first Black alderwoman and fought the city's housing discrimination by proposing open housing laws to the Milwaukee Common Council. In the four times she brought them to a vote throughout the Sixties, she was the only alderperson who voted yes each time. But no figure in Milwaukee at this time attracted both attention and controversy quite like the Rev. James Groppi. Practicing at the St. Boniface Parish that was located on North 11th Street on the city's north side, Groppi heard and saw firsthand the daily struggles of his many Black parishioners. Their struggles affected him, and his empathy toward them forced him into action. He became active in the freedom movement. He marched on Washington in 1963 and marched in Selma in 1965. He took on Barbee's cause to desegregate Milwaukee public schools with the MUSIC boycotts and grew into a civil rights leader himself.

Here was a white man of faith championing the causes of Black Milwaukeeans, a dichotomy in and of itself and a lightning rod for the growing tension that began to spill over into Milwaukee's white communities. Upon becoming the advisor to the NAACP's Youth Council in Milwaukee, Groppi organized protests that started with the protest against the Fraternal Order of Eagles and their whites-only membership during the summer of 1966. These protests continued on and off throughout the summer as Groppi advanced the group's activism and mission. The long, hot summer of 1967 saw a wave of riots that affected cities and urban areas throughout America, and Milwaukee was not immune. There was no single inciting incident, but rather a slew of dust-ups and scenes that lit the fuse for Milwaukee's Black community to say enough was enough. Rising racial tensions—especially with a Milwaukee Police Department that was increasingly preaching law and order—caused things to get out of control for four consecutive nights starting on July 30. Over those four nights, three citizens and one police officer were shot and killed. One hundred more people were injured and 1,740 were arrested. Compared to the riots in Detroit, Newark and elsewhere, though, Milwaukee was considered lucky. Milwaukee mayor Henry Maier instituted a curfew on the second night, declared a state of emergency and called in the Wisconsin National Guard to essentially shut down the city. Public transportation, schools and city-operated buildings all closed or suspended operations. The fear of another riot had done more than the riot itself. Maier was commended for his diligent response and for not letting things get to a full boil. But what he and the police department had done only put a lid on a simmering pot. Sooner or later, it was going to boil over and do so on a bigger scale.

Riding on the back of the riots, Groppi, the Youth Council and the Black Commandos—an all-male group designed to protect the Youth Council—started marching. On August 27, 1967, Groppi and his flock marched down the 16th Street Viaduct to Kosciuszko Park on Milwaukee's South Side and did so for the next 200 consecutive nights. That bridge has since been referred to as Milwaukee's Mason–Dixon Line, in part because of what occurred over those 200 nights. On the first night, the protesters marched along the bridge. They called for an end to housing discrimination. They chanted and carried signs, doing just what Groppi had done alongside Martin Luther King, Jr. They were nonviolently protesting. It wouldn't stay that way for long. The second night saw a crowd of competing protesters challenging Groppi, the Youth Council and the Black Commandos as they made their way to the South Side. They hurled racial slurs, threw stones and threatened violence before eventually acting on it. But for all the fear, violence, and lack of support they were feeling from a Milwaukee Police Department that was begrudgingly protecting them, Groppi and the marchers remained undeterred.

Groppi, the Youth Council and the Black Commandos continued to march down that bridge as the summer turned into fall and fall became winter. Groppi had allies such as Barbee, Phillips and other civil rights icons of the time to lean on in support and to march with. The marches and Groppi himself attracted attention on a national scale, and reporters marched with them every night to get a close-up look at a city dealing with its racial reckoning. Milwaukee's response to its growing Black population and their fight for civil rights and equality definitively shaped the city in the months and years to come.

3

Milwaukee's Second Chance

The NBA had left Milwaukee more than a decade prior, but the NBA's commissioner—Walter Kennedy—saw Milwaukee as a city ripe for an expansion team just as it was losing the Braves. He toured the city and even met with interested media. "Milwaukee has to be considered a good sports city," he said.[1] Suddenly, the flame reignited. After fraught times early on, the NBA was truly on the rise midway through the 1960s. Kennedy had been brought in to help the league land a national TV contract, improve the attendance of its existing clubs and to establish stability against the emerging competitors that set their sights on the NBA. Not too long into his reign, the NBA landed a national TV deal with ABC, the health of its teams improved and suddenly, by 1965, the NBA was looking to expand. The story of how Milwaukee even came to be thought of as an NBA city boggles the mind, though.

The Milwaukee Hawks were an NBA franchise from 1951 to 1955. It was owned and operated by Ben Kerner, who transformed the franchise from the Tri-Cities Blackhawks. Its home cities were Moline and Rock Island in Illinois and Davenport, Iowa, before coming to Milwaukee. The NBA was leaving the Tri-Cities setup behind, as well as the Oshkoshes and Sheboygans of the world, in favor of big cities just as Kerner was looking 200 miles north to Milwaukee. Lured by the state-of-the-art Milwaukee Arena, Kerner almost didn't come to an agreement with the arena board due to disagreements over rental fees. It was Fred Miller—of Miller Brewing Company fame—who came in at the eleventh hour and helped Kerner and the Hawks settle in Milwaukee. All Kerner had to do was put together a team, hire a coach and spread the word around about Milwaukee's new NBA team in the 41 days before their first game to kick off the 1951 NBA season. Despite the shotgun arrangement, the NBA welcomed Milwaukee with open arms. The Minneapolis Lakers wanted a more geographically friendly rival like Milwaukee within the predominantly East Coast–based league. Said Eddie Gottlieb, the owner of the Philadelphia Warriors, "Yes, we want Milwaukee because it has the necessary big arena and we feel it is a big league city.... This is Milwaukee's opportunity to get into the big time in a different sport but in the same league with major baseball cities like New York, Boston and Philadelphia."²

Kerner's reputation preceded him. He moved through players on a whim, cycled through coaches—including the legendary Red Auerbach—like they were chewing gum and constantly berated officials from his courtside seat. But what made Kerner dogged in the pursuit of his goal was that he cared so much about the Hawks and their survival in Milwaukee. The Hawks were his life and his sole business. He came into the NBA as an outsider and was one of the few owners who didn't own his home arena, which meant turning over every stone to try and get people through the gates for Hawks home games. There was no shortage of promotions that Kerner thought up just to get people through the doors. Like giving out a free pound of coffee during a coffee shortage, regularly scheduling doubleheaders with the Harlem Globetrotters and even handing out flyers that read, "WANTED! Basketball fans. No experience needed."³

But all of the time, energy and effort Kerner spent on the Hawks in his every waking moment couldn't help them on the court. Over the course of their four seasons in Milwaukee, the Hawks were 91–190. When all it took for a team to make the NBA playoffs during that time was simply not being last place in their division, the Hawks couldn't even do that. A losing product made it impossible for any franchise to put its roots down in one city for long. Eventually, the loser label that followed the Hawks became too big to shake and Kerner's promotional skills weren't enough to establish an interested fan base in Milwaukee. Fairly often, Kerner would look around the Milwaukee Arena during a home game and inflate the team's woeful attendance to make it seem more respectable. Years later, Kerner said there were three bad weeks in show business: "Holy Week, Christmas Week, and a week in Milwaukee… I can't incite nothing in Milwaukee. In Milwaukee they said the guy's a lunatic. This is a nut…. In Milwaukee, I could crawl on my knees, I couldn't get three lines in the paper. In Milwaukee I tell them that my biggest disappointment was that I was a failure in Milwaukee. I never knock. I got to tell the people they're great. I got to tell them they're a great sports town. They didn't know whether we were playing in the municipal league or on wheelchairs!"⁴

But it wasn't until the "Milwaukee Miracle"—when the Braves transferred from Boston to Milwaukee—that Kerner saw his future in Milwaukee dim by the day. The Hawks immediately played second fiddle to the Braves and Kerner was insulted by the preferential treatment the Braves earned, whether it was the ridiculously small rental fees that Milwaukee County Stadium negotiated with the Braves franchise or how Milwaukeeans welcomed the Braves players with a parade down Wisconsin Avenue

3. Milwaukee's Second Chance

before they had even played a single game in their new digs. Kerner had to fight for everything he earned—including the Hawks franchise itself—and it was still not enough to make it in Milwaukee. Always wishing for support within the community, he exhausted all of his options to make it in a city he knew and felt would support pro basketball. It was after the 1954–55 NBA season that Kerner and his Hawks were essentially evicted by the Milwaukee Arena. They couldn't guarantee Kerner home games in Milwaukee in the last couple of months of the season, including the playoffs. He promptly took his Hawks to St. Louis and the rest was history.

What Milwaukee lost was St. Louis's gain when Kerner found a city hungry for basketball and legitimacy in the growing world of professional sports. The Hawks were an instant hit, playing in the biggest arena in the league, and with the rise of the legendary Bob Pettit they grew into a championship contender, challenging Auerbach and his dynastic Celtics teams. Pettit was good enough to be named the NBA's Rookie of the Year in the Hawks' final season in Milwaukee, and he could have been the star that the Hawks needed to have stayed in Milwaukee. The Hawks won the 1958 NBA Finals and were one of the league's healthiest franchises up to and throughout the Sixties before Kerner sold the franchise in 1968. Meanwhile, Milwaukee had seen its Braves win the 1957 World Series over those mighty Yankees. Kerner's sway within the league grew alongside the Hawks' relevance. As the NBA was looking to expand the league and had its sights on being a 16-team league by 1974, Kennedy entrusted Kerner to be the head of the NBA's expansion committee, where he shaped the league in the years to come.

Even after all that had transpired in Milwaukee and all of the financial loss Kerner personally suffered, he saw the city as having a great appetite for the pro game. Much had changed in the NBA game since those Hawks teams called Milwaukee home. They played in Milwaukee before the days of the 24-second shot clock, and the league's television exposure was only beginning then. Kerner spoke well of the city's prospects and never once cried sour grapes about his failure to put basketball over in the city. While he acknowledged that he was not the one to establish Milwaukee as an NBA market, he always thought someone would come along who could. "Milwaukee is definitely one of the best cities available. It wasn't ready for pro basketball when the Hawks were there, but it is ready now. There is no question in my mind that whoever gets a franchise there will find it exceptionally lucrative."[5] Milwaukee always had Kerner's heart, but its prospects now had Kerner's head, too. He saw that one of the biggest cities in the country no longer had any major league representation. There was no competition and most importantly, Milwaukee had movers and shakers behind the scenes to run a franchise successfully. "One of the things I've always regretted was leaving Milwaukee, but I had no alternative. The Braves were so hot then, and pro basketball didn't have the stature it did today. Now Milwaukee is hungry for major league sports. It wants a major league identity. The population explosion is in its favor; money is no factor and it wants the excitement of backing a major league team."[6] Kerner's comments came just as the Chicago Bulls were set to play three games in Milwaukee during the 1967–68 season. A second chance in the NBA had done Chicago well, as it did Baltimore and St. Louis. Now, Milwaukee could show that it was ready for its own second chance.

For as much as the NBA valued Milwaukee by 1967, though, so too did the American Basketball Association. The ABA was born on February 2, 1967, and they were looking to do exactly what the AFL had done to the NFL and the world of pro football. They were going to challenge the NBA into a merger and do so by any means necessary. The ABA appointed George Mikan—"Mr. Basketball" himself—to act as the league's commissioner. The expansion fee to join the ABA for its inaugural season was $50,000 and Milwaukee had caught its eye.[7] And, sitting on the sidelines after seeing his dream of a pro football team in Milwaukee go bust, the ABA caught Fishman's eye. He saw how the league could challenge the established NBA. The ABA was looking for flash and for color, with their three-point line and their red, white, and blue–colored ball. He learned from his pursuits with the AFL to not seek entry in the league looking for legitimacy, though. The NBA was the one being hunted and not the other way around. Fishman wanted to get into action with the NBA.

He found an ally in Bulls owner Dick Klein, who saw Milwaukee as a worthy geographic rival to his Bulls. Those three games held in Milwaukee showed the city's growing appetite for pro basketball. A preseason game between the Bulls and the defending champion Boston Celtics on October 6, 1967, saw 6,029 fans come to the Milwaukee Arena, where Boston won 106–98. Another 5,048 fans saw the Bulls beat the New York Knicks 109–96 on Thanksgiving night. All of those fans came for a game that didn't have the name Milwaukee on either jersey. If Milwaukee wanted back into the NBA, Klein thought, there was no excuse for them not to go for it. "I think Milwaukee would be making a mistake if it didn't apply for an NBA franchise for the 1968–69 season…. If the people in Milwaukee seriously want professional basketball, I'd say they have as good a chance as anybody."[8] Momentum was building in Milwaukee's favor. It had the endorsements of the NBA commissioner, key owners and a fanbase that just wanted a team to call their own. Fishman chose December 7, 1967, for a face-to-face meeting with commissioner Kennedy. He had no prior connections with Kennedy, but got word from Klein that Kennedy would be in Chicago for a luncheon held in his honor. The day arrived with dreary and windy weather. Fishman came down with a cold and resorted to taking a $4 Greyhound bus to Chicago in hopes of getting a minute or two to present himself to Kennedy. Arriving late to the luncheon and soaked from the elements, Fishman approached Kennedy and got straight to the point. "Hello, I'm Marv Fishman from Milwaukee and I'd like to buy a franchise in the NBA. All the readings appear to be right, and I think I can put a franchise together," he announced to a surprised Kennedy.[9]

While he recalled the shock and confusion on Kennedy's face, Fishman remembered the commissioner being receptive to his pitch. The interaction didn't last long. Kennedy had to rush out and catch a plane to presumably stop in another NBA city. But that day and after each conversation with Klein, Fishman was more dogged in his pursuit to bring up an NBA team. In the coming weeks, he saw how his previous pursuits in football helped his case in all of the background checks that the league had to make on his behalf. In a week's time, Fishman had gotten further along with the NBA than he ever had with the AFL. He had lined up the requisite dates at the Milwaukee Arena that the NBA desired, lined up the initial investors behind the project and presented the NBA with a certified check worth $100,000 in his official application. In order to make the bid much more sound, though, Fishman sought a big-time investor to really help back the project. It had to be one who could support the team beyond the expansion stage. In relaying that to his accountant, Fishman got word of a man named Wesley Pavalon, who was very interested in Fishman's mission. Fishman had heard of Pavalon before, but couldn't place how he had. It wasn't until the two met in Pavalon's office, when they were going over Fishman's efforts to pursue an NBA team, that Fishman remembered how he first had heard Pavalon's name. The same architect had designed both of their offices. One day, Fishman received a call from his architect asking if he could help one of his clients. He was on the verge of having his license revoked after accumulating one too many traffic violations. If Fishman helped, Pavalon was offering a lifetime pass to a miniature golf course at Capitol Court in Milwaukee. Fishman did the favor and now it was Pavalon's turn to do one for Fishman.

Fishman couldn't believe what he saw when he read the top headline of the *Milwaukee Sentinel* on December 16, 1967: "City Applies for NBA Franchise."[10] He dug deeper. He found the top headline of the sports page in the *Milwaukee Journal*: "NBA Bid Monday Planned by Kohl."[11] Fishman was immediately crestfallen. He knew who Herb Kohl was, how he came from his family's conglomerate of grocery and department stores that were all over the city, the state and growing beyond Wisconsin. Fishman later referred to learning of Kohl's NBA bid as akin to being "flattened by a steamroller."[12] After all, Kohl had been on a similar track to Fishman in pursuing a pro basketball franchise over the last several months. It started with the ABA where Milwaukee was set to be the twelfth and final team in the league's inaugural season. The ball was plainly in Kohl's court. "I'm interested in bringing an ABA team here, but only if the community is interested, too. I need some time to sound out some people in town, to determine if others want this as I do," he said.[13] However, the deadline for Milwaukee to gain entry into the ABA came and went without Kohl having a franchise. The ABA was more than willing to start with 11 teams while Kohl sought more time than just two days to put his ducks in a row between rounding up investors and finding good dates at the Milwaukee Arena. The ABA dream came and went for Kohl, just like it did for Fishman. But Kohl had turned his sights toward the NBA. Kohl made inroads with the league through his role with the Milwaukee Brewers, Inc., group, headed by his childhood friend Bud Selig. The group was composed of influential Milwaukee businessmen and formed in the wake of the Braves moving to Atlanta. While the group's major focus was on trying to bring an MLB team back to the city, they also pursued other sports ventures like basketball and soccer. It was Kohl who had developed a relationship with Klein, the aforementioned owner of the Bulls, and had helped land those three Bulls games that effectively served as an audition for Milwaukee's second chance.

Kohl was front and center in trying to help Milwaukee gain entry into the NBA and was farther along than Fishman. Kohl became fascinated with the game of basketball and took in many Celtics games at the famed Boston Garden while attending Harvard University as he earned a master's degree in business administration. Even having the inside track, Kohl still played his cards close to the vest in regard to his enthusiasm to own an NBA team. "We are studying the situation, but it isn't an easy project to get into. There are a number of difficult problems to solve," he said.[14] Whatever difficult problems existed in Kohl's mind, it didn't dissuade him from putting in a bid for an NBA franchise three weeks later. Fishman was more than willing to concede to Kohl. He had no desire to drive up the price for either himself or Kohl. He knew that Kohl had the deeper pockets and appeared further down the road with the league. Fishman bowed out of the running and let Kennedy know that as well. He even expressed his interest in being a potential investor to Kohl when he encountered Kohl at a Marquette University basketball game, but the conversation didn't go farther than that. A few days later, Fishman received a phone call. It was from Kennedy and he asked whether Fishman was still interested in submitting an application. It quickly became clear that Kohl had dropped out of the running.

That news left Fishman dumbfounded. He felt that Kohl was the owner that the NBA was looking for. If *he* had not come to terms with the league, there had to have been a good reason why. Kennedy was not willing to share that reason, which left Fishman uneasy. It was Kerner who let Fishman know why negotiations had broken down between Kohl and the NBA. The biggest reason was that Kohl wanted a high draft pick in both the college and expansion draft, neither of which the league was budging on. They hadn't let expansion teams get the first pick in the college drafts before, and they weren't about to do so now. With Kohl no longer a factor, Fishman and Pavalon took up the baton. On December 29, 1967, just more than three weeks after that initial face-to-face meeting with Kennedy in Chicago, Fishman submitted their application for a franchise to the league's office.

The day finally came on January 22, 1968. With the NBA in New York City for that year's All–Star Game, the vote for expansion was held at the league's board of governors meeting. It was in this boardroom where Milwaukee was officially voted as one of two new members in the NBA, along with Phoenix. All for an expansion fee of $2 million for each club. The news quickly traveled back home to Milwaukee and there was no shortage of reactions from proud Milwaukeeans. Mayor Maier viewed Milwaukee getting an NBA team as proof that the Braves leaving Milwaukee did not irreparably damage the city's reputation as a desirable sports town. "The black eye some people said Milwaukee suffered from the loss of baseball to the southern television markets apparently didn't carry any weight with the NBA. No doubt they saw it as a cruel hoax," he said.[15] Selig took time out from his own pursuit of trying to bring an MLB team back to Milwaukee and congratulated Fishman and Pavalon for bringing the NBA back to Milwaukee. "Speaking for the Brewers, I'm delighted that Milwaukee is getting major league basketball. I wish them all the success in the world. Now I hope we can get Major League Baseball to help put Milwaukee on the map in all major sports," he said.[16] Kohl offered his congratulations, too. Instead of crying sour grapes over not being the one to bring the NBA back to Milwaukee, he saw the bigger picture for what this meant for the city. "I'm delighted. The important thing is not who owns the franchise, but that Milwaukee has one," he said.[17] After 13 long years, Milwaukee was finally back in the NBA. But more importantly, it was a major league city again. Fishman and Pavalon went to great lengths to ensure that what forced the Braves out of Milwaukee would not occur with their NBA franchise. They took a page out of the Packers' playbook and decided to sell shares of stock in the team that fans could purchase, becoming the first NBA team to do so, in a setup that was initially designed to make sure the Bucks would never leave Milwaukee. When shares eventually went to market a couple of months later, fans could buy a share for $5.[18] Demand was so high that the initial sale of 300,000 shares going to market was increased to 425,000 shares.[19] It eventually covered the cost of the expansion fee that Milwaukee Professional Sports and Services, Inc.—the operating company for Fishman and Pavalon—paid to enter the NBA.

Fishman was the representative to celebrate in New York on the day Milwaukee was accepted into the NBA. He bumped elbows with the invited New York press and celebrities. The next morning, though, as he bought and read as many newspapers as he could find around the city, Fishman found a much different reaction to the news that Milwaukee was back in the NBA. After all those many years of talking up Milwaukee as much as he could and trying to sell the city to the growing world of professional sports, Fishman found dissenting opinions from various columnists around the East Coast. He even had a memorable run-in with the legendary Howard Cosell, who remarked of Milwaukee's proximity to Sheboygan as a pejorative. Fishman just couldn't escape the skepticism of sportswriters on the East Coast, where pro sports were well represented and were treated as a God-given right. The Hawks had failed in Milwaukee and so did the Braves, they thought. What good would Milwaukee do for the NBA the second time around? "After studying the samples from my clipping service, I concluded that public opinion was not real high on the Milwaukee NBA franchise," Fishman said.[20] Pavalon faced a similar line of questioning from those fearing the same scenario with the Hawks and Braves coming to pass as Selig continued to push for a new MLB franchise in Milwaukee. In response to those doubts, Pavalon retorted, "It frightens me to think that certain individuals might be led to feel they've been right about Milwaukee when I know they're wrong. They say Milwaukee will only support a winner, but that's hogwash."[21] Fishman's trip to New York was not all bad, though. He took in the NBA All-Star Game, made connections with the other owners and various people around the league. He was ever the optimist, even in the face of a dubious crowd. He had imagined seeing NBA stars running up and down the court while wearing a Milwaukee jersey. Thanks to Fishman, that day was finally coming.

4

They're Called the Bucks

Among the biggest priorities for the club after they officially entered the NBA was to find a coach who would help bring the team up from dream to a reality. Both Fishman and Pavalon wanted a "Vince Lombardi" type[1] and there were eight months between the time when Milwaukee was back in the NBA and when they would be playing their first official game. While Fishman was in New York, he was reminded that he had the guy he was looking for in his own backyard. It was never the intention of Fishman and Pavalon to pursue Al McGuire—the head coach of the men's basketball team at Marquette University—when they brought an NBA team to Milwaukee. Fishman very much looked at it from a public relations perspective. Stealing away the coach of a Marquette fanbase that they were hoping to sell season tickets to would certainly be one way to rile them up, and not for the better. Fishman made connections with other owners and people around the league to see who might be willing to come to Milwaukee and coach the team. Names like Alex Hannum, Jack Ramsay, Dolph Schayes, and Paul Seymour came up and some even approached Fishman. But he left New York that All–Star Weekend knowing that none of them had expressed a real interest in uprooting to Milwaukee.

McGuire, meanwhile, had already cemented his image as a bombastic, larger-than-life coach who was bringing the best out of Marquette's basketball program. McGuire had been in the NBA and he had even played for his hometown Knicks during the 1950s. He followed up his brief playing career by becoming a coach, first as an assistant at Dartmouth and then getting his first head coaching gig at Division II Belmont Abbey College. When McGuire arrived in Milwaukee in 1964, Marquette showed a marked improvement and started vying for deep runs in the NCAA Tournament just as the NBA was circling back to Milwaukee. In many ways, it was McGuire's transformation of the then–Marquette Warriors that helped plant the seed for the NBA. It saw that Milwaukee had a much larger interest in the game of basketball. Success certainly has a way of doing that sort of thing. Word traveled through the grapevine all the way to Fishman that McGuire had grown tired of college ball and that he was greatly interested in making a jump to the NBA, excited by the challenge of coaching professionally and wanting to stay in Milwaukee. To pursue McGuire required a certain deftness from all parties involved. Fishman had backchanneled through McGuire's financial advisor to see whether this was just hearsay and it became clear that it was not. "I figured that McGuire considered the pro job a challenge," Fishman wrote. "McGuire always liked challenges. And I also had the feeling that McGuire had been thinking about the possibility of coaching Milwaukee's pro team ever since his good friend, Herb Kohl, had gone after a franchise. The thought occurred to me that one of the big attractions of an NBA franchise for Kohl was getting McGuire as coach."[2]

How everything followed from here is still subject to debate to this day. As McGuire's interest in leaving Marquette and jumping to the NBA ranks grew, he sought to be let out of the five-year contract he had signed the previous year. Father Raymond McAuley, the school's athletic director, had seemingly given the okay for him to do so. Before the Warriors' first-round match with Bowling Green State University in the 1968 NCAA Men's Basketball Tournament, McGuire held a meeting with his players and disclosed that this very well could be their last run together, if things all worked out. But a standoff between McGuire and McAuley developed from there. To anybody who was willing to listen, McAuley flatly denied that he had given any kind of permission or approval for McGuire to pursue an NBA gig. "As far as we are concerned, Al McGuire is our coach now, and he will be our coach next year," he said.[3] Oh, did Fishman and Pavalon step into something fierce! They certainly did make it very palatable for McGuire by offering a five-year contract that would have been worth $400,000—$200,000 in salary and an additional $200,000 worth of stock options.[4] All while McGuire was making $15,000 at Marquette. Years later, McGuire cracked wise as to why he was forced to honor his contract with Marquette and ultimately lead them to a national title in 1977: "The priests take a vow of poverty—and they expect you to abide by it."[5] McGuire had eluded Fishman and Pavalon's grasp and now the urgency mounted to find the best coach and general manager for the unnamed club.

Throughout their search to find a coach and during their failed attempt to woo McGuire, Larry Costello kept coming up as a name to pursue in conversations Fishman had with people around the league. It became so frequent that Fishman eventually thought it was worth reaching out to him, especially if he was this highly thought of. Costello was still an NBA player with the Philadelphia 76ers, though a sidelined one. He had torn his Achilles tendon after making a late-career comeback and moved down the bench alongside Hall of Fame coach Jack Ramsay during the 1968 NBA season. He wasn't a superstar, but in 12 seasons Costello had six All–Star appearances and attacked the game with a zeal and determination that were seen as hallmarks of a promising coaching career. There was no mistaking him out there on the court. His two-handed set shot that he launched from well beyond the key was his signature. He had an endless motor and was tough as nails defensively, by all accounts. Basketball and athletics had consumed Costello even before his starring days at Niagara University. He played in the NBA at a time when there was very little money and security in the game. Enrolling in dentistry school after getting drafted by the then–Philadelphia Warriors in 1954 didn't quash his desire to play professionally. A tour of duty overseas didn't derail his burgeoning NBA career a year later. To be an NBA player in those days was to take a leap of faith and Costello was standing right there, preaching the gospel of what it took to be an NBA player.

The day came for Costello to meet with Fishman and Pavalon at Eugene's Restaurant. Costello was picked up by Pavalon's black limousine at Mitchell International Airport. Fishman recalled how he saw Costello pop out of the limo with his signature crewcut and wearing a suit that looked one size too big on him. None of that mattered to Fishman. "I liked Larry from the start," he wrote. "I liked the way he walked like an athlete, the way he talked like an athlete. I even liked the way he dressed. He was the perfect no-nonsense guy. While everyone else was going to longer hair, Larry was still wearing his crewcut. He was too busy to worry about his hair.... I remember sensing total honesty about the guy. He didn't ask what the job was paying and he didn't try to negotiate price. He just said this is how much he needed and I remember thinking that his approach was quite reasonable and totally frank."[6] Costello jotted down notes on his yellow legal pad—soon to be a staple of his when patrolling the bench during his days in Milwaukee. It didn't take long for him to win over Fishman and Pavalon and for them to think he was the best possible coach available. All parties left the restaurant believing that they'd have a deal forthcoming. He may not have been their first choice, but Costello proved to be the best coach in the long run.

With Costello in place, Fishman, Pavalon, and company went back to the college route to search for a basketball mind that could build their expansion club. Enter John Erickson, the head coach at the University of Wisconsin. Erickson's basketball background was rooted in Wisconsin, from playing at Beloit College to coaching the Badgers men's team for nearly a decade. While Fishman admitted that those teams hadn't set the world on fire, Erickson was well thought of in basketball circles. The fact that he presented a "Mr. Wisconsin" image was a bonus, especially after the McGuire fiasco. On April 4, 1968, Costello and Erickson were unveiled to the press at Milwaukee's iconic Pfister Hotel. Before the crowd, Costello outlined the precise vision for how he wanted his team to play and the type of character he wanted from players in the expansion draft that was a month away. "I want players who love the game," he said. "A lot of them don't, and if you don't love the game, forget it. If I have my choice of a player with lots of desire and only average talent and one with lots of talent and little desire, I'll take the first one every time."[7] It was an historic day for the club and it was capped off by their later selecting Charlie Paulk, their first-round draft pick in the 1968 NBA draft. Yet, all of these moves that further established the organization paled in comparison to how the rest of the day evolved.

Just hours after Costello and Erickson were officially welcomed in Milwaukee on that April 4 day, Martin Luther King, Jr., was assassinated on the balcony outside a Memphis motel room. King's shocking death was an unhealable wound for a nation still steeped in the battle for equality. Amid civil unrest, immediate reactions were seen all over the country. In Milwaukee, King's death spurred a march of 10,000 to 15,000 people to memorialize the minister on April 8, 1968, and it's estimated to be the largest march ever held in the city. In Washington, D.C., the Fair Housing Act passed through the House of Representatives at the behest of President Lyndon B. Johnson. Further strides were made for civil rights, but all at an incalculable price. Just days earlier, Maier had been re-elected as the mayor of Milwaukee for a third term and won in a landslide victory. He won 86 percent of the vote over his challenger, a 31-year-old attorney named David L. Walther. That's a higher share than any U.S. president has earned throughout the history of the United States. In the first week of his third term, Maier asked the Common Council to adopt a fair housing ordinance similar to what Johnson had signed and put into immediate effect. When it went to a vote, Vel Phillips, who had first proposed the bill back in 1962, saw her supporters in the Council stand behind her. Milwaukee's fair housing law went into effect after a 15–4 vote after years of struggle and persistence from Phillips. Father Groppi, the Youth Council and the Black Commandos had stopped marching for the bill by then, though they were certainly present in the march after King's assassination. They had carried out their mission in ensuring that Milwaukee had fair housing laws. The prejudice, bigotry and hatred they faced in fighting for a basic American right for all people had been shown for the world to see.

Sales were climbing into the thousands for season tickets and stock shares were being bought by the Milwaukee public, which had learned they could make an imprint on the growing operation. A board of directors was going to preside over the Milwaukee franchise, even though Pavalon stood as the biggest shareholder of all and was promptly elevated from team president to chairman of the board. The team had a home, they had a fanbase that literally jumped at the chance to own a piece of the team and they would soon draft their first players ahead of their inaugural season. Now, all this basketball team needed was a name.

From the outset, Fishman and Pavalon wanted the public to be involved in choosing the name for the club. A contest sponsored by Coca-Cola was introduced two months after the initial announcement and the likes of Costello and Erickson represented the organization in the contest. The organization sought a name that would represent Wisconsin's image, that fit the sport of basketball and that was unique. After over 14,000 entries had been received, the Milwaukee Bucks was officially announced as the name of the team on May 22, 1968.

Of the 45 submissions for the Bucks name, the official winner was a Whitefish Bay man named R.D. Trebilcox. He submitted Bucks because they are "spirited, good jumpers, and agile. All exceptional qualities for basketball players too."[8] For his efforts, Trebilcox won a new AMC Javelin car, and Erickson even presented the keys to him. However, "Bucks" was far from the most popular submission in the contest. "Robins" held that honor, with 113 entries, followed by "Clippers." Other notable suggestions were Packers, Braves, Lumberjacks, Pioneers and, yes, Skunks.[9] Putting the cherry on top, the logo of an inviting cartoon deer spinning a basketball atop its hoof paired perfectly with the Bucks moniker. For the team's 34 home games at Milwaukee Arena, season ticket prices were set from as low as $85 to $153, depending on the choice of seats. Single-game tickets were set as low as $3.25 to $5.25 per seat. It quickly appeared that Milwaukee was backing its Bucks, even before they were called that in the first place.

5

Here Comes the Captain

All throughout the summer, the Bucks were locking down their selections in both the expansion and college drafts. The Bucks came away from both with some talent to work with. There were former and future All-Stars like Guy Rodgers, Len Chappell, Bob Love, and, yes, Larry Costello from the expansion player pool. Even as he was rehabilitating from his Achilles injury and taking on head coaching duties, Costello was initially preparing to act as player-coach in advance of the Bucks' maiden voyage. There were other burgeoning talents that intrigued Costello, Erickson and company. One such player was Jon McGlocklin, formerly of the San Diego Rockets. McGlocklin's inclusion in the expansion player pool was a shock to the Bucks brass and other decision makers within the NBA. The Indiana native was a former Hoosier and had yet to find his footing both with the Cincinnati Royals and the San Diego Rockets. He left both organizations in the same manner by being placed in expansion drafts in consecutive years. In Milwaukee, though, McGlocklin found a permanent home. An excellent shooter from all over the floor—even before the days the NBA had the three-point line—McGlocklin emerged as an immediate fan favorite. He scored the Bucks' first pair of points in their first game and went on to be the franchise's first All-Star selection during its inaugural season. He relished the chance to return to the Midwest after being selected by Milwaukee and was very community-minded from the beginning. McGlocklin earned the nickname "Mr. Buck" by giving back to fans, whether it was through speaking engagements or his appearances at summer clinics. Make no mistake, McGlocklin continued to make his mark on the Milwaukee community in the decades to come.

The college draft provided a sleeper talent who made a mark in the Bucks' starting lineup from the moment their first season tipped off. Greg Smith was a fourth-round selection—back in the days when the NBA draft went as long as 21 rounds—and came out of Western Kentucky. He easily could have stayed loyal to his Kentucky roots after having been selected by the Kentucky Colonels in the ABA. But a week after he was selected by the

5. Here Comes the Captain 31

Bucks in the 1968 NBA draft, Smith chose to sign with Milwaukee instead. At 6'5" and 205 pounds, Smith was a special athlete, thanks to his massive vertical leap and a knack for being able to play at any position on the floor. As a senior starring for the Hilltoppers, Smith hauled down 14.5 rebounds per game, which ranked among the nation's best that year. It was a wonder that the Bucks had been able to draft Smith in the first place. Nearly a year to the day when he signed his NBA contract with the Bucks, Smith was in a deadly car accident, along with his brother, Dwight, and their sister, Kay. Greg was driving the car from their hometown of Princeton back to the Western Kentucky University campus in Bowling Green. Both Dwight and Kay were asleep when Greg lost control of the car, which hydroplaned and flipped over in a ditch. It was a particularly rainy Mother's Day afternoon and it was determined after an investigation that the highway they were traveling down was covered in two inches of rainwater. Greg was able to kick out a window and emerge from the car, but both Dwight and Kay drowned. In 1971, Greg was awarded $10,000 in damages as the Kentucky Court of Appeals held the State Highway Department responsible for its negligence in the upkeep of the roads. At the time of his death, Dwight was close to being selected by the Los Angeles Lakers in the third round of the 1967 NBA draft. When Greg eventually met with Erickson and the Milwaukee press after the draft, he remarked, "If I was superstitious, I wouldn't be here today."[1]

As training camp drew closer and closer, only one holdout from their selections in both drafts remained for the Bucks as they built their inaugural roster. That holdout was certainly the biggest catch. There was no secret as to why the Bucks selected Wayne Embry first in their expansion draft. He had an air of legitimacy as a five-time All–Star and a recent NBA champion with the Boston Celtics. At 31 years old, Embry had been in the NBA for a decade. Would he go from the height of winning an NBA title to starting fresh in a city that was getting its second chance with the NBA? He had been under the assumption that the Phoenix Suns were going to take him in the expansion draft and was assured so by their owner. Instead, Embry learned that he was Milwaukee–bound after playing a round of golf on the day of the expansion draft. He knew Costello, knew of the Bucks' brain trust, but he was skeptical as to whether he'd play in Milwaukee, even after initial discussions with the organization. "I was not very enthusiastic, and they knew it. Larry told me they needed me for my leadership because they had drafted a lot of young players. He thought my experience would jumpstart the franchise. I remained non-committal," Embry later wrote.[2] As the second most senior player drafted by the Bucks—next to Guy Rodgers—Embry was a perfect candidate to play out the string by starting over in a new city. This was what life in the NBA was like for proven, established players who went unprotected in the expansion era. The more experienced you were and the closer you were to the end of your playing career, the more you were attractive to expansion teams that were eager to establish themselves. A proud player like Embry had more to think about than just getting the right contract for his services. It was also about uprooting his family to a new city, finding the right home and making sure his significant other and children found security in the face of big changes.

Embry's holdout dragged into June, into July and into August. All that was known was that the Bucks and Embry were struggling to come to terms on a deal. Meanwhile, as camp neared, Embry had gotten back into playing shape by exclusively eating a protein diet of eggs, meat, fish and cottage cheese. Eventually, a one-year, $40,000 contract was negotiated between the club and Embry and he officially joined the Bucks roster on September 12, 1968. Despite having given real thought to retirement and even lining up a fallback job at a printing company, Embry was swayed by the people who were in place in Milwaukee, and specifically by Erickson. "I was through until Mr. Erickson changed my mind. I'm at the age and the point in my career where I had to consider the long range possibilities. I'm playing from year to year.... But what influenced me quite a bit was the fact that I like the Milwaukee organization—the people I have met, the ball club we've got. I hope to be a contributing factor."[3] With Embry now in tow, the Bucks descended upon Milton College for their inaugural training camp. They set their sights on being the most successful expansion team in NBA history. That task was not exactly shooting for the moon, but Costello wanted to build a winning culture, no matter what people thought of the Bucks' talent. Costello decided early on that all players would room together alphabetically and regardless of skin color. "We just felt that rooming them alphabetically was the best way to do it. We're giving serious thought to using the same setup on the road during the season."[4]

Embry remembered getting ready for their first practice and thinking that these new Bucks would take to the court to start their drills. Instead, in came Costello carrying loose-leaf binders, along with his top assistant, Tom Nissalke. Costello called for the team to huddle up as Nissalke passed out personalized blinders to each player in the gym. It was Costello's playbook, which was filled with offensive and defensive sets, a set of team rules and a brief history of the NBA. In his 10 years in the NBA, Embry couldn't remember ever seeing anything like that. There was no question other players felt the same way, but they couldn't dismiss it out of hand. Costello expected all of his players to know that book inside and out and promised to quiz them periodically throughout the season. When drills finally got underway, Costello took off his warmups and kicked off practice with his

5. *Here Comes the Captain*

Wayne Embry (15) matched up against his former teammate Bill Russell in a game against the Boston Celtics during the Bucks' expansion season. Embry was the Bucks' first pick in the expansion draft and influenced the franchise before becoming the first Black general manager in professional sports. From the program for the Bucks' clash with the Celtics on December 3, 1968 (Milwaukee County Historical Society).

players. His pale skin compared to that of the players who sported summer tans led Embry to refer to Costello as "Casper the Friendly Ghost" to his new teammates.[5] This is how these new Bucks kicked off their run toward their first season in the NBA.

Embry had just a few weeks to settle his family in Milwaukee after deciding to play his eleventh season in the league. Staying in an apartment owned by Fishman in the suburb of Oak Creek, located on the south side of Milwaukee, Embry drove his wife, Terri, and their young kids to their new home. The 1968 presidential election was coming up and as they neared their apartment, they saw the signs advocating for Hubert Humphrey and Richard Nixon turn into George Wallace signs. Wallace ran as an independent and gathered a following in Wisconsin, specifically in the south side of Milwaukee. Upon starting his first term as the governor of Alabama, Wallace had introduced the motto "segregation now, segregation tomorrow, and segregation forever" as the University of Alabama was on the verge of accepting its first students of color, nearly a decade after the verdict of *Brown v. Board of Education*. When that day finally came, Wallace stood in front of the school's entrance to block the students, even after President John F. Kennedy had ordered that there be no resistance. Now that message took root up north and Wallace found a following in Wisconsin. When he ran as a challenger to Lyndon B. Johnson in Wisconsin's Democratic primary in 1964, Wallace received one-third of the 780,000 votes cast. As they unpacked their car, Terri Embry—who had marched from Selma, Alabama, with King—asked her husband, "Where on earth have you brought me?"[6]

6

Losing for Lew
(The 1968–69 Season)

There was a very real incentive for the Bucks not to be successful on the court that first season. There was a reason why 1968 was the year Milwaukee *had* to be in the NBA. Being the worst team in their conference, as Fishman and Pavalon were secretly hoping the Bucks to be at the end of the season, came with a chance to be truly great, as the last-place team in each of the two divisions would flip a coin to see which would get first pick in the college draft. Ferdinand Lewis Alcindor, Jr., was born on April 16, 1947, though the world later knew him and called him by a different name. His talent on a basketball court while growing up in Harlem and in the Dyckman Street projects was not apparent at first, though his height was. The only child of Cora and Ferdinand Lewis Sr., Lew Jr. went on to represent many things to many people: a champion for civil rights and Black people, the next great basketball superstar and a true humanitarian who was deeply rooted in finding his place in the world. For the Bucks, Alcindor represented salvation and acceptance, a symbol on which to pin their hopes of establishing themselves as a bona fide NBA franchise. This was during the days when no one dared to challenge the NBA's rule about waiting four years after high school before going pro, as it was still a couple of years before Spencer Haywood fought that head-on. That made the wait for when the big man turned pro one of the greatest spectacles in NBA history and something that only further established pro basketball.

Greatness and championships followed Alcindor wherever he went, first at Power Memorial Academy, a Catholic high school in New York, and then at UCLA, where he played for legendary coach John Wooden. Those Bruins teams with Alcindor down low were a successful machine, dating back to when his freshman squads obliterated the varsity teams before Alcindor even played an official college game. The NBA placed a premium on the big man. Alcindor was the next George Mikan, Bill Russell and Wilt Chamberlain, all rolled into one. The prospect of landing Alcindor was on the minds of Fishman and Pavalon as they combined forces. Pavalon had even openly talked to the press days after getting the franchise about the chance of pursuing Alcindor and what it might mean for Milwaukee. "Sure, I've thought about it," he said. "Because Alcindor is a junior, Milwaukee will certainly have a crack at him. This year, of course, it would have been impossible to get Alcindor if he had been a senior. We will have only the seventh or eighth pick. But next year? We certainly aren't looking forward to it, but if that should happen, well, I don't have to tell anybody what Alcindor would mean to the club."[1]

The chase for Alcindor required plenty of assurance from the league that Milwaukee would win the right to draft him if they had the chance—that there wouldn't be any funny business to see that he played for a big city, much bigger than Milwaukee. In fact, Kennedy went on record by saying that his biggest challenge for the 1968–69 NBA season would be making sure that games would be "played on the level" as Alcindor waited in the wings.[2] For all of the reasons why the Bucks desperately wanted Alcindor, so did the ABA. The league viewed Alcindor as a way to end any potential war with the NBA and to deal a crushing blow that would make the leagues think of merging faster than what either party thought was possible at the time. It didn't take too long to understand that the ABA was willing to deploy any advantage or unearth any information in their pursuit of landing the big man. Under the name of "Operation Kingfish," the ABA hired a team of psychologists, psychiatrists, private detectives and profilers to build their case for signing him. All of that for $10,000.[3] Alcindor loomed over everything the Bucks did in the course of their maiden NBA voyage. The idea of going through an expansion season where the Bucks would stomach plenty of losing was something that Fishman and Pavalon could go for. The big question was whether Milwaukee could support a team that was anything but a winner. The tension was palpable even before the Bucks took the floor for their first game at the Arena.

At last, the day arrived on October 16, 1968. It was only fitting that the Bucks hosted the Bulls for their first NBA game. Bucks management expected a crowd of a little more than 6,000 fans in attendance. That was shattered when the final count came up to 8,467, with one of those people being commissioner Kennedy. All those fans witnessed the Bulls get the better of the Bucks with a final score of 89–84. Milwaukee's opening night performance was marred by inefficient shooting and inopportune turnovers, despite limiting the Bulls to 89 points. Yet, everyone came away impressed by what the future held for the Bucks. Kennedy was the most enthusiastic of all as he referred to the Bucks organization as "top-drawer."[4] The NBA had returned to Milwaukee and the city embraced this second chance. Whether that would last as the season went on was the question. On opening night, it was a look at what could be. Chasing that first win proved to be more difficult than what the Bucks—namely Costello—could have imagined coming into the regular season after going 5–4 in their preseason tune-ups. The Bucks' loss to the Bulls was followed by losses to the Atlanta Hawks, New York Knicks, Boston Celtics and Baltimore Bullets. It took all of five games for Costello to receive an ejection—the first he ever received in his basketball career. Going 0–5 heading into Halloween night, the Bucks took out their frustrations on the Detroit Pistons to record their first NBA victory. The consistency and the cohesion that had been missing from the first five games were all there as Milwaukee triumphed in a wire-to-wire 134–118 win. With 6,694 fans in attendance, it was as if the Bucks won the right to advance in the playoffs or win an NBA title. The fans showered the players and coaches with a standing ovation at the final buzzer. The Bucks were led to victory by their captain as Embry led the way for scorers with 30 points. It left Costello glowing, having seen his team put it all together for the very first time. "This was our best overall performance," he said. "We shot better, we moved better, and when they put on their press, we used it to our advantage by getting the ball down the floor faster and breaking men for easy shots. I knew the first victory was coming soon, but I was beginning to wonder how soon."[5]

The win over the Pistons gave the Bucks the much-needed taste of victory after six tries. Savoring each and every win soothed the ever-maniacal Costello over that expansion season. Losses continued to pile up as the Bucks finished out the first month of the year. Yet, that did not do much to keep the people from showing up at the Arena. High-profile clashes against the star-studded Los Angeles Lakers in Madison and the Celtics helped the Bucks find their fanbase early, with only the Knicks, 76ers, and Lakers standing ahead of them in attendance figures.[6] The Bucks even had a small pep band and their own fight song: "Milwaukee Bucks! That's the name of our team. And they will win, with an effort supreme. Milwaukee Bucks! How they handle the ball. And they break great, whether they're short or tall."[7]

Announcing the action of Bucks games over the radio for WTMJ—Milwaukee's flagship radio station—was a 31-year-old disc jockey named Eddie Doucette. Doucette originally signed on with the Bucks as their publicity director as the team was building its roster and earned its "Bucks" nickname. Just months after his appointment, Doucette was also installed as the team's play-by-play man for the radio and served in both roles for the organization when they were starting out. When the season got underway, Doucette's work behind the microphone gave Bucks fans a lively and colorful personality to latch on to. Representing a team that was destined to take more lumps than earn wins starting out, Doucette made his broadcasts sing over the airwaves. Doucette's energy made him feel larger than life and he blurred the line between an objective and subjective observer by announcing games as if he was the Bucks' biggest fan. He had an endless reservoir of nicknames for Bucks players over the years that warranted a "Doucette dictionary" in order to keep up with who he was referring to at any given moment—"Captain Marvel" for Greg Smith, the "Cement Mixer" for Dick Cunningham, Wayne "The Wall" Embry— and exclaimed "Bango!" when Jon McGlocklin hit shots from long range. "Bango" went on to be the name of the Bucks' mascot years later. Doucette quickly made those broadcasts his own and it didn't take long for his style to influence the culture the Bucks cultivated in the years to come.

It wasn't until the arrival of Flynn Robinson that the Bucks found the spark they had been looking for. Robinson had already burned the Bucks in the two games they had played against their biggest rival, the Bulls. He was a speedy guard and led the Bulls in scoring, despite coming off the bench. Robinson welcomed the change of scenery and more playing time. He later recalled the effect that coming to Milwaukee and playing under Costello had on his career years later: "Milwaukee fans were behind the team and Larry Costello helped me a lot. He gave me a lot of confidence. He was the first coach to give me tips on how to be a better player. If a coach has confidence in you, you're going to play better."[8] When the Bucks acquired Robinson from Chicago, they were 5–11 in the standings. Robinson's arrival didn't put a stop to the losing. Far from it, in fact. Milwaukee was becoming undone by long losing streaks that further entrenched them as the dregs of the Eastern Conference. When the Bucks were in town, attendance had started to slip too. The novelty of having pro basketball back in Milwaukee again appeared to be wearing off at the gates. Elsewhere, the Bucks struggled mightily on the road, not winning their first road game until their tenth attempt. However, the Bucks were doing everything they could to ensure that they would be near the front of the line in the Alcindor sweepstakes. Fishman was assured by Kennedy and the league that they'd have the opportunity to land basketball's next big thing. The entire Bucks operation had learned just how much maneuvering was going on in the league behind the scenes. It started with rumors that the league would finally allow NBA teams to trade their first-round draft picks. The thinking was that if Alcindor said he only wanted to play in New York or Los Angeles, the Knicks or Lakers could come to Milwaukee to force their hand and give them everything they had to land the big fella. Three-fourths of the league had to vote in favor of it—but no such luck was given to the Knicks and Lakers.[9]

The bigger battle was being played out just 336 miles northwest of Milwaukee at the ABA's headquarters in Minneapolis. The ABA was

6. Losing for Lew (The 1968–69 Season)   39

coming after the establishment and after everything the NBA had built. The ABA was blustering a lot and upping the ante to do everything it could to land the big man. Mikan outlined the plan. All 11 ABA teams were going to pool their money together to make Alcindor the league's cornerstone player. In return, he'd have carte blanche to pick any team he wanted to play for and then some. It was all done in the name of weakening the NBA and to get the ball rolling on merger talks. This was "Mr. Basketball" against the NBA, the very league he had helped create when the Basketball Association of America and the NBL merged nearly two decades earlier. Such threats did not faze Kennedy and the NBA. "The same forces were mobilized to get Wes Unseld and Elvin Hayes," Kennedy said. "We plan nothing special to get Alcindor. We believe he'll see the light and pick the NBA just as Hayes and Unseld did."[10]

The fight to land Alcindor was one that Pavalon was more than willing to take up. If Fishman was the civic-minded entrepreneur whose dedication helped Milwaukee get back in the big leagues, Pavalon took a different tack, becoming known as the mastermind behind the Bucks. Nothing about Pavalon's journey to becoming a self-made millionaire whose wealth helped bankroll the Bucks followed any traditional blueprints. Pavalon was born on the North Side of Chicago to Russian–Jewish immigrants who changed their name to Pavalon from Pavalonsky. When Wes was 10 years old, his father left the family of six after one too many arguments with Wes's mom, Esther. The Pavalons ran a tavern on Chicago's sprawling Devon Avenue in order to support the family and they lived above an ice cream parlor. As he grew older, Wes was largely unsupervised and left to his own devices, and the streets of Chicago acted as his playground. There was nothing that Pavalon wasn't willing to do. He stole bottles from his family's tavern and cashed them in to start a newspaper stand to make money. He excelled in playing parlay cards at nine years old. In a drive to sell sponsorships for an intramural softball team one summer, Pavalon and his friends collected 217 sponsors and pocketed all the money for a team that never took the field. When Pavalon wasn't running the streets of Chicago or drawing up a get-rich-quick scheme as a teenager, basketball was his favorite sport to play at Green Briar Park. Pavalon was big, tall and hunted for rebounds. But he was so clumsy and had such a poor shooting touch that he was instructed by his coach to not take a shot during games. His experience playing basketball at Green Briar Park served as a refuge for Pavalon and led him to go down the path he would eventually chart for himself.

Pavalon was in the 10th grade when he dropped out of Nicholas Senn High School. He enrolled at Wright Junior College and when he was forced to produce his high school diploma, he bought one for $50. "Fortunately, no one at the college ever checked. But I sweated a lot there," Pavalon later said.[11] At 18 years old, Pavalon saw a help wanted ad in a Chicago paper for a TV repair teacher. Fresh out of completing a TV repair course, he arranged for an interview. The school wanted an experienced teacher for their course. Claiming to be 24 years old, he told them he was the man for the job. When pressed that 24 was a little young, Pavalon said that his father, who was about to turn 50, looked only a couple of years older than him. Pavalon got the job and six months later, he was running the school. Eventually, he looked to Milwaukee to start his own business, Milwaukee School of Television Services, Inc. Pavalon never recalled why he chose Milwaukee over cities like St. Louis, Cincinnati, or Indianapolis, other than that it was inexpensive to live in Milwaukee. He was 22 years old and with his new bride, Adrienne, Pavalon came to the city in 1954 with $1,800 and a handful of television sets and rented out office space in Milwaukee's Brumder Building on North Second Street.

A few years later, Milwaukee School of Television Services turned into Career Academy. Pavalon set his sights on building an occupational training school for anyone who dedicated themselves to any field of work. He worked 16-hour days and preferred to work during the evening and overnight. He commuted from Highland Park to Milwaukee for more than a decade before eventually moving to the city. Throughout the 1960s, Career Academy exploded into an incredibly profitable business. Pavalon's fortune grew as the operation expanded into major cities around the country. At its peak, Career Academy operated 15 schools in 12 cities, offered 11 home-study courses and had 18,293 students enrolled who collectively paid upwards of $15 million.[12]

In 1967, Career Academy went public on the New York Stock Exchange, which further catapulted Pavalon to lavish success. His wealth attracted all sorts of attention. *Sports Illustrated* described Pavalon as thumpingly rich, and he lived larger and larger.[13] A private Lear jet, a 68-foot yacht named *Marlinsue* for Pavalon's three daughters, a $25,000 custom Rolls–Royce and a new NBA team were all at his disposal. Pavalon employed a personal limo driver because he was a notoriously bad driver himself. Pavalon's self-made success extended into his running of the Bucks because he was the money man. His fortune reportedly grew to over $50 million as Career Academy's stock soared on Wall Street.

The ABA were talking a big game more and more, but Pavalon was right there to trade back barbs. "It's a lot of garbage," Pavalon said of the ABA's boasting that they'd land Alcindor. "And just how do these people think they are going to outbid the whole state of Wisconsin? If all they can come up is $1 million, they had better save it to buy themselves a one-eyed

6. Losing for Lew (The 1968–69 Season) 41

5'6" center out of Humpty-Dump State."[14] Nothing was going to get in the way of Pavalon's pursuit of what he felt was the piece that would put everything together. The war was brewing and Alcindor stood at the center of the battle, a battle between establishment and counterculture. The ABA was getting increasingly desperate as the days drew closer and slung many arrows toward the NBA. They had missed out on the top draft picks in the previous two years and Mikan was not going to miss out on Alcindor. "For the first time, we're actually in good position for the draft," he said. "Before this, we bid a lot of money and were beaten. I don't choose to be beaten again…. This man is a very outstanding player, one of the most exciting players coming out of college in a long, long time. The directors, the trustees, the owners of the league feel he is very important so that whoever gets him has a responsibility to pay him. We agreed this man is valuable. So, the league will put up a fund to make sure he gets his money, regardless of what happens."[15] The ABA went further with its mudslinging and alleged that the NBA had already staged a secret coin flip to win the draft rights to Alcindor. The ABA called the NBA's integrity into question whenever possible. The whispers and rumors grew so loud that commissioner Kennedy had to respond and deny ever holding a secret coin flip. "This is the most recent ridiculous statement about an alleged premature draft of Lew Alcindor by an NBA team," he said. "There has been no meeting; there has been no announced meeting, and the rights to Alcindor do not belong to the Milwaukee Bucks or any other club. There will be no determination of Alcindor's draft status until such time as the last place teams in each division of the NBA participate in a flip of a coin in the 1969 college draft—once those last place teams have finally been determined."[16] This episode led to the NBA deciding to televise the coin flip live when the two last-place teams were officially locked in.

The war between the ABA and the NBA heated up as Alcindor neared turning pro, and the Bucks had a problem on their hands: they started to win. The Bucks had won two straight games on four separate occasions in the first 62 games of the season. Over 12 days in mid to late February, the Bucks rattled off a six-game winning streak, set aflame by a heat check from Robinson. Three straight 40-point games propelled Robinson and the Bucks to the win column, which included him hitting a 30-foot game-winning shot to put the Bucks up over the Pistons. It brought up an uncomfortable question over whether the Bucks were becoming too good to tank for Alcindor. Milwaukee continued to rack up consecutive wins even as Robinson cooled off, and suddenly the Bucks had shrunk the Pistons' lead over Milwaukee to 3.5 games in the standings. Costello notoriously paid no mind to the worries that the Bucks were winning their way out of winning Alcindor. "All I care about is winning. I couldn't care less about the standings. I can't go out on the floor for a game intending to lose it. I've got to get excited and go all out to win. It's the only way I know."[17]

What Robinson helped spark, though, was the growing acceptance of the Bucks through attendance figures. Almost immediately in response to the Bucks' longest winning streak that season—and what was the longest such streak by any expansion team by that point—capacity crowds were showing up at the arena. The Bucks enjoyed their first sellout in their sixth straight win, a 126–117 victory over the Bullets on February 27, 1969. The Bucks came back down to earth as the NBA calendar flipped to March. The threat of overtaking the Pistons and leaving behind the chance to win the draft rights for Alcindor lessened, calming anxious fans. But before they could officially clinch last place in the East, the Bucks had one more night to celebrate.

The last Bucks home game in their expansion season came on March 10, 1969, when they hosted the San Francisco Warriors. That Monday night also served as a way to mark the final chapter in Embry's NBA career. Milwaukee stood as the last stop in his playing journey. The months of deciding whether he would play for the Bucks and the anxieties of moving to a new city that was embroiled in social unrest washed away. After consulting with his wife, Embry found peace in knowing that Milwaukee was it. The captain was bowing out as injuries had slowed him down by the end of the season and he knew that he had a fallback as the director of Boston's Parks and Recreation department. With the Milwaukee Arena just short of another sellout with 10,281 fans packed in, Embry was honored by the Bucks. With McGlocklin leading his cohort of teammates, Embry received a box of cigars, a wristwatch, and a bronzed replica shoe that commemorated Embry's infamous shoe size. He wasn't the only Buck honored that night. Robinson was named the Most Outstanding Bucks Player of that season after 5,000 votes were cast in a poll conducted by the Metropolitan Milwaukee Association of Commerce. The Bucks' 123–106 loss to the Warriors was secondary on that night. What the night stood for was the season-long vindication of Milwaukee's second pro basketball team. They did not have any stars, nor were they playoff-bound. That original Bucks team set the table for an exciting future at the Arena by winning more games than anyone thought possible, finishing the year with a 27–55 record.

Milwaukee had been building toward something long before the Bucks came into existence. Fishman had endured the failures of trying to attract a professional franchise to Milwaukee for years before he connected with Pavalon and the NBA. That nasty pit in the stomach of all Milwaukeeans upon seeing the Braves leave Milwaukee had created an inferiority complex that the city wanted to overcome.

Multiple Bucks players from their expansion season line up for a photograph outside General Mitchell Airport in Milwaukee before a road trip. From left: Eddie Doucette, Guy Rodgers, Flynn Robinson, Sam Williams, Jon McGlocklin, Greg Smith, Don Smith, Wayne Embry, Len Chappell, Dick Cunningham, Rich Neimann, trainer Arnie Garber and head coach Larry Costello (Historic Photo Collection/Milwaukee Public Library).

On a much smaller scale, the Bucks fought that same inferiority complex. Fishman and Pavalon listened to the skeptics who yammered on about how basketball couldn't work in Milwaukee. They were reminded time and again that Kerner was run out of Milwaukee because the Hawks had floundered both on and off the court, that the Milwaukee Arena and Auditorium board deemed the Hawks to be too much of a risk to invest in when home shows were a much bigger moneymaker. Fishman and Pavalon faced the same obstacles that Kerner had faced in locking down dates at the Arena that weren't marquee nights and in an older facility that was the smallest in the NBA. None of that mattered by the end of the season. The Bucks finished their home slate in Milwaukee with 212,362 fans in attendance over 34 games. Their average attendance of 5,942 fans over all of their 40 home games ranked seventh out of the 14 teams in the NBA that year. Pavalon glowed at how many strides the Bucks had made within their community. "The acceptance of our team by the fans has been marvelous.

I've never been so thrilled with anything in my life," he said.[18] Days after their home finale, Fishman was honored with the first annual Milwaukee Sportsman of the Year award, sponsored by the Joseph Schlitz Brewing Company, and he was showered with praise by Klein, Maier and former NBA player and Milwaukee native Dolph Schayes. The Bucks' first season was winding down, but before it could officially wrap up, there was one more matter to attend to.

7

With the Flip of a Coin

Wednesday, March 19, 1969. A date forever etched in history before and after the flip of a coin. The time was set for 11 a.m. in the league's office in New York. A three-way phone line between New York, Milwaukee, and Phoenix connected all parties, while Kennedy would do the honors on live television. And here Milwaukee was, waiting for yet another miracle. The Bucks officially clinched last place in the East on March 17, 1969, after the Pistons beat the Suns that night. Phoenix's fate was sealed weeks before as they were very clearly the worst team in the West, and they had already gone so far as to run a poll in the Phoenix newspapers over whether to call heads or tails in the eventual coin flip. Milwaukee may have come late to the party, but it was decided that Pavalon would be entrusted to call heads or tails, should he have the chance.

Kennedy outlined how the operation would go down. He'd draw between two cards that were placed on his desk to determine which team would choose heads or tails. When Kennedy drew the card, it came up Phoenix. Exactly how the Bucks had wanted it, according to Fishman. "Fine, I thought. Let Phoenix call," he said. "The old gambler's adage is to never choose on an even bet. The house never makes a choice. It is always safer to let the other guy choose against himself."[1] Still, all the Bucks brass who were in attendance brought along some sort of good luck charm that day. For Erickson—a Protestant—that meant bringing a kibbutz medal that his wife had gotten on a trip to Israel. Pavalon—who was Jewish—came into the office wearing a St. Christopher medal that one of his good friends had given him, and he was ritualistically chain-smoking cigarettes. Fishman had put a Winston Churchill silver coin in his left shoe. The three men appeared on a dais before the Milwaukee press corps, who were there to capture what was already the biggest moment in the franchise's 14-month history. Kennedy spoke over the phone line: "The card says Phoenix. What is Phoenix's pleasure?" "Heads," Suns owner Richard Bloch called into the speaker, honoring the wishes of Suns fans who voted in favor of heads by 51.2 percent in the newspaper poll. Kennedy was holding a 1964 John F. Kennedy half-dollar coin that he had received from the late Robert F. Kennedy (no relation to the commissioner). He flipped it in the air, caught it in his right hand, and slapped it over to the back of his left hand. He lifted his right hand and revealed it: "The coin flip has come up ... tails." Bedlam erupted in Milwaukee. Pavalon whooped and leapt up from his seat to bear-hug Erickson. He didn't even notice that he had burned Erickson's ear with the cigarette that he had been smoking in the run-up to the flip. Nor did Erickson care, not after the Bucks had gotten to pick Lew Alcindor. Media members in attendance were openly celebrating that the next big ticket coming into the NBA might be coming to Milwaukee. "Any further questions from Milwaukee?" Kennedy then asked.[2] Erickson responded that he would be in contact with the commissioner in short order. As the television cameras kept filming, Kennedy continued flipping the coin in the air, and it kept coming up tails.

Pavalon was pressed on what he would have called going into the coin flip. He said that he would have called tails. But that day was not the biggest coin flip he had ever participated in, according to Pavalon. "Yes, I won a hot dog when I was on the streets of Chicago and that was important then. And a year ago, I bought a farm in northern Wisconsin. We were $25,000 apart on the price, so we flipped a coin—double or nothing, too," he beamed.[3] The Bucks had won the flip, but they were diplomatic, choosing not to talk about Alcindor that day. It was far easier to do that knowing that they had the first pick in the NBA draft. Phoenix, meanwhile, was forlorn. The faces of general manager Jerry Colangelo and head coach Johnny "Red" Kerr said as much after Kennedy called tails. Suns players such as Gail Goodrich questioned the integrity of having a coin flip for the first pick altogether. "I think it's an injustice that they had to flip a coin at all," Goodrich said. "We obviously have the worst team in the league, so we should have the first choice. That's the way it is in football and baseball, why not basketball?"[4] To add insult to injury, that wasn't the only victory the Bucks had over the Suns that day. Milwaukee earned its 25th victory of the season by beating the Suns, 117–110, in Phoenix.

This was everything the Bucks had been building toward. The one voice curiously absent from the proceedings was that of Alcindor himself. It made sense, as he was leading the Bruins, which were in search of a third consecutive title and on another run to the NCAA championship. He was certain to be the first man to land a million-dollar contract before ever playing a professional game. Two leagues were fighting over his services and the months had been building toward his decision, which was about to change the professional game forever. Terry Bledsoe of the *Milwaukee Journal* went down to Louisville, Kentucky, in search of the story that was about to change Milwaukee forever and sought comments from Alcindor

7. With the Flip of a Coin

himself. UCLA was camped out there for the Final Four of the 1969 NCAA Men's Tournament. But the team notoriously had a policy against athletes talking to reporters, and that policy was upheld by coach John Wooden. Being two wins away from another NCAA title meant no distractions were going to be tolerated. Instead of talking to Alcindor directly, Bledsoe awkwardly addressed a few questions to Wooden, who acted as an intermediary for Alcindor and relayed his responses through the hotel telephone. The questions and answers went as follows:

> **BLEDSOE:** "What is [Alcindor's] reaction to Milwaukee's winning the flip to get the first draft choice?"
> **WOODEN:** "He says he doesn't know what to think about it."
> **BLEDSOE:** "How does he feel about the possibility of playing in Milwaukee?"
> **WOODEN:** "He says he has never been to Milwaukee, so he can't have feelings about it one way or the other."[5]

UCLA eked by Drake in an 85–82 victory and cut the nets down after a 92–72 victory over Purdue. Finishing with 37 points and 20 rebounds, Alcindor finished his time at UCLA with three titles, and an 88–2 record.

The Bucks had conquered the Suns and now it was time for them to conquer the ABA. No more jabs would be thrown from either side. Too much was at stake. It was put up or shut up time, and it came down to the man whose future would be decided one way or another. The mystique around Alcindor already existed back when he was a teenager starring for Power Memorial. So did the winning. He was called "The Tower from Power" and appeared on *The Ed Sullivan Show* after being named an All-American as a high school sophomore. He was friends with Wilt Chamberlain and saw him whenever Chamberlain was in New York playing against the Knicks. As schools and universities recruited and sought Alcindor, the calls and inquiries were so incessant that his parents made sure their phone number was unlisted.

There was a distance between the public and Alcindor well before he stepped onto UCLA's campus. He commanded intense media attention, and the shield that was in place between the media and Bruins players only heightened it. Once he was set to leave UCLA, Alcindor could no longer hide himself away. He'd have to stand firm on the decisions that would define the rest of his life.

He'd first experienced that when he boycotted the 1968 Olympic Games. The public met Alcindor's decision with hostility, seeing him as the next of the great Black athletes who disrespected the country by choosing not to represent it on an international stage. What they didn't understand was that Alcindor elected not to suit up for the Olympic team because of everything he had experienced and observed growing up in

Harlem. "Nothing in my whole life caused as unpleasant a commotion as the storm I got into over the Olympic boycott," he wrote in 1969. "My decision not to play was, in the end, one I made for myself; I felt I was right, I still feel I was right, and in the same circumstances I would do the same thing again."[6] Alcindor was shaped by racial incidents that he witnessed and experienced throughout his life. It was when he was sent to an all-Black boarding school right outside of Philadelphia as a fourth grader that he first realized who he was, and the significance of his skin color. "I never felt like I was Black until I was made to," he said.[7] He later returned to New York for schooling, but his parents knew that something had changed in Alcindor. His innocence was lost and he drove inward to find himself, especially as he grew in the public eye. His coach at Power Memorial, Jack Donohue, was once something of a father figure to Alcindor. That image shattered when Donohue, dressing down his players during halftime in a rare game that Power was losing, turned to Alcindor and called him the N-word. Donohue sought to rile up his players, but he almost lost Alcindor, who told his parents he wanted to leave the school immediately. He chose to stay, but he would never look at Donohue the same way again.

Alcindor's growing star and excellence on the high school court brought wins. Lots of them. He later recalled that after going undefeated in his sophomore year at Power and winning a state championship, his feelings toward basketball were changing: "Losing was unthinkable, and the game stopped being fun."[8]

Alcindor was no ordinary teenager—that much was clear. He soon learned, if he hadn't already, that everyone wanted a piece of him—whether it was a request for an autograph, a college assistant coach looking to recruit him, or even two professional sports leagues pulling out all the stops to woo him. This is the world that Alcindor had chosen, the road he traveled down. Seeking inner peace, he set out on a spiritual journey that would influence his decision-making for the rest of his life. The decision to either play for the Bucks in the NBA or the Nets in the ABA came with specific ground rules set by Alcindor himself. He was not looking for a long, drawn-out negotiation and wanted each side to submit one blind bid for his services. The Bucks were the first to meet with Alcindor at a hotel in midtown New York, with John Erickson, Bucks president Ray Patterson and Wesley Pavalon taking the lead. Lew was accompanied by his father and his two advisors—UCLA alumni Sam Gilbert and Ralph Shapiro—in a meeting that spanned four hours. It was over the course of that meeting that Pavalon connected with Alcindor on a human level and created a lifelong bond. "You're a human being with a birth certificate, and you can go anywhere you choose—anywhere that will make you happy," Pavalon said at one point in the meeting. "And you should be happy. But give us a chance to make you happy in Milwaukee. I believe in someone's happiness."⁹

The next day, as the Bucks made it official by announcing they'd be taking Alcindor with the first overall pick in the 1969 NBA draft, Alcindor and his advisors met with George Mikan and Arthur Brown, the owner of the Nets. Mikan and Brown offered a five-year contract, but with a salary that was substantially lower than the Bucks and NBA had offered. Alcindor and his advisors were surprised and asked whether that was Brown and Mikan's final offer. Mikan insisted on it and Alcindor promptly informed the Nets, the ABA and the NBA commissioner that he'd be playing in Milwaukee. "That morning, I had been wealthy and unconcerned, back in New York with the city spread before me and no budget or curfew to keep me off its streets," he later wrote. "By afternoon, I had been uprooted. I loved New York, but I would have to pass up a great deal of money to live there. Basketball was a business, that fact brought home to me my first day on the job. My first professional compromise: I chose Milwaukee."¹⁰ It didn't take long for Alcindor's decision to travel throughout the hotel. Other ABA owners reached Shapiro and Gilbert and upped the ante on the league's offer to the big fella, despite Alcindor's insistence that he receive a single bid from each party. The Nets and the ABA threw in everything, including the kitchen sink. They offered a five-year, $3.2 million contract that included annuity payments until Alcindor was 41 years old, 10 percent of the ABA's proposed TV contract and a 5 percent ownership stake in the Nets.

It wasn't as if Alcindor hadn't made it known that he'd rather play closer to home. Ultimately, that didn't matter to him, as he later recalled. "I was all tied up with respect and conviction and fairness. My religion taught me to abhor hypocrisy and right off the bat, I was faced with the choice between being where I wanted through double-dealing on the one hand and beginning a career honorably two thousand miles from nowhere on the other. I was pissed off. The Nets had the inside track and had blown it. I signed with Milwaukee."¹¹ News of Alcindor's decision to join the Bucks hit newsstands on March 29, 1969, which signified another win for the young franchise. The ABA didn't stop its pursuit of Alcindor and promptly filed an antitrust suit against the NBA, alleging that the NBA and its clubs had pooled money to ensure they'd land Alcindor—the very strategy the ABA had used in its efforts to land Alcindor. Upon receiving the UPI College Basketball Player of the Year award in Atlanta, Alcindor explained his decision to go to Milwaukee in front of the press. "I had to weigh two decisions, the ABA and the NBA, and the NBA seemed most solid and sound…. With all things being equal, it would have been easier playing in New York. It would have been different if the ABA had a better offer, but things not being the same, I went to the NBA... It was my decision and nobody else's not to get into a bidding war because it degrades the people involved. It would have made me feel like a flesh peddler, and I'm not that."[12]

After all of their bluster, the ABA and Mikan had squandered their biggest opportunity to be equal to, if not greater than, the NBA. Alcindor agreed to a five-year contract with the Bucks that was worth up to $1.4 million. Incentives included a signing bonus, annuities and more. Meanwhile, in a press conference that was thrown together quickly at the ABA's headquarters, Mikan was defiant and insisted that negotiations were open with Alcindor. At one point, the unshaven Mikan brandished a $1 million cashier's check like he was the head of Publishers Clearing House. He continued to insist that the ABA wasn't in a fair fight against the NBA and the Bucks. "Alcindor doesn't want to play in Milwaukee," he said. "He wants to play in New York. I'm not a good loser and never was. I want to tell you this. We're in business. We're damned mad. All we want to do is talk to the talent."[13] The Bucks headed west to grab Alcindor's signature and make his historic deal final on Wednesday, April 2, 1969. Putting pen to paper during a press conference held at a Hilton hotel in Beverly Hills, Alcindor discussed how he had never been to Milwaukee before but was eager to win and knew that his new head coach, Larry Costello, wanted to win too. Bucks officials raved about Alcindor's integrity in the discussions that had brought him to Milwaukee. It was Pavalon who said best what all this might mean for the city moving forward: "It's a dream come true—a beginning of a whole new era of Milwaukee sports. You know that coin flip with Phoenix for first choice was based strictly on luck. But it was poetic justice that we won, because we had a better record, better attendance and more fan support. We deserved it."[14]

It was a landmark moment for the Bucks, one that had been 15 months in the making. But for Alcindor, the inevitable had come to pass. He was set to make more money than he had ever made in his life. Pressure was increasing on his broad shoulders. Life in a new city would come with new experiences and a whole new set of challenges, more than he could have imagined. The ABA, meanwhile, had declared an all-out war on the NBA. Mikan lost the complete confidence of his ABA owners, and "Mr. Basketball" would soon be out of a job.

8

Alcindor Arrives (The 1969–70 Season)

From the moment he chose to sign with the Bucks, Alcindor divorced himself from his desires about how he wished for his professional career to go. In his mind, he had made a professional compromise, but a lucrative one at that. It was still one that was decided by the flip of a coin, though. He was a rich man and was heading to a city that was completely foreign to him and to a team that only had a losing year to its name. All that Alcindor knew of Milwaukee before he signed with the Bucks was that the Braves had won the 1957 World Series over his Dodgers' foe, the Yankees. Otherwise, he had no feeling toward the city that he was about to call home. Meanwhile, the Bucks had landed the face of their franchise, the very one they had dreamt of before they even entered the NBA. They invested heavily in his success, and the city had a superstar to rally around. Whether he would rally around them, well, time would tell. The same could not be said for the Bucks faithful, who exploded with excitement when it was made clear that Alcindor was en route to Milwaukee, of all places. The impact of Alcindor choosing Milwaukee was first seen in season ticket sales. The Bucks received more than 6,000 season ticket applications in the wake of his arrival. All previous Bucks season ticket holders had renewed their tickets in light of the news that Lew was coming to town. Everyone wanted a piece of Alcindor in light of his landmark decision. In some ways, the Bucks were just along for the ride. There were requests from upwards of 24 cities—including some as far as Mexico City—to have the Bucks hold an exhibition game there, just so fans could watch Alcindor. Bucks stock was soaring and even Alcindor emerged as a shareholder, along with other Bucks players, coaches and officials.

Alcindor made his first visit and introduced himself to Milwaukee on April 14, 1969, before nearly a hundred reporters in a packed conference room at the Pfister Hotel. The night before, he had spent hours in the hospital after injuring his right knee while trying to remove a corn on his foot.

As he towered over the podium, Alcindor let loose on a number of topics. He fired back against the NCAA and its anti-dunking rule, which came into effect after his sophomore season with the Bruins. He was no longer tied to an organization that clearly held him back and was looking forward to playing the game how it was supposed to be played. "It's very bad when you are legislated against. I guess the NCAA's the only organization that legislates against its attractions," he said.[1] The ABA was another target that came into Alcindor's crosshairs. Days after it countered its original offer, Alcindor said that he only heard about the $3.25 million offer from the ABA after reading about it in the newspaper. He conceded that New York was where he wanted to play, but said that the offer he had received from the Bucks and the NBA was easily the best he got. When asked whether he thought the ABA had demeaned itself with how poorly it conducted negotiations, Alcindor didn't hide what he felt about the league. "Yeah, I think they looked kind of bad," he said.[2] Now that he was financially stable, Alcindor sought to increase his involvement in social change. He had pushed for people of color to get better work and housing opportunities and hoped to do so in Milwaukee. "I am interested in the whole uplifting of the black community," he said. "There has to be some method of creating an upward spiral. The main thing is to upgrade the housing and education of the black people so that they have a better chance to help themselves."[3] At the end of the hour-long press conference, a cake was wheeled into the room to celebrate Alcindor's 22nd birthday, which was two days away. All the Bucks officials commemorated what was a great day for the franchise. It was only a year before that they were all in the same room to announce the hirings of Costello and Erickson. Now, Milwaukee officially added its newest attraction and Bucks mania was starting to set in, with Alcindor at the center of everything.

The Bucks had answered the big questions. They had secured their transformational player. Now it was time to fill out their growing roster and add more players to complement their superstar. They had hit it out of the park in the expansion draft and the college draft the year before. The later rounds of the 1969 NBA draft were no different. With the 45th overall pick, which was in the fourth round of the draft, the Bucks plucked a skinny forward from Norfolk State by the name of Bob Dandridge. Three schools had offered Dandridge a scholarship going into college, all of them in his home state of Virginia. He decided on Division II Norfolk State, a Historically Black College and University. Dandridge was incredibly prolific for the Spartans. He averaged a double-double in his sophomore, junior and senior seasons. As a senior, he scored 32.3 points per game and hauled in 17 rebounds per game. He often played out of position, as he slotted in as the team's starting center with their regular center getting drafted

8. Alcindor Arrives (The 1969–70 Season)

into the army. All of that should have gotten Dandridge on the NBA's and ABA's radar. Which he was, but not as much as one would think. In those days in the NBA, there was a stigma toward scouting Black players who were coming out of predominantly Black schools. They were often labeled by NBA decision makers as not being well-rounded. Dandridge did everything to buck those concerns and while he was a generous 185 pounds, his dependability, speed and IQ made him the steal the Bucks were looking for in the draft.

The first indication of how life had changed for Alcindor now that he had entered the pro ranks came over the course of the summer. He earned his history degree at UCLA, but made headlines for punching and breaking the jaw of an ABA player—Dennis Grey—during a pickup game in Los Angeles. Grey promptly sued Alcindor, the Bucks and the NBA for $750,000 in damages. The matter was later settled out of court. It was not exactly the rosiest backdrop for Alcindor as he made his way into rookie camp with the Bucks. Still, it made no difference in how ready he looked for the pro game in his first round of practices with the Bucks under Costello. Alcindor made a concerted effort to add more strength amid concerns that he was far too skinny to go up against the big, brutish centers in the NBA. He began lifting weights, but wanted to keep his mobility intact. He even sprouted another inch while in rookie and training camp. In a TV special that focused on his first experiences of professional life, Alcindor was asked by Eddie Doucette about the weight of expectations he carried and whether Bucks fans might be expecting too much of him in his rookie year. "Everyone realizes that this is the NBA and people realize this is the best competition—the toughest league and the toughest division of that league," he said. "So I don't think that too many people will be disappointed if we don't win every game."[4]

The centerpiece of that year's rookie camp was an intrasquad scrimmage on Sunday, June 22, 1969, at 8 p.m. in the Milwaukee Arena. It was the first glimpse of Alcindor in a Bucks uniform, and some fans were so eager to see his debut that they waited outside the Arena before the doors opened at 6 p.m. Tickets were sold on a first-come, first-served basis for $2 apiece. Before a sold-out crowd of 10,482 Bucks fans, Alcindor scored 35 points, grabbed 23 rebounds and had eight blocks to lead his side to a 125–118 win. Alcindor captivated the Milwaukee crowd long before the jump ball. He received a 40-second standing ovation when he was introduced by the PA announcer. He was asked after the scrimmage whether he had received a standing ovation before. "Yes, but not at an exhibition game," he chuckled.[5] The Bucks' prized rookie already had all of their fans feeling like they were walking on the moon weeks before Neil Armstrong became the first person to do so during the Apollo 11 mission.

The next rite of passage for Alcindor that summer came in August when he took part in the annual Maurice Stokes Memorial Basketball Game. The game was first organized in 1959 by Royals forward and Stokes's caretaker, Jack Twyman, in honor of his former teammate. Stokes had suffered a debilitating and harrowing brain injury that ended his promising NBA career with the Cincinnati Royals. Every year, the game was held at Kutsher's Hotel and Country Club in the Catskill Mountains and the event helped raise money to care for Stokes. The game brought together the league's biggest and best stars, and Alcindor was the next in line to take part in the hallowed tradition. It was his first time playing alongside Oscar Robertson. It was also his first time going up against Wilt Chamberlain, and he won the approval of his boyhood idol and contemporary. Alcindor was readying himself for the next step in his career and his journey. By the end of the summer, he felt confident and was sure that he was going to make it in the pros. Whether he was going to be able to make it in Milwaukee, that was another story.

The buzz and expectations surrounding the start of the Bucks' 1969–70 season reached fever pitch as they opened training camp at Milton College on September 18, 1969. They were already bracing for sellouts and were surpassing the attendance figures they set in their expansion season. In the Bucks' office, Erickson was eyeing a top-four finish in a crowded Eastern Conference that he expected to be a tight race. Elsewhere, the sky was the limit for what basketball observers thought of the new Alcindor-led Bucks. From *Sports Illustrated*'s season preview of the 1969–70 NBA season:

> Why waste words? Lew Alcindor can take Milwaukee from the cellar to the championship of the world.... Alcindor's value to Milwaukee is almost beyond reckoning. As he did at UCLA, he makes every man on his team a more effective player, not only through inspiration, but because his presence preoccupies rivals. He is—in no particular order—quick, agile, huge, smart, a good shooter, a team player, a winner. No, he is not as strong as Wilt Chamberlain, Nate Thurmond and some other centers—and he also cannot carry a tune as well as Mahalia Jackson or ride a horse like Braulio Baeza. But he comes as close as one man can to dominating a game played by 10 men.[6]

As expected, Alcindor was at the center position, where the Bucks could maximize their newfound potential. Costello expertly designed the team's offense to run though Lew by getting him touches down low in the post. Defensively, Alcindor would be key in protecting the rim, cleaning up on the boards and throwing laser outlet passes to get the Bucks running in the open floor. Alcindor's introduction to the NBA, though, was not the start that anyone expected he'd have. Of the Bucks' nine preseason games, Alcindor missed two due to a badly sprained ankle, fouled out in one and

8. Alcindor Arrives (The 1969–70 Season)

Team photo of 1969–70 Milwaukee Bucks taken during training camp. That season was Lew Alcindor's first year in Milwaukee and his presence was the catalyst behind the franchise's meteoric rise (Historic Photo Collection/Milwaukee Public Library).

was roughed up by opposing big men looking to send him a clear message that this wasn't college anymore. The Bucks went 5–4 in their preseason, but the excitement over the start of the regular season didn't dull one bit.

The NBA and ABC were equally invested in Alcindor's pro debut when the Bucks took on the Pistons on October 18, 1969. While ABC usually started its "Game of the Week" coverage on Christmas Day, the anticipation over the greatest men's college player making his NBA debut was too big to ignore, even in the face of college football dominating mainstream sports coverage during that time of the year. Alcindor's presence on the Bucks was the biggest reason why the team went from having zero games on national TV during their first season to having six in their second year. Alcindor didn't disappoint in front of a modest season-opening crowd of 7,782 fans as he helped lead the Bucks to a 119–110 victory over the Pistons that Saturday afternoon. He scored 29 points, grabbed 12 rebounds and dished out six assists over the 48 minutes of action. He still wasn't satisfied with his performance, however. Alcindor's perfectionism would inspire him to greater heights in the days, weeks, months and years to come. That night, at a dinner party hosted by Pavalon, Kennedy presented Pavalon with the John F. Kennedy half-dollar coin that he had flipped that led to Alcindor coming to Milwaukee.

Adjusting to the pro game was a challenge in itself for Alcindor. But that was just the tip of the iceberg. Alcindor was the center of attention, whether he wanted to be or not. He'd come to Milwaukee—and the 13 other cities he traveled to—and faced the same litany of questions wherever he went. All aspects of his life were fodder for the media and it was very clear that he was more comfortable speaking his truth in his own words, as he did for *Sports Illustrated* in the summer when he became a professional and graduated from UCLA. He was a constant subject of intrigue and attention from the Milwaukee press corps, but he didn't reciprocate those feelings. He increasingly had little interest in giving out money quotes or anything beyond four- to five-word answers. Word traveled fast that Alcindor was a tough interview, and he didn't hide his disdain for the routine of hearing the same questions over and over again while traveling from city to city.

Alcindor's uneasiness with the press certainly stemmed from the reaction to his boycott of the Olympic games in Mexico City and his decision not to represent his country. He was affected by the racial injustices that rocked the country throughout the Sixties, and it was specifically the bombing that killed four school-aged Black girls at the 16th Street Baptist Church in Birmingham, Alabama, on September 15, 1963, that lit a fire inside him. Not even a year later, while he was writing for the Harlem Youth Action Project newspaper before becoming a senior, Alcindor witnessed his neighborhood set ablaze by a riot that lasted nearly a week. A white off-duty policeman had shot 15-year-old high school student James Powell, who was unarmed. Alcindor saw the collateral damage unfold from the heinous act of one police officer. His racial awakening continued as the decade went on, more blood was shed and acts done in the name of white supremacy threatened to tear apart the country. For a person of his celebrity and stature, Alcindor's decision to forgo the Olympics was in line with the athletes-turned-activists who emerged over that decade. Alcindor sought inspiration from the likes of Bill Russell and Muhammad Ali, and he was the youngest among the 11 athletes at the legendary Cleveland Summit on June 4, 1967, supporting Ali's refusal to be drafted into the U.S. Army to fight in the Vietnam War. Alcindor was more than willing to stand on unpopular decisions as society expected him to fall in line. That didn't faze someone like Alcindor, who had been socially conscious from such an early age.

In reality, what Alcindor was greatly interested in and what he relentlessly pursued was spiritual enlightenment in the face of a tumultuous decade and as his superstardom grew on the court. He had gone to Catholic schools all of his teenage life, but when he arrived at UCLA's campus he stopped going to mass. During his freshman year, Alcindor read *The Autobiography of Malcolm X*. X had been assassinated months before, and that sent Alcindor down a path of exploring Islam. He delved further and

8. Alcindor Arrives (The 1969–70 Season)

further in Islamic teachings and regularly read the Quran as his time with the Bruins came to an end. The more he read and the more he discovered, he shed the inherent anger he held for all white people and instead sought greater equality. As he wrote in *Sports Illustrated*,

> The genuine Muslim bears witness that there is one God, that His name is Allah, and that all men—black and white—are brothers. There is no room in Islam for racial hatred of any sort, and I had come to realize that this was exactly the way I felt in my heart. I had worked past the age of rage. I could still become angered at individual acts of hostility and at the whole pattern of racial hostility. But I could no longer believe that the white man was inherently evil and cruel and black men inherently superior, as some of the other blacks are teaching nowadays. That is just the flip side of the old racism. I realized that black was neither best nor worst; it just was. I could no longer hate anybody. I could no longer afford to be a racist. If racism messed up a lot of people who had to take it, then it must also mess up those who had to dish it out. I did not want to be that kind of narrow man.[7]

When he was supposed to be playing in the Olympics down in Mexico City, Alcindor took his Shahada—his profession of Islamic faith—at a New York mosque on 125th Street. He recognized himself as Sunni Muslim, just as Malcolm X had grown to become. He was given the name of "Kareem Abdul-Jabbar" by his spiritual teacher, Hamaas Abdul Khaalis. This new name meant "noble and generous," "servant" and "powerful." It turned out that Khaalis had known Alcindor's father through the jazz outfit that both men played in during the 1950s before Khaalis's religious transformation. Initially, Alcindor chose not to make a big deal over whether his closest friends and his teammates referred to him by his new name. "I'm not going to make any issue out of my new name," he wrote in his *Sports Illustrated* article. "It's somewhat important to me whether you call me Lew Alcindor or Kareem, but I'm not going to blow my top if somebody does call me Lew Alcindor. It's a nice name: I like the sound of it; I admire other people who have borne that name. Call me Kareem; call me Lew. I'm not going to get uptight about it."[8]

Just as he did with basketball, Alcindor fully immersed himself in his new faith. He was searching for something and for some order in his life. It helped him reexamine himself, his thoughts on religion, on racial relations and society at large. By the time he arrived in Milwaukee, he was far down the path of self-discovery and he was living dual lives. In the world of basketball, the great amount of success he had already attained before he stepped foot in the NBA had made it no longer fun to him. Now, he was the golden boy of a growing NBA and Milwaukee was embracing him as one of its own, just as it had done when the Braves came to town years earlier. A door to a new world had opened before Alcindor. It maintained him and kept him balanced within his new surroundings. His faith made him despise hypocrisy and he carried himself as a man of honor. Honoring his word was the reason why he chose Milwaukee in the first place. Being the purist that he was, he viewed anyone who wasn't Muslim as a disbeliever, not to be trusted or even given the time of day.

There was another door that he was trying to keep shut both figuratively and literally. None of the customs and hallmarks that made Milwaukee famous were of interest to Alcindor, due to both his faith and his interests. After growing up in New York and going to college in Southern California, he didn't view Milwaukee as a real city. There were few jazz clubs for him to frequent and he certainly wasn't about to go to a bar to be mobbed by fans and drinkers. His religion didn't allow him to drink the beer that was brewed all across the city, nor did he have any urge to do so. Whenever he ventured out of his Juneau Village apartment—which had to have the door frames raised to nine feet to accommodate his stature—or traveled with the Bucks from city to city, Alcindor was easy to spot. For every admirer of his, there were many who would just gawk at the sight of his towering figure. He didn't have any tolerance for either. Entertaining anyone who approached him and wanted his autograph simply because of his fame was out of the question.

Serious culture shock settled in over his first few months in Milwaukee. In his home away from home, Alcindor braced himself for life in Milwaukee, just like anticipating the cold bite that fills the air when winter finally arrives. He was living on his own and his new religion was not just keeping him grounded, it was all that was sustaining him as he acclimated to his new environment and life in the NBA. He greatly valued his privacy and it didn't take long for him to forgo taking part in public speaking engagements or ceremonies celebrating him, the Bucks or the city of Milwaukee. The spotlight was shining more brightly on Alcindor. While he readily admitted that he didn't feel the pressure of living up to being the defining face of the NBA or society as a whole, Pavalon felt differently. "He's got such an image to live up to," he said of Alcindor's superstar status.[9] His every move, word and action were judged in the court of public opinion and by adoring fans. It shouldn't come as a surprise that the greatest shield that could be put up around Alcindor came from within, even as well-wishers came up to him in the rare times he was out in public. He told the *Milwaukee Journal*, "I like publicity. But it's as much of a burden than it is a blessing."[10] He became resigned to his new life and never thought that he'd be traded from Milwaukee.[11] The two things holding Alcindor together were his growing faith and being on the court, where he could focus on the task at hand. It wasn't long before the Bucks started winning. And winning big.

8. Alcindor Arrives (The 1969–70 Season)

If the Bucks learned how to crawl before Lew arrived in Milwaukee, he certainly helped them run far away from the competition. Success didn't come so easily to the Bucks at the start of the 1969–70 season. They were treading water and straddling the .500 line through the first month or so. Costello was tinkering and cycling through different starting lineups in search of the winning formula that could help elevate the team. Alcindor was the main attraction and he was drawing fans from all over. Not just in Milwaukee at the Arena, but on the road—especially when the Bucks made their trips to Madison Square Garden. The questions that Alcindor faced in his transition from the college game to the pros dissipated slowly. His skills did not translate instantly. It took seven games for him to have a 40-point game. But what he wasn't prepared for was the added toughness and physicality that was prevalent in the NBA in those days. Alcindor fouled out five times in his first nine games as a pro, and he felt every elbow that landed in his midsection as NBA veterans gave him their own welcome to the league. It all culminated in a November 21, 1969, game against the Seattle SuperSonics. The Bucks wound up winning 117–115, but not before Alcindor fouled out and was showered with boos from the crowd of 12,920 fans at the Seattle Coliseum. With 14 seconds left in regulation and the Bucks up two, Alcindor earned his sixth foul against his old friend and UCLA teammate Lucius Allen, who was in the act of shooting. As the jeers rained down on him, Alcindor left for the locker room and

Kareem Abdul-Jabbar preparing to take a free throw shot during a game. While it didn't take long for him to adjust to the NBA, living in Milwaukee brought a number of personal challenges. From the Bucks' *1971–72 Press, Radio and Television Guide* (Milwaukee County Historical Society).

spit on the floor in frustration. When a teenager taunted him as he made that walk back, Lew pushed the boy out of the way. Alcindor's anger could be his greatest fuel or undo him in such moments. He carried slights quite close to the vest and it took years for him to fully harness and rein in that great fury of his as a competitor.

Alcindor's presence on the court wasn't enough to guarantee success for the Bucks as they made their way through the season. This was still a young team, with an average age of 25 years. They had 32 NBA seasons of service under their belt, but Hall of Fame guard Guy Rodgers alone accounted for one-third of that time. However, you could tell that while the Bucks were still trying to find their sea legs as they fell to .500 through the first 20 games of the season, they were on the verge of a breakthrough. They entered the month of December with a 14–11 record. By the start of 1970, they improved to 26–14 and enjoyed a seven-game winning streak for two weeks up until Christmas. That was good enough to climb into second place in the East and they never let go of that spot. It took 82 games for the Bucks to win 27 games during their expansion season. It took them 41 games to reach that mark for the 1969–70 season.

Their 27th win was against the Knicks, who were cruising ahead toward the Eastern Conference title. That cathartic 118–105 victory was the first time the Bucks beat New York and their first win against them in five tries during that season. It certainly helped that it was nationally televised too. Unsurprisingly, Alcindor played a featured role in the victory as he put up his second 40-point game of the season. He finished with 41 points on 29 shots, 16 rebounds and three assists. The normally reserved Alcindor didn't hide how much he enjoyed beating his boyhood basketball idols. As the game neared its end and the Bucks cemented a comfortable victory over the league's best, he leapt triumphantly and raised both fists in the air, as if he just struck out the final batter in Game 7 of the World Series. It was the best game of his pro career to date and his emotions were high as he relished taking down the Knicks. "I've been wanting to beat them for a long time, especially after that one point defeat there the last time. The game meant a lot to me. It had to. A lot of friends of mine go to Madison Square Garden and root for the Knicks, but cheer for me. Now they're in a bit of a quandary."[12] No, the Bucks didn't catch up to the Knicks. Not by a long shot. New York had quickly asserted themselves as the league's best team from opening night and held what was then the longest winning streak in NBA history, with 18 consecutive victories. But the Bucks were getting used to the idea of seeing the Knicks much more often very soon. That win over the Knicks intensified the bad case of Bucks fever that was spreading all over Milwaukee. The Bucks were regularly playing to capacity crowds at the Arena. Everyone wanted to see Alcindor play in the flesh, and fans were becoming attached to a team that was clearly on the rise. This was a team destined for the playoffs. Which begged the question: Just where were the Bucks going to be playing their home playoff dates?

The Milwaukee Arena was booked when that year's playoffs were set to begin. The annual *Milwaukee Sentinel*-sponsored Sports and Home Show took precedence instead. With the Bucks on a winning streak and rising to the top of the division, it was very clear that any home playoff games had to be held outside of Milwaukee—with Madison the most likely choice. Being faced with such a predicament was normally a death knell for NBA franchises in those times. This same set of circumstances had forced Kerner to move the Hawks from Milwaukee to St. Louis. It'd be one thing for a team to just manage to squeeze into the playoffs and have to make arrangements on the fly to find a venue for a home playoff game. But the Bucks were contending for that year's title. The fact that they'd have to play their home playoff games outside of their home city had the makings of a true disaster in the sports business.

The Bucks' brain trust had foreseen this kind of jam when they were awarded the franchise. They played in the league's smallest arena, and Pavalon led the charge for a new arena that could give them the home dates they wanted rather than having to battle with the Arena and Auditorium board. "I plan to devote every fiber of energy in my body to getting a new arena for this city," Pavalon had declared when the Bucks originally appointed Costello and Erickson, more than two months after the birth of the franchise. "If they force us, we will do it privately."[13] When it was reported during the summer of 1968 that Milwaukee Brewers Baseball Club, Inc., had been promised a yearly $1 rental fee for Milwaukee County Stadium if and when it was able to secure an MLB franchise again, Pavalon was irate. "I'm tired of promises given to ghosts. Where is my $1 a year offer? Where the hell is my $1 a year offer?" he exclaimed during a press conference on June 21, after securing the rights to an international boxing franchise.[14] The push to build a new sports arena always lurked beneath the surface, and a study by Milwaukee County that went by the name of the Dineen Report recommended the construction of a new sports-convention center in downtown Milwaukee.[15] There were even proposals to build a so-called "Pladium" near County Stadium by the time the Bucks were making their run in their second season. The Bucks wanted preferential treatment and top priority for home games to make their operation even more successful than it had already been. There's no question that gaining Alcindor only increased their desire to play in a new, state-of-the-art facility rather than the oldest home arena in the league. Per the NBA commissioner, the league was under the assumption that the Bucks would only play in Milwaukee Arena for one season before building another facility. "It is, for one season," Kennedy said in 1968 when confirming that the Arena would be the Bucks' home. "But one of the reasons we moved into Milwaukee is the strong possibility a new arena will be constructed here."[16]

The NBA didn't hold them to that understanding, but the Bucks organization was more than willing to construct a new facility with the city and the county. Whether they were founded or not, rumors of the Bucks' relocation percolated and bubbled over as the fight dragged out in public, in Common Council sessions and market studies. The situation of not being able to play playoff games in their home arena only heightened concerns and forced comment from Bucks president Ray Patterson. "The fans have a right to know that somebody is looking out for their best interests to keep the Bucks in Milwaukee. Everyone in the organization is dedicated to finding ways to help the Bucks stay.... I hope that within five years, the officials of Milwaukee will recognize this problem. There is no question in my mind that if someone sat down and talked about this, they could justify a new building."[17] Leave it to the public to show which side they stood on. Bucks fans and season ticket holders filed a petition as threats of relocation jockeyed between the organization and local government over the second half of the season. Some even picketed before games. By the final few weeks of the season, 35,411 signatures were gathered, adding more urgency to the matter. This was just the start of Bucks fans' effort to see their team play where they belonged—Milwaukee.

The matter of building a new arena wasn't going to be solved overnight, but calls were rising to tend to the question of home playoff dates. For the Bucks to play in Madison required both the approval of the University of Wisconsin and the Big Ten Conference, and it probably helped to have someone like Erickson in their corner for that. Still, a Milwaukee county supervisor named Gerard B. Skibinski took it upon himself to offer a solution to the Bucks' problems. For Milwaukee's Parks and Recreation Committee, Skibinski drew up a proposal that would have the Bucks play their home playoff games in County Stadium. How could Skibinski justify the Bucks playing basketball in an outdoor stadium in late March and early April given the Wisconsin climate? The linchpin to his plan was to not just build a portable court over the vacant baseball field, but to build a bubble-like dome that would enclose the court to keep players, coaches and officials warm during the game. That would mean the Bucks fans in attendance would be sitting on ice cold, steel bleachers and braving the elements. Skibinski reasoned, though, that if Packers fans were willing to do that when Green Bay played its home games as late as December, Bucks fans could do the same. The project was estimated to cost $100,000, and, whether due to the cost or the feasibility of the project, Skibinski had

8. Alcindor Arrives (The 1969–70 Season)

reservations about the bill passing, especially in short order. "I doubt if I can sell them [the county Parks and Recreation Committee] on the idea. I guess it takes a little too much imagination," he reasoned.[18] Skibinski had been through this before. In fact, this was the third time he introduced a bill to enclose County Stadium and make it a year-round venue rather than have it continue to stand vacant, save for the handful of games that the Chicago White Sox had played in Milwaukee in both 1968 and 1969. Skibinski even asked the architect who designed the Mitchell Park Domes in Milwaukee to render a sketch of a dome that would function in County Stadium and solve the Bucks' problem of not having a permanent home from the moment they entered the NBA. Skibinski was used to failure, but when a newspaper cartoon was published that made fun of his bubble idea, he was not happy. Specifically, he was not happy that the cartoonist had put the bubble in the wrong place, so he paid an artist $15 to produce a sketch that put it in the right spot. Eventually, the proposal was shot down by a 20–5 vote. Skibinski was praised for his ingenuity and for bringing more urgency to the matter of finding the Bucks a permanent home. "It would be a very embarrassing situation to have a championship team and not have them play in a championship city," declared fellow county supervisor Fred Tabak after the vote.[19] In due time, County Stadium would be full again. Bud Selig's never-ending quest to bring an MLB team back to Milwaukee led to the bankrupt Seattle Pilots officially transforming themselves into the Milwaukee Brewers a week before opening day of the 1970 MLB season. With that, Milwaukee was back in the big leagues and, once again, no longer a one-team town.

Temperatures may have been falling over the month of January in Milwaukee, but nothing was cooling down the Bucks. They kept up their winning pace and went into the All–Star break with a 33–16 record. That All–Star Weekend featured the first of Alcindor's 19 All–Star appearances. He was joined by fellow Bucks teammate Flynn Robinson. While he was not voted to be a starter for the East team, playing in that year's All–Star Game gave Alcindor an opportunity to play among the stars. He shared the floor with Robertson, he backed up Willis Reed and he aimed to soak up the experience of being in the league's biggest showcase for its stars. But it was an opportunity that he ultimately found dull. "It's no big thrill.... The other fellows aren't excited about it either. Actually, it's a little boring. I'm really interested in getting back to action with our team and trying to win as many games as we can."[20] The Bucks were the latest team to enjoy the fruits of Alcindor's excellence. But they were proving to be a great team beyond their seven-foot superstar center. Dandridge, in his own right, had hit the ground running—first as a super sub and then forcing Costello's hand and getting into the team's starting lineup—even though Dandridge preferred coming off the bench. He found moving to the pro game to be an easier transition than he had anticipated, as he relied on the very skills that had made him a star at Norfolk State: hustling for second chances, running the floor and hitting opportunistic shots when the Bucks ran plays designed for him.

The Bucks played exactly how Costello wanted them to play. He remained vigilant about finding the perfect formula and the perfect rotation, almost to an overbearing degree. But the results were resonating loud and clear. The Bucks had set their goal on simply making the playoffs that season. They easily surpassed that target as they racked up win upon win. The same went for smashing their attendance record set in their expansion season. They were 33–16 when they went into the All-Star break. They won 13 of 16 games in January and emerged as the second-best team in the NBA that year, standing just behind the Knicks. Onlookers saw a dynasty in the making, one only made possible by newcomers like Alcindor and Dandridge. Twyman, the longtime NBA veteran-turned-broadcaster, summed it up best as the Bucks continued their rise into February: "There is no telling how far this club can go. They're getting better all the time, and they're still basically a young and inexperienced team. If they continue to improve as fast as they have already this season, they will be a power in this league for many years to come."[21]

The Bucks earned their 46th win with a 140–127 victory over the SuperSonics in Portland on February 21, 1970. It was a celebratory night, not just for the fact that Alcindor finished with the first 50-point performance of his NBA career—he did that 10 more times over his Bucks stint. It also served as a fitting way for the Bucks to clinch their first playoff berth, and they did so with 15 games left in the regular season. Milwaukee's aspirations had changed once they surpassed their win total from the year before, secured their first winning record and clinched a playoff berth. Expectations had also changed. It wasn't enough to have booked their first trip to the playoffs, and neither was winning a series. The Bucks set their sights on something much bigger. As they sprinted down the final stretch, they announced they had topped the $1 million mark in ticket revenue for that season. They trailed only the Knicks and Lakers in that regard. The Bucks reached 50 wins by beating the Cincinnati Royals 120–114 on March 1, 1970. They clinched second place in the East when they beat the Celtics 138–134 with six games to go in the season. They finished the regular season with 56 wins and 26 losses—a year after going 27–55. Going from a 32.9 winning percentage in their expansion season to a 68.3 winning percentage in 1969–70 still stands as the sixth-biggest jump in winning percentage year over year. Alcindor went on to be named that season's NBA Rookie of the Year, and he finished third in MVP voting,

8. Alcindor Arrives (The 1969–70 Season)

behind Jerry West and Willis Reed. Meanwhile, the Bucks finished the regular season with an average attendance of 9,491 fans over their 38 home dates, along with 13 sellouts. The Bucks were valued at $6 million with the boost that came from Alcindor, their high marks in attendance and their incoming sum of expansion money after the NBA announced three new teams for the 1970–71 season. The Bucks were living large, and a long playoff run would only assure a bigger fortune.

Milwaukee knew who their first-round opponents would be long before they clinched second place in the East or even before winning 50 games. The 76ers—the very same club where Costello was a player for a decade and had even coached before leaving for Milwaukee—had trudged through a 42–40 campaign. The Bucks had beat the 76ers in five of the seven games in which they faced off against one another during the regular season. Still, many of the players on the 76ers' roster had played through long playoff runs, despite no longer having Chamberlain. The 76ers were just three years removed from winning an NBA championship. The Bucks didn't exist in 1967 when they won. Philadelphia was going into the playoffs playing in the friendly confines of the Spectrum. The Bucks were dispatched to Madison, where they split their time between the Dane County Coliseum and the UW Field House. It was fair to wonder just how the Bucks—with their playoff inexperience and their lack of a home court advantage—would respond going into their first playoff series as a franchise.

They did not alleviate those concerns in what ended up being a 125–118 Game 1 victory in favor of Milwaukee. The Bucks played tight most of the way through before opening up and taking control of the game late in the fourth quarter. In his first playoff game as a pro, Alcindor finished with 36 points and 20 rebounds, though he fouled out with 18 seconds left to go before the final buzzer. Game 2 was no better as the 76ers evened up the series with a 112–105 win in Wisconsin's capital city. It was the shot in the arm they needed as the series shifted over to Philadelphia. The 76ers were bearing down on the Bucks. They brandished a level of physicality that the Bucks had to adjust to, especially amid the playoff atmosphere. Punches were thrown and brawls ensued, and it wasn't surprising to see the Bucks stumble initially after taking a few hard jabs. Game 3 in Philadelphia served as a litmus test for how these young Bucks could overcome these difficulties. They needed to build on what little home court advantage they had possessed.

Milwaukee responded by pulling off one of the most dominant victories in playoff history. Backed by Alcindor's 33 points and with seven players scoring in double figures, the Bucks drubbed the 76ers on their way to a 156–120 win. The Bucks' 156 points stood as an NBA playoff record that lasted for 20 years. They shot a blistering 60.9 percent from the field on 110 shots. Costello marveled at his team's performance and he took relish in putting the pressure back on the 76ers. The 76ers players, too, even in defeat, were left in awe at such a showing. The Bucks had rallied together. They put their foot down and showed their might in front of a hostile crowd. From that point on, the Bucks didn't look back. Despite a 50-point game from Sixers forward Billy Cunningham, the Bucks captured Game 4 in Philadelphia with a 118–111 win. Back in Madison, the Bucks finished the job by taking Game 5 with a 115–106 victory, led by a 46-point outing from Alcindor. Clutching the ball, Pavalon walked into the locker room after the game and handed out $1,000 bonuses to the Bucks players and coaches as they advanced to the Eastern Conference finals. Now, all the Bucks had to do was await their next opponent, and Alcindor made no secret after the game as to who they wanted: "I think everyone wants New York. Everyone wanted to play New York again as much as they wanted the regular season to end."[22]

The Bucks were not being careful about what they wished for. While they believed they matched up well with the Knicks, New York made it very clear why they were the league's best that season. The Knicks had finished the season with 60 wins, had a +9.09-point differential and had taken four out of the six games they played against the Bucks during the regular season. The Baltimore Bullets had pushed the Knicks to seven games in the first round of the playoffs and the Bucks were no doubt looking to pounce on a tired Knicks team that had been pushed to its limit. This was very much a little brother trying to take down his big brother. The Knicks had fallen short the year before by winning a spot against the Celtics in the 1969 Eastern Conference finals, only to fall in six games. They sought to get a playoff-sized monkey off their collective backs, and this was a good chance to win their first championship in the franchise's history, even as the league's heir apparent to Wilt and Russell had come along. Alcindor—a New Yorker—badly wanted to take down his beloved Knicks and achieve the unthinkable in his first professional season: to bring his Bucks from being the worst to finishing first.

The Knicks were having none of that. Game 1 was a test of rest versus rust for the Bucks, as it had been over a week since they had taken care of business against the 76ers. New York, meanwhile, was looking hard into how they could slay the NBA's new king and tear apart the Bucks from within. They pressured the Bucks' ball handlers all over the court as they fed the ball to Alcindor. It was Reed's job to push and body up Alcindor as far away from the hoop and the paint as he could all series long. Game 1 saw that strategy fluster the Bucks, and it was the key to New York striking first by notching a 110–102 victory. Game 2 was much more frustrating for how agonizingly close the Bucks came to leaving New York with a game in hand. A pair of missed free throws by Alcindor with 52 seconds left and a one-point deficit in the fourth quarter did the Bucks in. He did that while amassing a triple-double of 38 points, 23 rebounds and 11 assists. The Bucks were finally returning back home to Milwaukee, but were returning in an unfamiliar situation. They had only lost back-to-back games on one occasion since the beginning of December. The pressure was on them to take two straight games while on their home court—all while facing an opponent that was doing everything possible to stymie them.

New York was the more complete team. They had the big man in Reed who could bother Alcindor, the forwards to outmuscle the young Buck forwards on the glass and the well-rounded guards who trapped the likes of Robinson, McGlocklin and Freddie Crawford. Robinson particularly had a rough series as he was playing with a groin injury against both the 76ers and the Knicks, and Costello looked to any solution he could find on the Bucks bench to alleviate Robinson's workload. The Bucks put a stop to the bleeding in Game 3. They racked up a 101–96 win to put the series at 2–1. For his part, Alcindor finished with 33 points and hauled in an astounding 31 rebounds. Confidence was restored and, with a little wind in their sails, the Bucks were bullish on evening up the series in Game 4, which was to be played in Milwaukee. With Alcindor proving to be a handful, the Knicks felt the urgency of the moment. Their owner, Ned Irish, said, "If we don't beat them this year—well, I think it will be the last time anybody will have a reasonable shot at them. Yes, I really believe that."[23]

Game 4 saw the Knicks meet the moment head-on. They raced out to command the game from the opening tip and entered the locker room with a 20-point halftime lead. The Bucks gave it a go in the third quarter by outscoring the Knicks 34–17 in the period and coming within one possession to tie the game at multiple points throughout the quarter. Ultimately, though, they never broke through. The Knicks wrestled back control and finished with a 117–105 victory to go up 3–1. The Bucks never got any closer than that, and with Game 5 at Madison Square Garden, the Bucks' phenomenal ride that year reached its final destination. The Knicks put together a 132–96 demolition that had the 19,500 fans at the Garden singing and hollering all night long. With their team up 40 points with a few minutes left to go, Knicks fans singled out a target to serenade as they booked their trip to the NBA Finals. Alcindor heard the Knicks faithful take extra delight in seeing him watch the end to his first season from the bench all throughout the final frame. From the stands, Knicks fans boisterously sang, "Goodbye Lewie, we hate to see you go." The scene left a sour taste in Alcindor's mouth after the game as he rationalized it and the team's finish to the season: "How do I feel about it? I can't feel about it. That's their problem. If they want to act like that…"[24]

The Knicks were bigger, faster and stronger than the Bucks. More importantly, they were familiar with these moments. They had the talent and they matched that with the playoff mettle that carried them to their first championship in franchise history. The Bucks had gotten their franchise star and saw just how much he had carried them to success. The Knicks, though, were the model for which the Bucks needed to put everything together and take that next jump. To go from good to great. Costello marveled at the Knicks' performance and recognized just how they had torn apart the Bucks with their mix of veterans, outside shooting and ace defensive work one through five. Nonetheless, he saw the future as very bright for the Bucks. "We'll be back in these playoffs next year. And we'll be back a lot of years after that. And we'll be better."[25]

For Alcindor, the season was over and he was looking forward to leaving Milwaukee for the summer. He had spent all winter withdrawn in his apartment. He racked up hefty phone bills with long distance calls. He immersed himself in Islam, but there was no sanctuary or any community in Milwaukee to involve himself in. Instead, he isolated himself in his Juneau Village apartment. "It was a pretty lonely experience and I didn't see it getting any better," he summarized later.[26] Before he left for the summer, Bucks officials vowed to Lew that help was on the way. In fact, they had it all arranged just as their season ended in New York. The arrival of a sure-to-be Hall of Famer was in the works. Life was about to become a lot easier for Alcindor on the court. The struggles and difficulties that he faced off the court in Milwaukee, though, only grew. He had made a compromise by coming to Milwaukee and he learned just how much he had conceded once he settled into his new surroundings. In truth, he never fully shed feeling like a stranger in a strange land while he was in Milwaukee.

9

Here Comes the Big O

The chain of events that led the immortal Oscar Robertson to come to Milwaukee on April 20, 1970, was years in the making. Although he was born in Charlotte, Tennessee, and grew up in Indianapolis, Robertson was a Cincinnati institution. It was as a University of Cincinnati Bearcat that he became the NCAA's all-time scoring leader, a title he held for over a decade before "Pistol" Pete Maravich came along. The Cincinnati Royals selected Robertson as a territorial pick, under a rule that the NBA put in place to keep talented players within the same region where they had played college ball. Throughout the decade that Robertson was a Royal, he was the constant performer that the Cincinnati faithful could count on. His individual brilliance—whether it was becoming the first player to average a triple-double over an entire season, his being named MVP, or the laundry list of awards and honors he earned—elevated the Royals to where they could compete within the East. In a league dominated by big men and that saw success as having a quality big man, Robertson was the antidote. There had been only a few examples of small guards such as Bob Cousy breaking through and becoming a star in a big man–driven league. With his wide array of skills, his size, and his athleticism, Robertson was the first "big guard" and the complete package of what the NBA was growing into at that time.

There was no getting over the hump against the dynastic Celtics, and the Royals always fell short. Robertson was the poster boy of falling short in the eyes of NBA observers, his greatness be damned. Eventually, Robertson alone wasn't enough to keep the ship steady for the Royals. After the team had fallen to the Celtics one too many times, the tenor of Robertson's relationship with the Royals—and eventually Cincinnati—began to change. The reality of the situation was that there was always something holding the Royals back. Sure, having to face the Celtics to get out of the East didn't help. Neither did the fact that Royals ownership and management began to make basketball decisions in terms of dollars and cents and not in search of going all-out for a championship. Robertson witnessed this firsthand when he renegotiated his contract with the Royals in the summer of 1965. His original contract had ended and the new one was littered with incentives that were unique to Robertson's contract at the time, from earning a percentage of gate receipts at Royals home games to the security of having a no-cut and a no-trade clause. Robertson was one of the first athletes to be represented by something close to an agent. In his case, it was his friend and attorney J.W. Brown. With the help of Brown's expertise, Robertson didn't give an inch or compromise from his singular vision, just as when he was running a play on the court. It didn't take long for Robertson to realize that if an athlete let someone take advantage of them once, it was going to continue for the rest of their career.

As the NBA began to establish itself as a league of note throughout the 1960s and at the height of his powers, Robertson was asked to be president of the National Basketball Players Association. He was flattered and accepted the position when asked by his peers Jack Twyman and Tommy Heinsohn, as well as little-known attorney Larry Fleisher. The NBA's players union was formed by Cousy in 1954 and was the first of its kind for any of the major sports leagues in North America at the time. Fast forward a decade later to when Robertson was named president, and NBA players were still fighting for better wages, a better investment in lodging and traveling and more security as they sought to make a living for themselves. NBA owners were reluctant to recognize the players union. Many of them were even unwilling to meet and negotiate with the players who sought a better way of life in the NBA. The tension and conflict between the owners and players naturally grew as the NBA grew in stature. The 1964 NBA All-Star Game is still infamous for marking the point when the players stood up for what they felt was owed to them. This was the first All-Star Game to be televised live in NBA history, and the players saw it as the ideal platform to send a message to the owners and the league. The game eventually tipped off after a slight delay and an unprecedented standoff between the players, owners and the NBA commissioner. A locked door to the players' locker room was the only thing standing between the parties before the players won out. The players hit the floor for layup lines with no one in attendance thinking the game could possibly have been cancelled in a boycott.

The truth is there was no better person to help further establish the players union and its fight against NBA owners than Robertson. The business of professional basketball was changing. The NBA was expanding and doing so at a rapid pace. The arrival of the ABA and the threat it posed to the NBA increased the need for players to fight for the power that they sought. More significant was the fact that the demographics of the players were changing. The NBA was becoming a more predominantly Black league, and while integration was occurring throughout the Sixties, progress was still very slow-moving in the basketball world, on and off the court. The NBA was going to be expanding into cities and markets that were resistant to racial and social progress in many cases. Suddenly, the Black NBA players were forced to carry the torch for inclusion and equality and to do so in a very public way. It was a significant reason why Robertson was asked to be president in the first place by Twyman, Heinsohn and Fleisher.

Robertson took on his new role with zeal and he never missed a meeting until his reign ended in 1974, when he retired both as a player and as president of the players union. Fleisher and Robertson were aligned with one another. From their individual experiences, both were inherently distrustful of NBA owners' interests. Issues such as the need for a better pension plan, going down to playing 10 exhibition games a year and being paid for those games, having a true All–Star break and instituting an 82-game regular season were the first to be implemented on Robertson's watch. Nevertheless, he wanted to tackle bigger issues, and the biggest of them all was the reserve clause. The reserve clause was not just a problem in the NBA, but for the NFL, MLB and NHL. In essence, when a player signed a contract in those days, his rights were solely tied to his team. All of the power lay on the side of the teams, and with no free agency in place players had very little recourse if they were unhappy with their contract. Sure, they could hold out, but doing so garnered criticism and smear campaigns from management, the press and fans alike. The players had to stand up for what they wanted, and it always came at a price.

The longer Robertson spent with the Royals, the more the slights added up. He couldn't stand how management was not willing to spend to build a roster for a championship. He saw teammates like Wayne Embry, Adrian Smith, Bob Boozer and Jerry Lucas get shipped out as their window to contend drew shut. The holdouts that Robertson engaged in for better contracts—which he won after every negotiation—saw him be labeled as a troublemaker and a malcontent, labels that still follow him to this day. Robertson had a thick skin, but he certainly never forgot where the slights came from. It was the arrival of Cousy in the summer of 1969 that was the final straw for Robertson. Cousy was hired as the Royals' head coach, and after having missed the playoffs in 1967–68 and 1968–69, he was given carte blanche to reimagine the team however he saw fit. Since retiring from the NBA in 1963, Cousy had been a successful coach at Boston College, but when a "Godfather" offer from the Royals came to him, he couldn't refuse. A three-year contract for over $100,000 was simply unheard of for coaches in those days. But no other coach had the last name Cousy, either. If mistakes were going to be made, it was Cousy who would make them.

In what Robertson described as the worst year of his professional career, Cousy and his superstar point guard never once got on the same page. It started with Cousy asking Robertson to not be as ball dominant as he always was with the Royals. Furthermore, Robertson dug up things Cousy had said of him in the past. Things that weren't all that flattering, to say the least. One such instance was when Robertson had entered the NBA and Cousy was asked for his opinion of who would be more successful, Robertson or Jerry West. The resulting headline read, "West Could Be Best, Oscar Could Be Royal Letdown."[1] Cousy didn't have the winning formula to fix the Royals once the season got underway. He thought coming out of retirement might do the trick, but that experiment was short-lived, lasting only seven games and a total of 34 minutes. There was no magic trick to solve the Royals' woes as they struggled to tread water all season. Robertson assumed the role of an innocent bystander. The Royals didn't feel like his team anymore and he and Cousy clearly didn't see eye to eye. The frustration grew as the team declined and the Cincinnati press portrayed Robertson in a negative light. The Royals needed to somehow become more successful again, Robertson was seen as standing in the way of that progress. "In life, sometimes you get into a situation where you let fate decide your course of action. I hadn't done anything to create this situation. So I figured why should I try to solve something I had no control over?" he later reflected.[2] Soon enough, Robertson discovered his likeness wasn't on the team's promotional advertisements. He even remembered showing up to the Royals' home arena to play the Bucks on January 28, 1970, and a parking attendant showing him a newspaper ad featuring every player and coach lined up in a grocery store. Every Royals player except Robertson. The parking attendant asked, "What's the matter, Oscar? Aren't you on the Royals?"[3]

Two days later, the Royals suffered a 108–103 loss against the Celtics. Robertson pulled his groin muscle and struggled to walk around the locker room afterwards. As he labored in pain, he was approached by a reporter inquiring about a trade. The reporter was soon led away by the team's PR staff, but Robertson contacted his attorney. It turned out the Royals had agreed to trade Robertson to the Baltimore Bullets for Gus Johnson, a high-flying forward who was close to being sidelined by injuries. Johnson had a much lower salary, and he'd help the Royals save money. Robertson knew that his time with the Royals was coming to an end. This wouldn't be the way he would go out, though. The next morning, Cousy explained to Oscar that he was heading to Baltimore for Johnson straight up in the deal. Robertson said it wasn't so cut and dried. That afternoon, Robertson, Cousy, and the rest of the Royals management met in Brown's office. Brown explained, "Well, ... unfortunately, Oscar doesn't want to go to

Baltimore. And I guess you haven't read his contract lately. Oscar has the right of veto over any trade." Robertson likened the reaction to a bomb exploding in the office.[4] Management pled with Robertson and Brown to reconsider, but Robertson would only go through with the deal if he was assured more money. Bullets management wasn't about to acquiesce to that, and the whole deal was on life support after it reached the press. The Royals had to save face and challenged Robertson and Brown to agree to any deal they would put forth. In return, Robertson made it clear that he would welcome a move, but it would have to be done on his terms.

The trade between the Royals and the Bullets was vetoed by Robertson, and after the dust settled he announced that the 1969–70 season was going to be his final year in Cincinnati. "I wanted to play the reminder of my years in Cincinnati," Robertson told the press. "But I feel that I cannot play for the Royals under any circumstances after this year. It's to the point now that I have to leave."[5] The final few weeks of the season saw the Royals slip out of playoff contention and afforded fans their final glimpses of Robertson in a Royals uniform—on the bench, that is, with nagging muscle injuries. It was suggested in the press that he wasn't hurt and that he was sitting out the rest of a disappointing season. It only added to the sour grapes for Robertson. Happy endings rarely come for players synonymous with a franchise, even players as great as Robertson. The city of Cincinnati didn't experience the glory of winning an NBA championship, but Robertson had become synonymous with the city itself. From the moment he announced that he would be leaving the Royals, it wouldn't take long for the Royals to leave the city altogether. That day came when they announced on March 14, 1972, that the franchise would relocate to Kansas City and be rebranded as the Kings.

In his last weeks playing in Cincinnati, Robertson grappled with plotting the next step of his career. Of course, there were all sorts of teams interested in him and he had his pick. The big-city teams like the Knicks and the Lakers were obviously interested. So were the upstart Suns. He even had the chance to return to Indiana and play for the Pacers in the ABA if he wanted to. But the criteria for his next home was clear to Robertson. The basketball fit was a top priority and so was his and his family's preference to stay in the Midwest. He and his wife, Yvonne, liked the change in seasons. He also wanted his kids to get a good education and to live in a good neighborhood. While he was weighing all of these factors, Robertson got the idea of moving up north. "I just might like to play in Milwaukee," he remembered telling Brown.[6]

Brown sought a three-year, $700,000 contract that included all of the same stipulations Robertson had with the Royals. The wheels that brought Robertson to Milwaukee went into motion on the very night that the

Knicks bounced the Bucks out of the playoffs. In negotiations, Robertson saw how much the Bucks and Pavalon valued him and what he would bring to the team. "We want to pay Oscar what we think he is worth. Milwaukee had a fine season, used lots of young players and all they need is Oscar to join with those kids," Pavalon said during negotiations with Brown.[7] The Bucks met Robertson's terms and all that was needed was for the Royals to get on board. As the two teams haggled over which youngsters would be thrown into the deal, Oscar assured Yvonne that while things would be different, they would be good for the family. They were leaving Cincinnati—the place where they had grown considerably, where they met, and where they started raising their family. Events had taken their toll on him and his wife that final year, and they were on the same page about seeking a fresh start. There was a lot to leave behind. Oscar made it clear that he wouldn't make the move to Milwaukee if Dandridge was included in the deal. Ditto for Greg Smith. The Royals' hands were tied and they had already bungled their first attempt to move Robertson. They settled on veteran guard Flynn Robinson, who had previously been drafted by the Royals, and Charlie Paulk, the Bucks' first-ever draft pick, the same year he was drafted into the army. Just hours after the Bucks left Madison Square Garden after that Game 5 loss, they announced that they had acquired Robertson.

Bringing Robertson to Milwaukee simply wouldn't have happened without the help of Embry. While working in Boston's Parks and Recreation department and as an announcer for the Celtics, Embry served as the conduit between Robertson and Bucks management. In the Bucks, Embry saw the ideal opportunity for Robertson to not just contend for the championship that was missing from his career, but finally win one too. He remembered telling Robertson, "You're the greatest player ever to play the game, but there's one thing you haven't achieved. You deserve a championship ring."[8] Embry's help in securing Robertson eventually parlayed him into getting the role of administrative assistant with the Bucks' front office.

There were many questions that came Robertson's way when he made his first public appearance with the Bucks before the Milwaukee press on May 1, 1970. Inquiring minds wanted to know of his relationship with Cousy and the Royals, why he chose Milwaukee, what he thought of the opportunity to play alongside Alcindor and how the two superstars were going to co-exist. The latter question was the biggest one facing the Bucks. The Bucks had spent Alcindor's rookie season designing ways to get him the ball and run the team's offense from the inside. Now, here was the NBA's greatest assist man—Mr. Triple-Double himself—and finding that the right balance in incorporating two ball-dominant figures sounded like a potential problem on paper. That was, to anyone but Pavalon. "I don't think Oscar realizes how good [Lew] is, and I don't think [Lew] realizes how good Oscar is. They've never played together, except one time at Kutsher's, and until they do, they won't be able to realize how great this thing

Oscar Robertson stands at the podium before the Milwaukee press corps during his introductory press conference at the Pfister Hotel in downtown Milwaukee. Sitting beside him is Larry Costello. From a program commemorating Oscar Robertson Day at a March 26, 1974, game against the Kansas City–Omaha Kings (author's collection).

can be," he told reporters. Likewise, Robertson didn't see any problem in figuring out how his relationship with Alcindor would work on the floor. "Getting the ball in to [Lew] won't be an adjustment. It'll be a pleasure," he said.[9]

Perhaps an even bigger question was how the Bucks would be able to maintain such a high payroll, with their top two players earning 20 percent of the team's gross income. To Pavalon, the gamble was a simple financial calculation on top of it being a good basketball fit. "It's a sound step for several reasons," he said. "I think we could assume we could be contenders for several years as we were—with Lew and the men we had. If this move makes us more of a contender, if it gets us farther in the playoffs, if it helps sell some of the seats we weren't selling in the early part of the season— then it's justified."[10]

The same week that Robertson was traded to Milwaukee, he filed an antitrust lawsuit against the NBA on behalf of the players union. Rumors intensified of a merger between the NBA and the ABA. The war between NBA players, NBA owners and the league itself had begun and it was Robertson who bore the burden by having his name head up the lawsuit, along with 13 other players—including the Bucks' own Jon McGlocklin. Robertson testified before Congress as the players sought to abolish the college draft and put an end to the reserve clause that bound them to their team from the moment they entered the league. "There can be no merger until issues such as free agency and 'freedom of movement' are settled," the union's statement read.[11] Even as the players filed their lawsuit against both the ABA and the NBA, the two leagues voted to merge on June 18, 1970. The ABA unanimously voted 11–0 in favor of the move, while the NBA voted 13–4 after a five-hour meeting with the league's board of governors. The NBA would adopt the ABA's 11 teams to create a single 28-team league and Kennedy would operate as the league's sole commissioner. The plan called for the leagues to fully integrate no later than the 1973–74 season, pending the approval of Congress. And the NBA emphasized the urgency of the matter for the sake of the ABA. "Unless legislation permitting a single league is enacted, disintegration of the A.B.A. is only a matter of time," the NBA declared.[12]

Robertson had gotten his fresh start, symbolized by the number he wore upon joining the Bucks. Of course, McGlocklin was already synonymous with no. 14 in Milwaukee and if anyone thought that Robertson would fight for the same number he wore in Cincinnati, they were sorely mistaken. "Jon doesn't have to give it up. That was it for the number for me in Cincinnati. I don't care to wear it anymore," he announced.[13] Robertson was adopting Milwaukee as his new home town, and with the help of Bucks stakeholders he found a house on Kenboern Drive in Glendale, a suburb north of the city. It was a brick multi-level home, with cathedral ceilings and a fountain in the foyer. News quickly traveled through Glendale that the newest star for the Bucks was going to be living there and a petition was circulated among homeowners that sought to prevent it. The petition cited the effect on property values, but when it reached Robertson's future neighbors, they instead welcomed the Robertson family and created a friendship that lasted for decades. It wasn't until later that Robertson learned of the petition. It didn't take long for him to be seen on the streets of Milwaukee in his recognizable Jaguar convertible with license plates that only featured the letter "O."

10

Marching Toward a Title (The 1970–71 Season)

Nowadays, it is common to see NBA stars join forces with one another. Star power catches the attention of everyone, even those who may be stars themselves. The advent of free agency has made player movement a lot easier in the NBA than it was in 1970 and while all of the focus is on the bigger, glitzy markets on either coast, a smaller market can get lucky through the draft and eventually become a perennial contender. Milwaukee defied that earlier trend with the addition of the league's greatest guard. Robertson needed the Bucks as much as they needed him. At 31 years old time was not on his side, and he had learned that no one can do it by himself. This was a legacy play, and just how much joining the Bucks would help extend his playing career was the big question. Expectations swelled even bigger for a club that had won 56 games the season before. Reed—the leader of the team that put an end to the Bucks' season—was glad that the Knicks got one while they could. In his mind, "the [Knicks] might not have had a chance later."[1]

Robertson's presence brought a level of command and respect that the Bucks sorely needed to maintain their ascension toward the top of the league. It didn't take long for Alcindor to take note of what life was going to be like teaming up with one of the best players in the NBA. But it'd take years after playing with Robertson for Alcindor to appreciate what the legendary guard did for him. "Had I known that what he added to my game would come only once in my professional lifetime, I might have stopped to savor the pleasure of working with the best. I'd never known anything but the best, though, so while I enjoyed playing with Oscar, it wasn't until several years later that I appreciated him fully."[2] The Bucks had two stars, defined by the past and present. Robertson was far more settled in his personal life and had the agency to choose where he wanted to be. Alcindor, meanwhile, was grappling with life in Milwaukee and lived in isolation, often at his own choosing. They came up through very different paths and

10. Marching Toward a Title (The 1970–71 Season)

joined the league at very different entry points. Finding common ground would have to take time, even in a pressure cooker. Still, Robertson saw how he, Alcindor and Costello all had a shared vision of success. "We both had reserved personalities, and, I think, we each felt isolated from the mainstream, middle-class world," he later wrote. "We weren't close at first and didn't spend time talking, on or off the court. But along with Larry Costello, we shared certain traits. What I think mattered the most was that we agreed that being as efficient as possible cut down our chances for errors. We had professional attitudes and approaches to the game. No nonsense."[3]

The first indication of how the season would be for the Bucks came at training camp at Carroll College in Waukesha. It started with conditioning, fundamental drills, daily scrimmages and Costello continuing to quiz his players on their basketball acumen. The Bucks weren't done with managing their roster, though. In came Lucius Allen and Bob Boozer from the SuperSonics in exchange for forward Don Smith. Allen was a teammate and roommate of Alcindor's during their time at UCLA and he brought with him more ball-handling, speed and a budding scoring ability. Likewise, Boozer played with Robertson on the Olympic team that won the gold medal in 1960 and in Cincinnati with the Royals. Boozer brought more scoring punch and another veteran presence. Allen and Boozer first met with the Bucks not at Carroll College, though, but in paradise. It had been decided before the Bucks bowed out of New York at the end of the last season that they would spend a large portion of their training time in Hawaii. The backdrop of the beautiful beaches, clear blue water and bright sun in the North Pacific suited the Bucks, even though it was anything but a vacation. While in Honolulu, where they practiced two-a-days, Costello named Alcindor and Robertson as co-captains of that year's squad. It was his decision to make, but there was no objection from any of the players either. The signs of what was about to brew this season continued in Honolulu, where the Bucks had scrimmages with the Lakers and the San Diego Rockets. Their first preseason game featured all reserves in the starting lineup, and the Bucks beat the Lakers by 13 points. The second game against the Lakers—this time with their starters—ended in a 129–111 win for Milwaukee. A dominant 115–88 victory over San Diego rounded out their Hawaiian voyage. When the Bucks returned to the mainland, they brought their dominance with them. They finished their preseason a perfect 10–0 and were the only team to go undefeated in the preseason that year.

For his part, Robertson saw the makings of something special happening before his eyes. It was hard for a seasoned pro like him to get too high or too low based on preseason results, but much had changed for the

Big O. Here he was, with a brand-new team and playing alongside some of the most talented players he had ever played with. He was the conductor behind the Bucks' attack that hit the ground running back on that Carroll College campus. "'We're going to win it all,' I told the guys. Over and over, during practices, I said it," he recalled.[4] Even with the additions of Robertson and Boozer, the Bucks were still very young and inexperienced. With an average age of 24.6 years old, the Milwaukee players were only starting to feel their potential. Going from good to great was a massive challenge and Robertson took it upon himself to not lose sight of the main goal. The start of the 1970–71 season saw the Bucks switch conferences with three new expansion teams coming into the NBA. The Bucks moved to the Midwest Division in the Western Conference and set themselves up for regular meetings against nearby rivals like the Bulls, the Pistons and the Suns.

For the second straight year, the Bucks started off ABC's national NBA coverage. Milwaukee opened their season in Atlanta against the Hawks and the top pick of the 1970 NBA draft—"Pistol" Pete Maravich. As glowing as their performance was during the preseason, the Bucks had some early-season kinks to work out when they tipped off their regular season. They rallied from being down as much as 16 points in the first half before they went on to spoil Maravich's pro debut with a 107–98 win. They followed that up with a one-point loss to the Pistons three days later. In their home opener, Milwaukee had to go to double overtime to outlast the Bullets 122–120. Costello constantly worried and tinkered with the team's fast-breaking offense, their starting lineup and how to cater to Alcindor and get him the touches he needed. He wanted Robertson to shoot more and was waiting to see a killer instinct develop within the team and on the court. The balancing act between the coach on the sidelines—Costello—and the coach on the floor—Robertson—wasn't something that could be easily achieved after just a preseason and the first handful of regular season games.

The Bucks scuffled out of the gate in their first few games after their undefeated preseason, but they quickly found their footing after that home opening win against Baltimore. For the next month and three days, the Bucks won their next 16 games, by an average +14.6-point differential. They catapulted themselves to the top of the West by beating up on a very favorable slate of teams that helped keep them sharp and rested, with their first nine games being played over 32 days. The cohesion that was developing in the starting unit of Robertson, McGlocklin, Dandridge, Smith and Alcindor was palpable, with their mix of speed, athleticism and balanced scoring. The ingredients were coming together in their fast break, their suffocating defense and a bench unit that could support their stars when needed. It was hard to ask for a better start on the court and off it. The

10. Marching Toward a Title (The 1970–71 Season)

Bucks head coach Larry Costello (left) draws up a play on his always-handy yellow legal pad during a huddle. In his eight and a half seasons coaching the Bucks, Costello finished with a 410–264 record, made two trips to the NBA Finals and won an NBA championship. From the program for Oscar Robertson Day, March 26, 1974 (author's collection).

Bucks welcomed sellout crowds for their opening set of home games. Even the hard-driven Costello attempted to loosen the reins and enjoy what was being built before him.

The Bucks had a chance to come within reach of the longest winning streak in NBA history when the Knicks came to town on November 27, 1970. Of course, the Knicks themselves had just set that record the year before. There was no doubt they were invested in keeping it intact and to make sure the Bucks weren't about to touch it. The Knicks had gotten off to a hot start in their own right with a 19–7 record and stood atop of the

East going into this rematch. With that said, they were certainly showing the effects of their long run to the title. Their roster had been thinned out due to the expansion draft. The Bucks had a score to settle and with a home-and-home scheduled on back-to-back days. This was their first chance to get revenge on the team that had sent them packing just seven months earlier. But if the Bucks wanted to show the Knicks that they were a team to be feared—now with an upgraded roster headlined by Alcindor and Robertson—they didn't show it on that Thanksgiving weekend. They blew a nine-point lead after scoring a franchise-low 11 points in the fourth quarter on the Friday afternoon game, which ended in a 103–94 win for New York and ended the Bucks' winning streak. The next night in Madison Square Garden, the Knicks rallied from a 14-point deficit with six and a half minutes remaining in the fourth quarter to win 100–99 in a frantic finish. Costello had lamented earlier in the season that the Bucks hadn't developed a killer instinct, despite the overwhelming victories they were securing.

In the Bucks' two biggest games against their biggest nemesis, Costello was vindicated in his thinking. Those games also opened Robertson's eyes as he wrestled with the Bucks' collective inexperience all across their roster. He later observed,

> What we needed, though, was a killer instinct. For many players, I knew, this came with experience—most of our guys who were getting playing time hadn't been in the league long enough to really suffer or know what it meant to want to win. They'd almost made it to the finals the previous season, and that was pretty good. But this was my 11th year in the league and I'd never made it to a championship. Every game took a little bit out of me that I couldn't get back, and I didn't know how many chances I was going to have. I wasn't messing around out there. It was my responsibility to get this team mentally ready. From this point forward, I was more aggressive. If someone screwed up, or didn't want to play, we talked the situation out. People who weren't rebounding, guys who weren't playing defense, they needed to realize that we had to get the job done.[5]

Robertson was unbending and fully took hold of the reins, leading the team in his own way. He was no longer just reading the room and diagnosing where the problems lied. From the moment he walked into that locker room, his voice carried weight. His teammates sensed his urgency, and the pair of losses to the Knicks showed everyone just how far they had to get to reach the Knicks' level. Robertson was the Bucks' leader and the guiding hand when the pressure tightened, when defenses were taking away what the Bucks did best and when Alcindor was crowded in the post. Robertson held his teammates accountable for mistakes made, whether they weren't digging down on defense or not going after rebounds—the little things that could make the difference between winning a championship or not. To get the Bucks to where he wanted to go, he was going to be the voice bearing down on them and cursing them out on the floor and in huddles, even as Costello was shouting similar messages from the sidelines in his three-piece suit. Alcindor was more than happy to cede this role to Robertson, as he later told *Sports Illustrated*: "Oscar respects people that can perform. Sometimes I think that's all Oscar respects. If you don't put out, you lose Oscar's respect fast. He curses guys out right on the floor! For not putting out. For acting flaky. He tells 'em. And that's good. Because a team has to have somebody like that. I won't do it, myself. I'm a little too humanitarian. But Oscar doesn't have that problem."[6]

Milwaukee quickly got back to its winning ways after the Knicks series, though lapses were scattered throughout the month of December. Whenever those occurred, though, the Bucks came back playing harder and angrier. Their responses after slipping up were devastating for those teams that stood in their way. They entered 1971 with a 29–7 record that was good for the top in the Midwest Division and in the West. Talk of making a run at the 76ers' record of 68 regular season wins surfaced when the Bucks reached 30 wins and beyond. But they were tested once again by the biggest thorn in their side when the Knicks came to town on January 7. Every one of the meetings between these clubs felt like a preview of that year's NBA Finals. The Knicks had routinely gotten the better of Milwaukee, whether it was in the regular season or the playoffs. All the Bucks needed to do was show that they could give it back to the reigning champs. But from the start, nothing went as planned. Alcindor was saddled with foul trouble midway through the first quarter. The Bucks had targeted Reed with limited success, despite his battling a flu bug. With no Lew for large stretches of the game, the Bucks had to adapt or meet their all-too-familiar fate against the Knicks. Costello entrusted Robertson with leading the way and designed the team's half-court offense to have Oscar run as many pick-and-rolls as possible. In turn, Robertson upped his aggressiveness. He looked for his own shot and knew when to hit open teammates if the Knicks' defense was slow to react. Robertson put on a master class. He was in total control and operated with total efficiency. While the Bucks had wilted when the Knicks made their fourth-quarter rallies earlier in the season, Oscar put a stop to that this time around. He splashed in shots from all over the floor and diced up the Knicks' defense. The Bucks survived the 23 minutes when Alcindor was on the bench and outscored the Knicks 51–48 during those minutes. When Alcindor was on the floor, he helped deliver a decisive 116–106 victory for the Bucks.

For all his efforts, Robertson fell one rebound short of tallying his first triple-double in a Bucks uniform, but 35 points on 19 shots and 13 assists was more than good enough to do the trick. Robertson may have downplayed his ability to turn the clock as he had, but his teammates and rivals marveled at the manner in which he carried the Bucks to such a symbolic win. Costello wished for Robertson to play like that more often and his wishes would come true as the season went on. To his credit, though, Robertson knew exactly what he was doing. There was a real urgency to capture that first NBA championship. But the season was still a marathon and not a sprint. He was no longer a one-man show and he had adjusted his game to suit his teammates and his fellow superstar. The Knicks hovered over the Bucks' season as they looked to defend their title, chasing them in winning streaks and for that year's championship. For that night, the Bucks showed they deserved to be mentioned in the Knicks' company, just as Robertson essentially declared to a sold-out crowd at the Arena. He was still capable of supporting a team on his shoulders. The Bucks went into the All-Star break with two more wins and sent Alcindor, Robertson and Costello to headline the West squad in San Diego. Their place at the top of the NBA had been reserved for the three biggest figures responsible for the team's success. And they were loading up for their playoff run by adding another veteran forward into the mix with the addition of McCoy McLemore from the Cleveland Cavaliers.

As the Bucks maintained their position at the top, Alcindor remained in isolation when there were no games and when he wasn't at practice. He attracted the spotlight and his presence lifted the Bucks into relevancy—not just in Milwaukee, but for curious basketball fans across the Midwest in places like Minnesota and Iowa, areas that the NBA had not yet broken into. Fan mail came into the Bucks' office from all over the country and from as far away as Europe and Africa. Some of that fan mail was published in the *Milwaukee Journal*, which reported that he received over 13,000 letters in his first two seasons in Milwaukee.[7] Inquiring minds wanted to know more about the reserved Alcindor. Eventually, the Bucks printed a letter on special stationery with the Bucks emblem fixed on it and sent it to every well-wisher. The letter read, "Thank you for your wishes. An autographed photo is enclosed for you. Best regards, Lew Alcindor."[8]

Chuck Johnson, the sports editor for the *Milwaukee Journal*, accompanied the Bucks on a road trip out West to get a better sense of what Alcindor's life was like on the road. What he found was just how taxing it was for Alcindor to walk among a sea of people when he wasn't afforded the luxury to hide among the crowd. He was ill at ease with his celebrity and the idolization of young boys and fans as he moved through airports when the Bucks flew commercial airlines in those days. He was always reminded of who he was at all times and his teammates and Bucks officials always remarked on how unrelenting it was for the big man. That was

10. Marching Toward a Title (The 1970–71 Season)

life on the road. Back in Milwaukee, Alcindor was still reluctant to call it home, as he preferred life in big cities such as New York, Los Angeles, and even Boston. In Johnson's profile, Alcindor opined, "I still feel the same way about Milwaukee. The Midwest is not my cup of tea. I haven't met a lot of people in Milwaukee. It's a good town for factory workers." Johnson pressed Alcindor further on whether it mattered to him where he lived during the season. He reasoned that while half his time would be spent in the 16 other NBA cities, Alcindor sought comfort. "Sure. I want to be comfortable where I live. I'm not comfortable in Milwaukee. There's nothing to do," Alcindor said.[9]

When the story was published, Alcindor's comments about his life in Milwaukee and specifically on it being "a good town for factory workers" drew attention and even some ire. Alcindor was never one to mince words and he spoke matter-of-factly in those rare moments when he let down his guard. On one hand, Alcindor was referring to Milwaukee as the place where he performed his job—the city where he played basketball, and that's it. On the other hand, he was holding up a mirror to what he felt about the city. He was still a stranger in a strange land. If he was going to be reminded of who he was constantly, he would remind Milwaukeeans who they were in his mind's eye. The fervor generated by the story and the published reactions and editorials from readers and staff of the paper grew so intense that Alcindor felt the need to clear the air. "It's just that people misunderstood what I wanted to say," he told the *Journal*. "Milwaukee is not the type of place I like to live—that's right. But people are taking it personally, and I didn't mean it that way. There are nice people and some not so nice, just like any place else. But I still contend that the fans are great, and that the satisfaction I do get from Milwaukee comes from being appreciated by the fans."[10] Alcindor wanted to make sure nothing he said was taken personally. If anything, though, the episode reinforced just how out of place Alcindor was in Milwaukee and in the world he traveled in.

If the Bucks' 1970–71 regular season was defined by anything, winning streaks topped the list. The Bucks had three stretches where they won at least 10 consecutive games. They made a run at the NBA's longest winning streak at the start of the season and they were hungry to surpass the Knicks' 18-game win streak after scuffling following the All-Star break. It all started on February 6, 1971, when the Bucks breezed to a 111–85 victory over the Warriors at the end of a nine-game road trip. They kept on winning, and winning bigger and better than ever. Soon enough, they reached double digits once again, and they captured the Midwest Division title and the top seed in the West with their 13th straight victory when they beat down the Rockets 139–104 on February 24. The Bucks bagged a $50,000 bonus for those two feats and got within reaching distance of the 76ers' all-time record. The Bucks climbed into March with their 16th straight win and matched the streak they had built over the first month of the season. A 112–97 win over the Lakers on March 3 put them at 17 straight wins, and a tight 116–113 win over the Buffalo Braves tied them with New York's famed 18-game win streak. A night later while in Detroit, the Bucks set an NBA record for 19 consecutive wins by beating the Pistons 108–95 at Cobo Arena. This normally reserved Bucks group didn't hide how they felt about making history. "I'm so happy I don't know how to describe it. In three years, we did something it took New York 24 years to do," Costello beamed after the game.[11]

The Bucks tacked on one more victory over the SuperSonics to reach 20 consecutive wins and they soon were faced with a dilemma. They were on the precipice of glory at 65–11 and three wins away from matching the 76ers' 68 wins. But Costello saw the long game that was ahead and he didn't want to risk going for a short-term goal when the greatest glory was within reach. "We could do it if we wanted to, but if we went real hard and Lew or Oscar got hurt, I'd have to live with that for the rest of my life. Winning the title is the thing," he preached.[12] Meanwhile, some Knicks players lamented the fact that their hard-fought streak had been broken just one season after they compiled it. "I know that records are made to be broken, but I would rather it had lasted longer than one season," said Reed.[13]

The Bucks' ascension couldn't have been timed more perfectly. Bucks fever was hitting its peak and they racked up sellout crowds as the Bucks came closer to Philadelphia's record of 68 wins. In the locker room, confidence was soaring and the almost unshakable Robertson was not going to let all of this fall by the wayside. He saw how his teammates had sharpened themselves to conquer their opponents on a nightly basis, and he was uncompromising in the pursuit of perfection. He felt that this was the most beautiful basketball he had ever been a part of, but he became even more demanding of his teammates. "When I look back now," he later wrote, "I also understand how much this perfection affected me…. Maybe I acted this way because I saw how good a team we were becoming, maybe because I finally had a chance at a title and did not want things to go sour."[14]

Milwaukee's win streak was stopped at 20 games when Chicago prevailed over the Bucks in a 110–103 overtime loss on March 9. The last week of the regular season saw them drop four of their final five games. Milwaukee finished out flat, but there were more than enough milestones achieved and their pursuit of a title was not compromised. An historic season ended in a 66–16 record and what still stands as the second-largest point differential in NBA history (+12.2). For his part, Alcindor earned the first of his six Most Valuable Player awards after averaging 31.7 points per game, shooting 57.7 percent from the field, 16 rebounds per game and 3.3 assists

10. Marching Toward a Title (The 1970–71 Season)

per game for the season. The Bucks finished the year as the second-biggest attraction in the NBA, with a total attendance of 883,985 fans watching their games both at home and on the road. They averaged over 10,000 fans for all of their 41 home games, split between the Arena and in Madison, and it was in Madison that their second straight playoff run began.

"What happened in the past doesn't mean a thing," Costello sermonized as the Bucks opened their 1971 playoff run against the Warriors.[15] In their six regular season meetings, the Bucks had beaten up the Warriors routinely, as evidenced by their +18.1-point differential in those games. San Francisco was 41–41 and rode the line of mediocrity. There was enough, though, to give the Bucks trouble. No player demonstrated that more than Nate Thurmond, the Warriors' long-limbed center, who possessed a defensive presence so bothersome that Alcindor referred to him as the toughest center he'd ever go up against throughout his NBA career. Costello, meanwhile, always bordered on being maniacal in wanting his team to play the right way in pursuit of perfection. Like Robertson, the closer the team got to achieving a level of basketball dominance, Costello didn't want to let it go. The Bucks were raring to go after an eight-day layoff, and the series was starting in the Bay Area due to previous conflicts at the UW Field House in Madison. Would being forced to give up their opening home court advantage spell doom for the Bucks?

The series starting on the West Coast made no difference to the Bucks as they ran off with a 107–96 win over the Warriors. They were powered by Robertson and Alcindor, who combined for 57 of the team's 107 points. For Game 2, the Bucks continued to keep the Warriors at bay in their home away from home. A dominant 29–16 third quarter gave them a 104–90 win and put the series at a 2–0 lead in favor of the Bucks. Not even foul trouble for Alcindor limited the Bucks for the night, and their starting lineup combined for 85 of their 104 points. Game 3 once again saw the Bucks hold serve with a late flurry to put the stamp on a 114–102 win. With the series at 3–0 and moving to San Francisco, it was going to take a miracle for the Warriors to get one over on the Bucks. Milwaukee had an answer for every one of San Francisco's responses, even if the Bucks weren't playing their most composed and dominating brand of basketball. They had a way of demoralizing the opposition even when they weren't operating with peak efficiency—the true mark of a team that isn't to be trifled with. But the Warriors got their miracle in Game 4. Thanks to a 43-foot shot made by Joe Ellis with one second left in regulation, the Warriors avoided a sweep and enjoyed a 106–104 win to put the series at 3–1. The Bucks played a flat game, especially by their own measure. Costello lamented after the game that they had taken the Warriors too lightly. "Now that these guys have won a game, they may start thinking they can win the whole damn thing," he said.[16]

That loss rattled Costello. He lamented that the Bucks had taken their foot off the gas. Three days after losing Game 4, the Bucks accomplished one of their biggest feats of the season by running the Warriors off the floor with a 136–86 win to advance to the conference finals. It still stands as the franchise's biggest playoff victory. According to Costello, there was one key element behind the swift and decisive victory: "Maybe it was just a matter of steak and eggs." Costello revealed that all the Bucks players and coaches had convened to eat together before the game, something they apparently had never done before that season or even in their first three years as a club.[17] Milwaukee had to wait for the Lakers to outlast the Bulls in seven games to advance to the conference finals, and that gave the Bucks five days of additional rest. This was to be the hotly anticipated series where the mentor and the protege would finally face off against one another.

Alcindor had crossed paths with Chamberlain as he was discovering his basketball potential. Chamberlain walked the road that Alcindor followed a decade later. They shared enough of a relationship that by the time the Bucks and Lakers met for this series, the two giants had a falling out. Chamberlain represented the old guard and Alcindor represented the new. At the center of their hard feelings were the principles and the racial awakening that defined the two generational talents. Chamberlain was a supporter of Richard Nixon in the 1968 presidential election and Alcindor increasingly championed civil rights at the time of his boycott of that year's Olympics in Mexico City. It's a good thing the series was billed as the battle between Alcindor and Chamberlain because the Lakers didn't have much else to work with. They had lost Jerry West to a knee injury earlier in the season and while they had proven to be veterans capable of stepping up in his absence, they knew they'd be outmatched by the Bucks' dominance.

Before the series started with Game 1 in Milwaukee, Alcindor was presented with his MVP trophy in front of Pavalon, his parents and a crowd of Bucks faithful who cheered him for this first of many honors throughout his career. Milwaukee dominated the first two games and raced out to a 2–0 lead on their home floor. A 106–85 victory in Game 1 and a dogged 91–73 win in Game 2 showed their breadth and how they were able to win in the playoffs. In fact, the 73 points the Lakers scored in Game 2 were the fewest scored by a team in a playoff game for 16 seasons. Los Angeles struck back with a 118–107 victory, supported by the 17,334 fans at the Forum for Game 3. Costello acted as if the world was falling around him once again. "We've got our work cut out. This isn't going to be a cakewalk, that's for sure," he demurred to reporters.[18] For all of the work the Bucks had cut out for them, they responded with a 117–94 win in Game

10. Marching Toward a Title (The 1970–71 Season) 89

4, which they played on Alcindor's 24th birthday. The birthday boy led the way with 31 points and, yet again, all the Bucks starters hit double figures. They got a big lift from Boozer with his 16 points off the bench, helping put the Bucks over with a complete showing.

Game 5 came back to Milwaukee. That April 18, 1971, afternoon had the makings of a celebration. The Bucks had been the better team and despite some nagging injuries to Robertson, they proved to be the healthier team, too. That day, they won the West and advanced to the NBA Finals with a 116–98 victory over the Lakers. It was Smith's turn to lead the Bucks with 22 points and it was the first time since high school that he had led his team in scoring. Pandemonium swept over the fans in the Milwaukee Arena as the minutes and seconds ticked down with the Bucks putting away the Lakers for good. The Bucks prevailed over a banged-up Lakers team.

In a rare moment of graciousness, the Milwaukee crowd paid tribute to the Lakers' valiant fight. When Chamberlain was subbed out of Game 5 with 2:25 remaining in regulation, all 10,746 fans in attendance gave him a standing ovation. It was a gesture that left Chamberlain feeling honored. "It was wonderful," he said. "I can't recall if this ever happened to me before. You give whatever you have to give, and when it's appreciated, it's gratifying…. It shows you that basketball fans have come a long way, just like the players." Alcindor noticed the good faith that Bucks fans had toward Chamberlain, too. "The fans here are more decent than those in New York. They give you credit where credit is deserved," he said.[19] Almost to the day a year ago, the Bucks had been wiped off the floor by the Knicks and certainly their fans. Alcindor could still hear the fans in the Garden singing "Goodbye Lewie," and how they razzed the hometown kid. Now the Bucks had won the West and they awaited their rival to join them in the NBA Finals.

The truth is that the Warriors and Lakers were only footnotes in the Bucks' path toward a championship. Bucks players and officials felt there was only one team that was worth knocking off on their way to the title. They didn't hide how much they wanted to face the Knicks. Alcindor had his personal motivations for why he wanted to conquer his hometown team on the way to his first NBA title. McGlocklin wanted the Knicks for the simple fact that if the Bucks didn't face the reigning champs, he felt, "they were never going to acknowledge us in the East."[20] Only Smith went on record as being indifferent to who the Bucks would play, the Knicks or the Bullets. The Knicks had been the biggest thorn in the Bucks' side all season long. Five of the Bucks' 16 losses came at New York's hands. There would be no better way to show how much the Bucks had grown than by knocking off the reigning champs on their way to an NBA title. It was treated as so much of a foregone conclusion that the Bucks had already printed up programs for a finals battle between the two best teams that season: the Bucks and the Knicks. But the Bucks would have to continue to wait for the Knicks to join them. While Milwaukee made it out of the West, a grinding battle between the Knicks and the Bullets saw Baltimore come out on top.

It looked as if the Knicks were going to make quick work of the Bullets, going up 2–0 in the series after hosting the first two games. The Bullets fought back by taking the next two tilts quite handily to even up the series. The Knicks outlasted the Bullets 89–84 in Game 5, but Baltimore blitzed the Knicks right back for a 113–96 win in Game 6. In a do-or-die Game 7 on their home floor, the Knicks found themselves in familiar territory. They made a run late in the fourth quarter and even took a brief lead with under three minutes to go in the fourth. They had done this so many times in the past, especially against the Bucks. It was the greatest measure of championship equity—being able to pace themselves and striking in those big moments because they had been there before.

A new champion would be crowned for the 1970–71 season when the Bullets knocked the Knicks out with some big buckets late in the fourth to take a 93–91 victory that propelled them to their first of four trips to the NBA Finals that decade. They did so with a 42–40 record and the gap was wide between them and the Bucks, even as Baltimore had given the Bucks their biggest taste of defeat with a 30-point victory earlier in the regular season. The Bucks responded in kind by beating the Bullets by 52 points one month later, and they had taken four out of five games in their season series. It was as much of a shock to the Bucks as anyone that the Bullets had beaten the Knicks. Robertson later revealed just how much of a foregone conclusion they felt it was that they were going to play the Knicks: "We honestly didn't think Baltimore would beat the Knicks. They'd won two consecutive series in deciding seventh games. But because of scheduling quirks and expansion, we hadn't played them in more than three months. Coach Costello and assistant coach Tom Nissalke had to lock themselves in the film room and watch tapes of the Bullets, going over each of their playoff games in order to properly scout their tendencies."[21]

The Bucks weren't about to downplay the Bullets, especially after seeing the hard path that they traveled to get to this point. Costello noted just how explosive they were on offense, and their improvements defensively had been key to getting past the Knicks. But they had paid a price to make it to the NBA Finals. Their biggest stars—Earl Monroe, Gus Johnson, and Wes Unseld—were all nursing injuries suffered during the Knicks series or earlier. With the top billing on the marquee outside the Milwaukee Arena belonging to the World Championship Wonago Rodeo, the Bucks hosted

10. Marching Toward a Title (The 1970–71 Season) 91

the Bullets for Game 1 of the 1971 NBA Finals on April 21, 1971. Early foul trouble sent Alcindor to the bench for much of the first half, disrupting the Bucks' bid for control to set the tone for the night. Midway through the second quarter, Robertson got some extra motivation to win his first NBA championship. Fred Carter was the Bullets' sixth man and was coming off a terrific series against the Knicks. He had played hero for the Bullets when he sank the 20-foot shot that proved to make the difference in their Game 7 win over the Knicks just days earlier. During a trip down the court in the second quarter of Game 1 against the Bucks, he saw that Robertson had matched up on him. Whether it was his growing irrational confidence or the uber-competitiveness he possessed, he immediately shouted, "Get me the ball. I've got Oscar on me."[22]

In that moment and for the rest of the finals, Robertson made it a point to humiliate and best Carter any time the two were matched up on either side of the floor. Robertson remembered any slights directed toward him, both on and off the court. When Carter saw that Robertson had switched onto him and made a big show of wanting the ball, he embodied for Robertson everything he had battled against throughout his pro career. He was getting closer to accomplishing the only thing he hadn't done in his 11 years in the league, and it hung over him greatly. He was as good as anyone who had come through the NBA, yet it still wasn't enough to stop the questions: whether he was good enough to win it all, whether he could fight off his age when he joined Milwaukee, whether he and Alcindor could co-exist on their way to a championship. Robertson was four wins away from truly immortalizing himself. He may have been the Big O, but Carter wasn't about to cower in respect to him. With Alcindor in and out of the game, Robertson steadied the ship. He played the most minutes out of any Bucks player during the opening game of the series and finished with 22 points, seven boards and seven assists in his first finals game. A 16-point third quarter from Alcindor accounted for half of his 31 points of the game, and the Bucks left the Arena that night with a 98–88 win and a 1–0 lead.

It was a far from perfect performance—the kind that had come to define their season in general. The Bucks finished with 23 turnovers and after the game Costello bristled at the team's sloppiness. It was clear there was some meat left on the bone and that they had to be sharper to see out their mission. But confidence was at an all-time high—with Alcindor figuring that the Bullets were fatigued, battered and bruised. He saw a sweep or series victory in five games as the likely outcome. "Possibly, but I don't want to say we'll beat them in four or five. They were a little let down in the first game after that tough series with New York, and I think their play is going to pick up," he said.[23]

Jon McGlocklin (left) attempts to defend a layup from Baltimore Bullets guard Fred Carter (center), while Lew Alcindor (background) extends his reach to block Carter's shot. The Bucks swept the Bullets during the 1971 NBA Finals in what ended up being a lopsided series and the second championship sweep in NBA history (Historic Photo Collection/Milwaukee Public Library).

10. Marching Toward a Title (The 1970–71 Season) 93

Three days later, the Bucks descended on Baltimore for Game 2. Once again, the Bullets matched the Bucks bucket for bucket throughout the first half, and the Bucks went into halftime with a 49–45 lead. Whatever words were had behind closed doors stayed there, but coming out of the locker room the Bucks emerged as the dominant force they had been earlier. By the end of the third quarter, they held an 18-point lead and took the wind out of Baltimore's sail. They steered their ship into Baltimore's harbor and took Game 2 with a 102–83 win and a 2–0 series lead. The normally reserved Bucks couldn't contain their excitement anymore. Costello shouted throughout the locker room after the win, "Two down, two to go. Now all we've got to do is tie the knot. We can't let them get off the hook now."[24] Some players including Smith and McGlocklin entertained the idea of putting up a clean sweep over the Bullets. Robertson was quick to pull back on that notion, preferring to keep his eyes on the prize. But the thought of Milwaukee capturing the championship became widespread. The Bucks were too overwhelming for the Bullets to handle. The Bucks' best players were playing some of their best ball when it mattered the most and their confidence was oozing down to the role players. It was inevitable that the hammer would fall down hard enough to sink the Bullets whenever they came close to upsetting the order of things. When the Bucks returned home after winning Game 2, they arrived at Mitchell International Airport to find a thousand fans cheering them on.

Back at the Milwaukee Arena for Game 3, the Bucks were led by Dandridge. Foul trouble limited Robertson right when it looked like the Bucks had a comfortable lead over the Bullets midway through the third quarter. A 16-point lead dwindled down to a 70–68 edge in the span of four and a half minutes. Robertson promptly returned and the Bucks quickly reopened a double-digit gap. Dandridge and Smith provided some much-needed hustle and movement off of the Bucks' stars to break loose toward the rim and put down some needed buckets. As did Alcindor, who manned the middle on both sides of the ball. When it was time for Milwaukee to shake the Bullets loose, Robertson helped finish the job, four fouls be damned. In the locker room afterwards, though, very few Bucks players were ready to hang the banner or pop the champagne yet. Costello complained that his Bucks team wasn't all that sharp and that they hadn't even played well offensively all series long. Alcindor was clear in saying he was far from excited, even this close to the finish line. "No, I'm much too involved to get excited. You do that after it's over. When you get excited, you start to lose. Right now, it's a lot of hard work."[25]

That wasn't all of the talk involving Alcindor. Just hours earlier, Bucks president Ray Patterson, appearing at the Wisconsin Club where he and the Bucks were being honored for their community service, let it slip that Alcindor was on his way toward getting married that summer. After the Bucks' Game 3 win, Alcindor was pressed for more details by inquiring reporters, and that exchange went as follows.

> REPORTER: "Congratulations, Lew. I hear you are engaged."
> ALCINDOR (on his way to the shower): "Huh?"
> There is a pause of perhaps five minutes while Alcindor showers. He returns.
> REPORTER: "I hear you are getting married next summer. What is the girl's name?"
> ALCINDOR: "I can't tell you that. There's nothing for sure. There are too many variables. There's no date. Something might happen. Nothing's set."
> REPORTER: "I heard you were looking for a house here, that you like Milwaukee, and want to live here."
> ALCINDOR: "Who told you that?"
> REPORTER: "Ray Patterson announced it at a dinner tonight."
> ALCINDOR: "Well, I didn't tell him that."[26]

April 30, 1971. The forecast for Baltimore was a lovely spring day with a high of 63 degrees. The Baltimore Civic Center was packed with 11,842 Bullets fans who knew their team was making its last stand. The Bucks were as poised as ever, entering the night knowing glory awaited them with a victory. The stage was set for Milwaukee to become the fastest team to go from being a new franchise to winning an NBA championship in the NBA's first 25 years. There was only one man who was going to be steering the ship. It couldn't have been anyone else but Robertson to set the tone for the night. He had it rolling from the jump. He was hunting for his own shot, he set up his team on the break and was looking to slow down any of the Bullets guards on their way to the basket. Twenty-one of Robertson's 30 points came during the first half. The Bullets were fighting back. Literally. First, it was Monroe who squared up against McGlocklin after disputing a foul call and who even set his sights on Embry, who was seated courtside. Then, it was Jack Marin and Dandridge swinging at each other. Dandridge connected an absolute haymaker on Marin's face that left both with technical fouls. Baltimore hung in there enough to close the gap down to single digits not long into the start of the second half. But the Bucks woke back up. They dialed up their defense by smothering Bullets players as they looked for any daylight. With more and more stops, the Bucks ran and ran. They put the Bullets more out of reach and made the inevitable a reality. The minutes started counting down to five when some fans in attendance headed for the exits. With 2:42 remaining and with the Bucks up 113–97, Alcindor took a seat. But not before briefly raising his arms in triumph and being embraced by Robertson as he headed to the bench. The clock

10. Marching Toward a Title (The 1970–71 Season)

Jon McGlocklin (left), Bob Dandridge (center), Oscar Robertson (arms raised) and Greg Smith (right) celebrate the Bucks winning the 1971 NBA championship right as the buzzer sounds at the end of Game 4 against the Baltimore Bullets. It all came only three years after the Bucks were founded by Marvin Fishman and Wesley Pavalon. From the Bucks' *1971-72 Press, Radio and Television Guide* (Milwaukee County Historical Society).

continued to wind down and the Bucks reached the final stop in their journey. The normally reserved players were starting to crack. They showcased the emotion and joy of a team that had eyed one singular goal.

In his first NBA Finals, Robertson averaged 23.5 points per game, shot 52.3 percent from the field, dished out 9.5 assists and brought down five rebounds. Alcindor was named MVP of the series after he averaged 27 points per game on 60.5 percent shooting from the field, and 18.5 rebounds and 2.8 assists per game. And not for nothing, Dandridge made his mark on the sweep by averaging 20.3 points per game on 52.2 percent shooting from the field, 9.8 rebounds per game and 3.3 assists per game. Just as they had done all season long, the Bucks' "Big 3" of Alcindor, Robertson and Dandridge powered the team's dominance. In fact, the same went for the Bucks' entire starting five when you factor in Jon McGlocklin and Greg Smith, as all Bucks starters averaged over double figures in scoring against the Bullets. Make no mistake, this was a complete effort from a complete team, just as they had shown over the entire season.

Once the final buzzer sounded, the pandemonium began. Bucks players, coaches and staffers all mobbed each other across the court as they made their way to the locker room. TV cameras awaited the Bucks stars as they entered the locker room. Robertson bear-hugged Jack Twyman as the two celebrated Robertson finally breaking through and becoming an NBA champion. Robertson put up his index finger and shook his head in disbelief. All of the years full of anguish and heartache that he encountered over

A celebratory Oscar Robertson (center) hugs Lew Alcindor as they are interviewed by ABC television broadcaster and former NBA player Jack Twyman on the heels of the Bucks winning the 1971 NBA Finals. From the program for Oscar Robertson Day, March 26, 1974 (author's collection).

his time with the Royals. The playoff disappointments. The growing failures from ownership and the disconnect between him and the organization. The incessant questioning over whether he was truly great enough to capture an NBA title. All of that noise just vanished into thin air. The Bucks' decisive sweep of the Bullets made that possible, as did their season as a whole. Dating back to their undefeated preseason where they won 10 straight games, the Bucks finished their championship season with a 66–16 record and had only lost two playoff games, finishing with a combined 78–18 record. They were the second team in NBA history to have a clean sweep on their way to a title. They dominated their competition all year long. The team everyone expected them to meet in the NBA Finals fell one game short of doing so. But as the old adage goes, you play who is in front of you. And the Bullets stood as the Bucks' last team to wreak havoc on that year.

The champagne flowed throughout the locker room, with all but

10. Marching Toward a Title (The 1970–71 Season)

Alcindor sipping from the bottles of bubbly. Robertson raised his glass in the air and beamed, "You know this is the first champagne I've ever had, and it tastes mighty sweet."[27] For some, it was a chance to reflect on a long journey and how all of that hard work and dedication to their craft had led to this moment where they could stand and be referred to as NBA champions. McGlocklin knew a lot was riding on this season and relished this milestone after coming to Milwaukee as a castoff in the expansion draft. Boozer—who won gold at the 1960 Olympics along with the Big O—called the title the "ultimate thrill."[28] Costello had won a title as a player and now as a coach, and both felt enormous in his mind. And then there was Smith. He was incredibly overjoyed with how he—a fourth-round pick in the Bucks' first draft three years earlier—had now become an NBA champion. "I'm so happy I can't explain it," he said. "This is a long way from a small town in Kentucky. Princeton's the name, man, and be sure to spell it right. I started out just wanting to make the team. I figured if I could last a year, I'd be happy. This is too much for me to believe it's true."[29]

The Bucks celebrated long into the night knowing that they each had an additional $17,000 in their pocket after winning that year's championship. The city of Milwaukee celebrated, too. A convoy of cars packed Wisconsin Avenue well after the victory was over, with fans celebrating up and down the street. It was only a precursor of the scene that awaited the team when they arrived in Milwaukee at Mitchell International Airport at 2:15 p.m. the next day. The Bucks got off the plane and were greeted by over 10,000 crazed Bucks fans who were overjoyed to see their team on top of the basketball world. Mayor Henry Maier and other Milwaukee County officials were on hand to welcome them back to the city. Chants of "We want Lew! We want Lew!" echoed throughout the crowd. Those chants went unheard by Alcindor, though, as he stayed back east in New York to celebrate the latest and greatest achievement in his young NBA career. So, too, did Costello, who did not fly back with the team that day. Robertson and his wife, who had played host for the wives of Bucks players for Game 4 on Friday night, drove back to their house on Kenboern Drive to see a sign hung up on their driveway. In black spray-painted letters, it read, "Congratulations, O!"[30] This was the same neighborhood that had gone so far as to draft up a petition to prevent them from living there.

The Bucks' return from Baltimore and the warm reception they received from their fans at the airport was the closest thing they had to a championship parade. Why the Bucks' dominance and glory didn't warrant a parade is unknown. It was the kind of thing that could have brought the city together—a city that had been embroiled in social and racial unrest right before the team was born. Their triumphs on the basketball court could have been seen as a way to unite a city that had grown divided.

The Bucks reflected how the city's makeup had grown and changed. Making it to a championship win as fast as the Bucks did furthered Milwaukee's reputation as a good sports town and gave the city its next generation of stars and fan favorites to support as they ascended to the top of the NBA. They followed in the footsteps of the Braves and mirrored how that team also catapulted to success upon winning the 1957 World Series. The Bucks restored the city's pride after some wayward years, but unlike the Braves, they were given no grand parade down Wisconsin Avenue. There's no doubt the city of Milwaukee would long for the chance to celebrate a champion in the years to come.

Perhaps fittingly given how fast it came together on the court, Bucks players and coaches went their separate ways after a job well done. After a long season and plenty of pacing back and forth on the sidelines, the Bucks coach finally relaxed. Costello took that time to reflect on what was the key ingredient behind the team's play and concluded it was their togetherness. "Togetherness, that's what did it," he said. "Some teams only dig a deeper hole for themselves when they run into the weaker moments. They start looking at each other and pretty soon somebody says, 'It's that guy's fault, or that guy's fault.' Usually, it isn't the fault of anyone in particular, just something that catches up with a ball club."[31] Costello could have been talking about the Bucks' origin story. It all started with Fishman's mission to bring Milwaukee back into the world of pro sports. Fishman eventually brought Pavalon into the mix and the two gave life to an NBA franchise that climbed its way to the top faster than anyone could have imagined. Fishman couldn't believe it and he shook his head in disbelief as he saw Bucks players and officials celebrate throughout that Friday night and Saturday morning in Baltimore. Pavalon, on the other hand, saw it as the natural fulfillment of his original timeline.

From the moment he joined forces with Fishman, Pavalon had envisioned this timeline. It started with wanting a winning team on the court and building it to become a champion team in a short time. That timeline netted a talent like no other in Alcindor, which caught the eye of Robertson. The foundation the Bucks built grew with a strong supporting cast made up of players at the start of their careers. Castoffs who were deemed expendable by the other teams in the NBA made for a special chemistry that brought the Bucks to the promised land. Seeing it all come together was hardly surprising to someone like Pavalon. That didn't mean he didn't take satisfaction in achieving such greatness. "This has made a lot of people happy and that makes me happy. I see happy people all around, and that makes the whole thing worthwhile," he told the *Milwaukee Sentinel*.[32] "The team is my release. I'm not the establishment guy in Milwaukee, and I don't go to the opera and culture things like that. But I have given the city a performing art,"[33] he declared to Baltimore reporters as he and the Bucks celebrated this great achievement.

Everything had come together for Pavalon on the court and with the Bucks. Everything else in his life, though, had unraveled. His business—Career Academy—had expanded across the country, but its accounting methods were called into question. The company was accounting for the full price of each franchise as soon as contracts were signed. Eventually stock analysts started sniffing around and took a long, hard look at the books. They determined that the company's profits in 1968 were actually one-half of what had been reported. The company's stock price tumbled dramatically at the turn of 1970. Pavalon tried to steer the ship out of financial ruin, but it was too late. He filed for Chapter 11 and in 1975, Career Academy declared bankruptcy. Making matters worse, Pavalon's marriage had ended bitterly just as the Bucks began their championship season. He traded his possessions and the lavish lifestyle he had built for himself for a life of reclusiveness, settling on a site aptly called Hidden Valley Farms, just outside of West Bend, 45 minutes northwest of Milwaukee. Pavalon may have lost his vast fortune, and his dream of a sports empire with a professional basketball and hockey team was only half fulfilled. Still, there was no question as to what would be his greatest legacy.

On June 4, 1971, just over a month after having captured an NBA championship, Costello, Robertson and Alcindor sat before the press in Washington, D.C. They were about to represent their country by doing a tour of Africa on behalf of the State Department and the NBA. Spreading the gospel of basketball, the three Bucks figures were set to go on a six-nation trip with stops in Algeria, Senegal, Nigeria, Tanzania, the Somali Republic and Mali. Each had his own reasons for going on the trip. Costello and Robertson had made similar trips overseas before on behalf of the State Department. The inclusion of Alcindor was curious, though. He was just three years removed from his Olympic boycott, skipping the games that would be made famous by Tommie Smith and John Carlos when they held their black-gloved fists in the air after winning their medals, in the name of Black Power and in protest against their country's racism and inequality—the very things that Alcindor identified in explaining why he chose against representing his country on a global scale.

Things had changed dramatically for Alcindor in the month since winning his first NBA title. Days earlier while in the nation's capital, he had married his wife, Habiba, at the Church of Islam at 4 a.m. in accordance with Muslim law. Those in attendance had to be practicing Muslims according to his spiritual leader, Hamaas Abdul Khaalis. That meant Alcindor's parents were forbidden to see their son get married, causing much friction between him and his family. After having been prevented from seeing the ceremony, his mother didn't stay for the reception afterwards.

When Alcindor sat before the press on that day to talk about his impending trip with Robertson and Costello on behalf of the U.S., he only wished for one thing: to be called by his Islamic name. "When I'm speaking and holding news conferences, I want to use my Islamic name. I hope to get respect from my countrymen," he said. For Abdul-Jabbar, the opportunity to travel to Africa was a deeply personal one. It was a chance "to return to the fountainhead," as he called it.[34] He explained that while his grandfather was from the West Indies, he spoke Yoruba, the language of Nigeria—the country he believed he descended from. Abdul-Jabbar had spent the last several years reclaiming his history and reinventing his own place in the public eye. Yes, he may have been given his new name by someone else, just as he was named Lew by his parents. But Abdul-Jabbar's path toward self-discovery had led him to the point where he no longer needed to lead a double life. He had hidden his faith from a public that couldn't tell the difference between a Black Muslim and a Sunni Muslim—the latter of which Abdul-Jabbar practiced as and identified as.

At long last, this was Abdul-Jabbar finally announcing to the world who he truly was. It was on the world to respect his wishes and to respect his choice to be a member of the Islamic faith. The split between Kareem and Lew was no longer hidden in the Bucks locker room, his home or a mosque. Now, he had decided to fully reveal himself to the public and, as he would say, it was on all of us to accept his truth. For some, that acceptance took longer than it should have—even within the Bucks' own locker room. He followed up his landmark announcement by purchasing a $78,000 house in Washington, D.C., for the use of Khaalis and the Muslim community, so they would have a sanctuary where they could worship. He and his new wife took a detour during their trip to Africa, visiting Tunisia and Saudi Arabia, and eventually made their pilgrimage to Mecca. Kareem was finally living the way he wanted to, and it would be on the Bucks organization to help keep that possible.

11

Dynasty in the Making? (The 1971–72 Season)

When the Bucks won their first NBA championship on April 30, 1971, it was seen as a warning shot to the rest of the NBA. The NBA was about to be dominated by the men in forest green and red. Fishman had picked an emerald for the Bucks' championship ring that year, thinking they'd use a diamond for the title the next year and a ruby for the year after that. Players of that era even expected that the Bucks would capture titles for the foreseeable future. You could see the thinking behind this. The Bucks had the greatest and brightest superstar in their grasp and he was already the league's Most Valuable Player by his second season. Robertson's gambit to take his talents to Milwaukee helped him capture that elusive championship that once hung like a millstone around his neck. The Bucks were young and had already learned how to win in record time. It's hard to fault anyone who penciled in the Bucks to play in every NBA Finals for the rest of the decade.

More than 50 years later, hindsight colors the picture to help us see how and why the Bucks failed to extend their title into a dynasty. Some reasons are more obvious than others: age and plenty of miles finally catching up with Robertson; the bad breaks and poorly timed injuries during playoff runs; not landing one of the greatest players in the game, Julius Erving, when the NBA was truly in the Wild Wild West. The funny thing is that the very circumstances that are thought to have contributed to the Bucks' downfall faster than anyone could have foreseen only tell half of the story. The fault lines had already appeared as the Bucks were on top of the basketball world, and eventually the foundation cracked. The constant tension between players, coach, management and ownership was at the heart of why the Bucks became so successful so fast and why they ultimately failed to win another championship for the next half century.

The Bucks stood atop the NBA during that summer of 1971, making them a powerful entity within a league that was seeking to end the war between the NBA and the ABA. As players were fighting tooth and nail to prevent a merger from happening, arguing it would lead to a monopoly, the Bucks stood as one of the rare NBA clubs whose management also opposed a merger, along with the Warriors. The players associations arranged an All–Star Game between the NBA and ABA for May 28, 1971, out of season; it would mark the first time that players from both leagues played on the same court and was meant to show that the leagues could play against each other without a merger. Threats of fines and suspensions came from many owners in both leagues—but not from Milwaukee. "The owners refuse to present any game between the two leagues without such a merger. By such refusal, the owners' sole motivation should be clear—money. What should be of interest is the fan and the quality of product he sees. The players share that interest, and because of it, they will meet the public's desire for a super game," Robertson stated when promoting this landmark event.[1]

The Bucks also never had a greater amount of sway and capital for their ongoing battle for a permanent residence within the city. The plan to develop an arena next to Milwaukee County Stadium fizzled out, but the state was in the middle of working out plans for a new facility in State Fair Park. It was located just seven miles west of downtown Milwaukee, where the Bucks could be the major tenant. Rumors of relocation rumbled—especially as the Bucks brought Milwaukee a championship—and the public's interest in securing the franchise's roots in the city where it belonged grew and grew. No one wanted to see what happened to the Braves happen to the Bucks. In the mind of Milwaukee's mayor, the Bucks belonged in downtown Milwaukee. "I think it would be a detriment and a loss to this community if it were any other place other than downtown Milwaukee," Maier said.[2]

Meanwhile, for his work leading the Bucks to a championship, Costello was handsomely rewarded with a new three-year contract. It made him one of the highest-paid coaches in the league, with an estimated total of $150,000. Bucks assistant coach Tom Nissalke left for the ABA to coach the Dallas Chaparrals. Dandridge went public with his demand for a better-paying contract. "Management tells me to hold my head high, and be proud I'm a world champion. I am. But championships won't buy me food when I'm old. Money will," he told reporters in the middle of his pay dispute.[3] All Dandridge wanted was more financial security and to get what he thought he was worth for a team that won a title. He got that when the Bucks handed him a three-year, $200,000 extension to sign as he worked toward finishing his degree and prepared for the start of camp.

It was a relatively quiet summer for the Bucks in terms of who'd be coming and going. As the start of camp neared, the lineup that contributed

11. Dynasty in the Making? (The 1971–72 Season)

to that championship was no longer intact. First, the Bucks shipped off backup center Dick Cunningham to what was now called the Houston Rockets. Boozer then went out on top and retired after an 11-year NBA career. Cunningham had been there almost from the beginning of the Bucks' formation and was well-liked within the locker room. He and his wife contributed a thank you letter to the *Milwaukee Journal*'s editorial section after he was traded: "Three short years we've lived here, but in our 25 years of life these years will be memorable. We've drunk your brew, we've gained many pounds at your family restaurants and have enjoyed all of your beautiful sights. We even brought our two children into the world in wonderful Milwaukee. What we will miss most of all is all the wonderful, friendly people in Milwaukee. Thank you, Milwaukee, for making these past three years so very pleasurable."[4]

The names were starting to change within the roster, but the ambition and the team's overall goal did not. That was made very clear by Abdul-Jabbar, who announced his desire to win another championship at the start of camp. He declared, "I just want to do it again. I can't do too much more."[5] After a summer full of travel and personal changes, Abdul-Jabbar now had a companion as he settled back into the Milwaukee area, in the suburb of Mequon. He found that married life only sank him and his wife further into isolation. His connection to mainstream America—strained by the growing reaction to his name change and now-public devotion to Islam—had atrophied. "Although my wife was with me, my family and friends were at a distance; I was living in a Midwestern city that supported me without sustaining me. I had few acquaintances and wasn't spending time with those I had. All I had was my work, and I threw myself into that," he later shared.[6]

As the machine was ramping back up for the Bucks, Robertson tended to bigger matters. On September 22, 1971, he appeared before the Senate Subcommittee on Antitrust and Monopoly and was one of two NBA players to testify, along with Dave DeBusschere. Before the subcommittee, Robertson proclaimed, "Our opposition to the proposed merger is total. The players recognize the unfairness of a system of professional basketball which allows them to negotiate with only one team."[7] Robertson faced a long line of questioning from senators who pushed against the idea of players' rights and the bidding wars that pitted the NBA and the ABA against one another. When the topic of salaries came up, Republican senator Roman Hruska of Nebraska pressed Robertson. Hruska asked, "You seem to have done very well for yourself. Do you think you are worth more than the $100,000 you are getting?" Robertson replied, "To be honest and frank, I think so."[8] Robertson's answer brought laughter from the senators on the subcommittee as well as those in attendance in the gallery. But he wasn't smiling. Robertson approached his testimony with the same steely determination that he brought to the basketball court. His fight for what he thought was fair for the players had brought him this far and even after he went back to the camp, nothing stopped him from continuing the fight.

The Bucks didn't go on to enjoy an undefeated preseason for the second straight year. Instead, they went 8–4. When the regular season opened, though, they went into high gear, returning to the high standard they had established during their championship season. They opened the season by winning their first seven games before falling to the Celtics. And then they immediately rattled off a 10-game winning streak to improve to 17–1 over the first month of the season. If the Bucks were a team of destiny on their way to another championship, they were showing what the next few years could look like for the NBA. The staff at *Sports Illustrated* even thought they were shaping up to be the best NBA team ever in light of their latest fast start to the season, writing, "None of today's professional basketball teams can approach the Bucks, and if one recognizes a steamroller when it comes down the road, probably few teams of the past could match them, either."[9]

Even as they were at the peak of their powers, the Bucks—namely Abdul-Jabbar—courted controversy. The biggest instance came after a rare 106–103 home loss—their first loss at home in 24 straight games—to the newly rebranded Golden State Warriors on November 30, 1971. It was early in the fourth quarter when Abdul-Jabbar snapped on Warriors forward Clyde Lee. The two were tussling for position in the post, where Abdul-Jabbar always set up shop. One too many elbows and too much jockeying for position led to Abdul-Jabbar audibly cursing out Lee on the floor and flashing both of his middle fingers at him. The heat of the moment had gotten to the big man, as it did a few times before and after that game. But the *Milwaukee Journal* ran the picture of Abdul-Jabbar flipping off Lee on the front of its sports section and it took on a life of its own. It stirred plenty of reaction, not just from *Journal* readers around Milwaukee, and the paper's sports editor, Chuck Johnson, justified why he ran it on top of the page: "The hope here is that [Abdul-]Jabbar, the Milwaukee Bucks and the National Basketball Association will decide at once that enough is enough."[10] Bucks officials like Patterson quickly came to Abdul-Jabbar's defense. "I think it's a shame that somebody should see fit to take advantage of something Jabbar did in the heat of competition," he said.[11] Even Maier chimed in, continuing his crusade against the *Journal*—he had barred the outlet from his press conferences because of criticism aimed at him and his administration—and expressed his outrage for running the photo: "It is a great sport of The Journal Co. to take advantage of a public figure in an intense moment of a hard fought game. It is not very

11. Dynasty in the Making? (The 1971–72 Season)

sporting, considering what Kareem and the Bucks have done for basketball in Milwaukee."[12]

The Bucks were 25–4 when the next and biggest piece of their championship puzzle was removed. On December 10, 1971, Milwaukee dealt away their iron man, Greg Smith, to the Rockets for Curtis Perry and the Rockets' first-round pick in the 1972 NBA draft. It was a gut-wrenching blow for Smith. Arriving at Milwaukee as a fourth-round pick in the 1968 NBA draft, he had blossomed into a rotation regular and then an indispensable cog within the team's starting five. "It's part of pro sports and you accept it. The hardest part is saying goodbye to all the friends my wife and I have here. We had three fine years and had bundles and bundles of friends. If there's any city I had a choice to live in, I'd love to come back to Milwaukee. I really loved this city," Smith said in his parting message to reporters and fans alike.[13]

Bucks president Ray Patterson admitted it was a move that was incredibly tough to make, but the future flexibility and a top draft choice was too good for the Bucks to pass up. It still didn't make up for how devastating it was to the Bucks' best player. Abdul-Jabbar revealed that Smith was his best friend on the team. They bonded together through their love of movies and Kareem found that he could talk to Smith about anything going on in his life. That wasn't normal for the usually reserved seven-footer. When Smith was traded to Houston, Abdul-Jabbar saw the move for exactly what it was. He later wrote:

> I was very upset. I'd never had a friend forcibly removed before by some management whim. It was typical, wrong-headed owner thinking… What they didn't understand was that Greg was a key ingredient in the special chemistry that had made us champions. His selflessness, his continual movement, his leaping and defense, all were blended into a team that knew exactly how to win. We had become close as a team on and off the court largely because of his bright and affable personality. We'd just become champs, why break us up?[14]

The machine hadn't slowed down. The Bucks still had the likes of Abdul-Jabbar and Dandridge ascending and the steadying presence of Robertson kept them organized in their march toward repeating. Costello was growing more and more restless as success was almost guaranteed. But the connective tissue that had brought the players together was fading. The personnel moves suggested that a longer view was required. Perhaps they would be the very moves that could extend the team's era of glory if things panned out the right way in the draft. Time would have to tell, but the players certainly noticed the messy way things were handled and the lack of grace extended to those who had helped the organization win a title.

Out west, the Bucks saw a new threat emerge. Well, it wasn't exactly a *new* threat at all. The Lakers had responded to being beat down and battered by the Bucks in the playoffs the season before. They may have gone through the first three weeks of the 1971–72 season with a 6–3 record, but they won on November 5. And kept winning afterward. They won every game they played for the next two months and built their winning streak to 33 games—still an NBA record to this day. Suddenly, the Lakers were the main story of the NBA and they stole away the spotlight from the defending champions. They had surpassed the Bucks' 20-game winning streak, doing the very thing the Bucks had done to the Knicks during their title run. The Bucks did everything they could to keep pace with the Lakers and posted a 32–7 record by the start of the new year. Fans of the Bucks, Lakers and of the entire NBA circled January 9, 1972, on their calendars as the second time the two teams would clash that year. ABC had the rights to broadcast on national television what genuinely could be deemed as the biggest regular season game in the NBA's history. It was such a big deal that the city of Milwaukee would not be blacked out from seeing the game live, as was normally the case for Bucks games at that time.

The Bucks rode high on confidence and they had the bragging rights of being the defending champions. Costello called his shot days leading up to the clash by declaring that the Bucks would beat the Lakers. "We can beat them all if we play our game, and we're going to beat the Lakers, too," he said. "We're the champs, they aren't. They've got a winning streak, but that's all. We're the champs until they beat us."[15] It should come as no surprise that Costello was locked in about beating the Lakers' streak. He flew down

Oscar Robertson (right) loads up to shoot a jump shot over legendary Los Angeles Lakers center Wilt Chamberlain. The Bucks and Lakers had a number of high-profile meetings during the regular season and the playoffs during the Bucks' formative years. From the program for Oscar Robertson Day, March 26, 1974 (author's collection).

11. Dynasty in the Making? (The 1971–72 Season) 107

to Atlanta to see the Lakers pick up their 33rd consecutive win just hours after the Bucks had taken down the Pistons in Detroit. In watching the Lakers dismantle the Hawks with a 44-point victory, Costello saw a way to prevent them from running wild in Milwaukee. In order to win, the Bucks had to crash the boards to stop Chamberlain from throwing devastating outlet passes down the length of the court. There was no question the 10,746 fans in attendance at the Milwaukee Arena got their money's worth seeing the two powerhouse teams go back and forth that Sunday afternoon. The Bucks did what they planned and bothered the Lakers up and down the court. Los Angeles made plenty of errors with the ball and the Bucks feasted on those miscues. It wasn't until the fourth quarter that the Bucks broke away from the Lakers and gave them that feeling of impending defeat for the first time in more than two months. When the final buzzer sounded, the scoreboard read: Bucks 120, Lakers 104.

The Bucks had done what the Lakers' last 33 opponents couldn't do. After the game, Costello almost sounded like a man indignant. He continued to remind everyone what the Bucks had accomplished just months earlier. "I'm glad Atlanta didn't beat them Friday night, so we could have the chance. We're the world champions; they aren't," Costello shouted to anyone who was listening.[16] Even Abdul-Jabbar—who had become cynical about winning since it was all he had known in his basketball life— felt excited by the notion of putting an end to the Lakers' winning streak. From then on, Costello was the one to sound the horn when NBA observers crowned anyone other than the Bucks as the favorites for that season's championship. Until the Bucks were knocked off, there was no point in penciling in the likes of the Lakers, the Knicks and so on.

The subject of winning and success was one of disillusionment to everyone but Costello within the Bucks locker room that year. The Bucks had grown accustomed to winning big and humiliating their opponents by gaudy margins. After winning a championship, they were wired to turn it on when the lights were the brightest, which was best embodied in that streak-busting win over the Lakers. They had championship equity, but Costello despised the notion of complacency and was still obsessively searching for the perfect game. McGlocklin put voice to it when he explained the difference between experiencing the success the Bucks had during their championship season and defending their title: "Winning the title with a third-year expansion team was the miracle thing. We showed more emotion. This is not an over-emotional ball club and I wish we were…. But Milwaukee has become accustomed to having the big winner to root for. They had the Braves in the World Series, the Packers in the Super Bowl, and then the Bucks getting to the top so fast. Now we're expected to win, instead of people hoping we can."[17] The Bucks were no more than four years old and the concept of winning—to most if not all players on the team—had become so routine that the joy of competition had disappeared. Perhaps that came down to the principal figures involved, whether it was the workaholic coach, Costello, who had no problem drilling down on players day in, day out, or Abdul-Jabbar and Robertson, who still stood as the reserved leaders who weren't getting too high or too low after the outcome of a game. This established some checks and balances, but there was certainly something being lost in the day-to-day life of the team. That sweet taste of victory had grown stale to the Bucks as they marched toward defending their title.

After breaking the Lakers' streak in early January, just past the halfway mark in the season, the latter half of the year proved to be a much bigger challenge for the Bucks. They still hummed along and Abdul-Jabbar was arguably never better than he was during that season. He raced ahead to clinch the season's scoring title by averaging a career-high 34.8 points per game while making 57.4 percent of his shots and hauling down 16.6 rebounds per game. Abdul-Jabbar's extraordinary play was becoming even more necessary to the Bucks' success. Their floor general, Robertson, was slowed down by an abdominal injury. It debilitated him for the rest of the season and, after missing 18 games that year, robbed him of his ability to run at full speed.

Change continued to sweep through the Bucks as they geared up for the playoffs in the last few weeks of the season. Out was Patterson, who moved from the Bucks to the Rockets. Houston offered a deal that was too good to pass up and, sensing that he had accomplished everything he could in Milwaukee, Patterson was eager for a new challenge. The Rockets—just like the Bucks—were looking to secure a brand-new arena to play in and proved successful in that quest after bouncing around in their first few years in Houston. Patterson had championed the cause for a new arena more than anyone else associated with the Bucks. When he announced his intention to leave the organization, it set off alarm bells. The threat of relocation always hovered over the Bucks as they signed short-term leases to play at the Milwaukee Arena. The endless studies and lobbying from the city and the county painted a picture of the Bucks being obstructed by government bureaucracy. However, Patterson made it clear that his exit didn't dim the Bucks' long-term future in Milwaukee. "Absolutely not. This doesn't mean a thing. The Bucks' future is bright in Milwaukee, and I'm confident that they will always be there," he assured reporters in February after announcing his coming departure.[18] Patterson's resignation was effective April 30 and the Bucks had big shoes to fill. Luckily, they didn't wait all that time to find Patterson's replacement and turned to a man wearing size-17 shoes.

12

The Captain Makes History

Wayne Embry got a call from Patterson, who relayed that Wesley Pavalon wanted to see him in his office on Monday, March 6, 1972. The upshot was that the man who had been the first captain in Bucks history became their next general manager. The news left Embry dumbfounded and speechless as Pavalon broke it to him, accompanied by a few key Bucks board members. Embry was 34 years old. He was almost three years removed from his playing days and had been serving as an administrative assistant for the Bucks since he facilitated the trade for Robertson. He had been the longest holdout from the Bucks' expansion team, and the organization's brain trust had made a major impression on him during his last season on the court and his post-playing career.

Pavalon awaited any questions from Embry while he sought to compose himself. The gravity of the moment was hitting him. He'd be breaking barriers as the first Black general manager in any of the major sports in North America. He would be doing it in a city that was far from the most progressive place in the country. Embry remembered arriving in Milwaukee for the start of his final NBA season as a player and encountering houses that had signs advocating for former Alabama governor and hardened segregationist George Wallace as he ran for president in 1968. Milwaukee was a few years removed from the riots and the open housing marches, but the fight for integration in Milwaukee public schools and the class and racial divides still remained. When the shock wore off, Embry asked Pavalon what his job description would be. Most importantly, he wanted to know whether he'd have the authority to make the kinds of decisions that other NBA general managers had made before. Embry was not about to make history only to become a figurehead.

For all that Pavalon represented to the Bucks—a larger-than-life character with excessive wealth and stories straight out of a Mark Twain book—he never forgot where he came from. Pavalon hustled for all that he earned and eventually lost. Growing up on the North Side of Chicago and living in a lower-class community made up of all sorts of different cultures made him very sympathetic to those who were discriminated against, especially during those times. According to Embry, Pavalon didn't like being referred to as an owner because he "disliked the notion that any one person can own another."[1] It wasn't out of the ordinary to see Pavalon wearing a dashiki or flashing the Black Power sign after the riots in Milwaukee. Pavalon's progressivism stood out at a time when culture clashes between players and owners were part and parcel of the world of pro basketball. "You know, there are still owners in the league who have trouble accepting blacks. Think directly, not indirectly. Who created the black problem in America? Obvious, right? The whites. But people think indirectly. They blame the victims for being victimized. So in basketball, you hear checkerboard. Don't play five black men. Checkerboard. Different colors," Pavalon said of the NBA's handling of race at the turn of the 1970s.[2] Pavalon had even consulted with Father Groppi over the Bucks' nickname during the team's naming contest due to the connotations the word had during the days of slavery.[3] Embry was well within his rights to be initially skeptical of his promotion, but there were no strings attached from Pavalon and the top of the organization. Embry would be empowered by his new role and it meant that he'd be another ear for Pavalon's 2 a.m. phone calls.

A press conference was scheduled for the next morning and Embry kept his initial statement brief. He thanked Pavalon and the Bucks' board members for this opportunity, even though he had realized overnight what an undertaking it all would be: scouting for the draft, negotiating with players, overseeing ticket sales and managing the health of the business overall. The very first question asked of Embry was an obvious one: "How does it feel to be the first black general manager in professional sports, and do you think that is significant?" Without missing a beat, Embry replied, "It is significant, only if others think it is significant."[4] It turns out others did think it to be significant. The NBA had seen players become coaches or player-coaches almost from its inception. Not only was Embry breaking racial ground, though, he was also breaking ground as a former player turned executive. Embry was being hailed as a pioneer, but it didn't make the weight of his new role any more bearable. He later wrote, "I could not fail, because it would be a setback for blacks. Forget the fact that hundreds of white general managers had been fired and no one thought twice about hiring another one. What I tried to get across was that we as blacks should be given the same opportunity to fail as whites. That would be significant, but it would be more significant if I succeeded—as Jackie Robinson did."[5]

Not all the reaction to Embry's appointment was positive, of course. Embry remembered accusations that Pavalon had hired him as window dressing. Hate mail came to the Bucks offices and Pavalon made sure the worst of it never came across Embry's desk. But Embry knew it was there.

12. The Captain Makes History

More threats followed Embry over his years in Milwaukee. It didn't take long for him to block out all of the negative noise, just as he had done throughout of his life. To be a trailblazer was to build a path for others to follow. All along, Embry had the qualifications and experience to be in this role and help define the franchise's next phase. He felt the responsibility of having to maintain a championship-caliber roster for Kareem and Oscar immediately. The requirements for Embry to succeed were far different than for the GMs who came before him. The Bucks had ascended to the top and it was Embry's job to keep them there. That meant doing it with less valuable draft picks, because the Bucks were fighting for the best record in the league in those days. The budget to operate the team was far different and less lavish than it had been when the Bucks were pursuing the likes of Abdul-Jabbar and Robertson. It was going to be hard to reimagine a roster that was losing its youth in favor of experience and the drawbacks that come with that. Embry had to do all of this while starting from scratch in the front office, as many Bucks staffers had followed Patterson to Houston.

Back on the court, the Bucks finished the 1971–72 regular season with a 63–19 record. They clinched the Midwest Division with a 109–98 victory over the Portland Trail Blazers with seven games left in the regular season. When asked about capturing another division title after the game, Abdul-Jabbar remarked, "I'm just glad it's over. That's about it."[6] For the second straight season, Abdul-Jabbar was voted as the league's Most Valuable Player. But even as mighty as he had been throughout his third NBA season, the Bucks were leaving observers unimpressed. They weren't throttling the opposition with the same vigor and fury that came to define their run to the championship one year earlier. Furthermore, Robertson's health status was still a big question mark. No one else had quite the ability to break down and diagnose opposing defenses in the manner that Robertson could, even at less than 100 percent. It was the Lakers—not the Bucks—who were being tabbed as the favorites to win that year's title as the playoffs began. Los Angeles finished the season with an NBA-record 69 wins, besting the mark set by the 76ers during the 1966–67 season. The Bucks may have held onto their bragging rights by beating the Lakers and breaking their 33-game winning streak, but the Lakers bested the Bucks in the four other matchups they played against each other during the regular season. The clubs were on a collision course to face off against one another in the conference finals that would determine who would take the West. This time, there weren't any detours.

For the second straight year, the Bucks opened their playoff run by meeting up against the Warriors. The Warriors were stronger than a year before and still had some of the same players that bothered the Bucks, the biggest being Nate Thurmond. They were looking to flip the script this time around and they gave the Bucks quite a jolt by taking a 117–106 victory in Game 1 on the Bucks' home floor. Golden State outshot, outhustled and outsmarted a lethargic Bucks team during their comeback win and Costello was quick to point out that it was a wakeup call for the Bucks. They answered that call by taking Game 2 with a 118–93 win. A runaway 122–94 victory followed in Game 3 for the Bucks as the series shifted to the Bay Area. Slowly but surely, the Bucks were flexing their old muscles and showcasing the dominance that had become so routine with them. Games 4 and 5 weren't as one-sided, but Milwaukee did away with the Warriors in five games, just as they had the previous year.

Awaiting them were the Lakers, who swept the Bulls in four games. For the second straight year, the team to come out of the West was either going to be the Bucks or the Lakers. Unlike the previous year, it was Milwaukee that was more banged up. Robertson's durability had taken a hit and McGlocklin had missed the Warriors series with a back injury. The Bucks needed to be at their best to take on what was the league's best. It was Kareem versus Wilt, West versus Robertson. The lovable losers versus the new dynasty of the NBA. There was much more at stake than the Bucks simply defending their title.

The Western Conference finals started on April 9, 1972, exactly three months after the Bucks broke the Lakers' 33-game win streak. It was another Sunday afternoon and the Bucks put in an absolutely smothering performance that ended in a 93–72 win. The Bucks put the clamps down on the Lakers by limiting them to 27 percent shooting from the field and only eight points throughout of the third quarter. The 72 points the Lakers scored were the fewest the Bucks had allowed as a franchise up to that point. Needless to say, it was quite the opening statement the Bucks made. Abdul-Jabbar gave a reminder of who the Bucks were and what the Lakers aspired to be. "We don't need too much to fire us up, because we're the champs," he boasted in a rare fit of emotion afterwards.[7] The Bucks weren't looking to take just one game in Los Angeles as the series opened. They were regaining their swagger and were talking more confidently than they normally would. They felt and believed they could take the first two games. They had regained their motivation and, most importantly, their hunger once the calendar turned over to the postseason. Speaking about this, Dandridge said after the game, "I guess it was because we won the title last year and didn't have the same motivation. But now we're in the playoffs and those are what really count in the NBA. We have a lot of pride on our team. We're the world champions and we're playing like we did last year.... We'll remain the world champions until someone dethrones us, and that will be tough to do."[8]

The Lakers responded in Game 2 to pull out a 135–134 win by the skin

12. The Captain Makes History   113

of their teeth and with some unforeseen help. A late game possession saw Abdul-Jabbar trapping West down the floor in hopes of forcing a turnover with the Bucks down 133–132 as the clock ticked down the last 20 seconds. Abdul-Jabbar got a hand on the ball, dislodging it from West, only for it to bounce off of referee Manny Sokol. West regained possession, but Abdul-Jabbar came back and knocked it loose again. West retrieved the ball in the backcourt and zipped it up the court to Happy Hairston, who slammed it home. It left the Bucks with quite the gripe. "It's unfortunate when an official gets involved in a key play, one that will affect the outcome. I wish I had lots of money and then I might say a lot of things," Costello bristled after the game.[9] The series shifted to Milwaukee for Game 3 and the Lakers emerged victorious yet again. A 108–105 victory for L.A. came down to the final minute, in a game in which the prevailing takeaway was an unsuccessful bomb threat being called in during the second quarter. Game 4 saw the Bucks even up the series with a 114–88 win that restored order, at least for one night. As much as they tried to fight it, though, things had caught up to them. Robertson wasn't moving well enough to kick off a fast break. The injuries were piling up and plaguing the Bucks. And yet, Costello was more than willing to make the case that this series should have been over by now. "We should have won this thing in four games. But I'll tell you one thing: We're only going to Los Angeles once. None of this return trip stuff. We're going to win it in six," he declared between Games 4 and 5.[10]

You couldn't fault Costello's logic, or his "win in six" prophecy. The Bucks had won two one-sided contests and the Lakers had eked out both of their wins in the final minute. The Bucks had outscored the Lakers by 43 points through the first four games in the series. They still had the extra gear that made them the defending champs. It was as if Costello was baiting the Lakers to put forth a more complete effort, and they showed it in Game 5. With a 115–90 victory, the Lakers ripped through the Bucks over the course of the second half. It was apparent Robertson didn't have the manpower to be on the court for how much the Bucks needed him out there. He was limited to just 29 minutes and finished with nine points. West certainly took notice of Costello's prediction, too. "I think our players saw his comment that they would win it in six. Anytime a coach says anything like that, the guys on the other club are going to find out about it. I wonder if he still likes the Bucks in six," he commented to reporters after the win.[11]

Costello didn't back down and kept believing in his side. He didn't believe the Bucks would quit, and they would be playing for their playoff lives on their home court in Game 6. After a much needed four-day layoff to regain some energy, the Bucks had to win or go home for the final

Oscar Robertson backs down Jerry West in the post during a game between the Bucks and Lakers. Robertson and West's careers were intertwined from when they were drafted no. 1 and no. 2, respectively, in the 1960 NBA Draft and retired weeks apart from one another in 1974. From the program for Oscar Robertson Day, March 26, 1974 (author's collection).

time. It was a tight contest all throughout the first half and the Bucks went into halftime with a one-point edge at 51–50. They created some breathing room over the course of the third quarter and eventually held their biggest lead at 85–75 with nine minutes left to go in the fourth quarter. The Lakers kept on coming, but the Bucks held strong with a 96–91 edge with under three minutes to go. From there, the wheels fell off. The Bucks players afterward lamented the fast shots they took that they missed. The Lakers capitalized on some quick possessions to whittle away at their deficit. They eventually overtook the Bucks with 1:34 remaining and didn't look back. When the final buzzer sounded, the scoreboard read: Lakers 104, Bucks 100.

12. The Captain Makes History

There went the Bucks' title defense. Their series against the Lakers was defined by missed opportunities: their inability to close out Games 2, 3 and 6—two of which were on their home floor—and Robertson laboring under plenty of pain. Costello had to go as far as to limit Robertson's time on the floor to seven minutes for Game 6 and cited the Bucks' need for more speed on the floor. As expected, the Bucks players were dejected at seeing their season come to an end and in the manner it did. No one summed up better than Costello their bewilderment at where all of the magic had gone: "We weren't as hungry as last year. We played as hard, especially during the playoffs, but I don't think we did it with as much emotion."[12] Costello found an ally in McGlocklin, who echoed, "We definitely didn't have the same hunger. I know that's a natural tendency after you win the championship, but it's still no excuse. We didn't play like we should have. There was a difference in attitude on the team—a difference in intensity. We weren't as intense as we were last year. Last year, we felt like we weren't to be denied. This year, it seemed like we felt we could be denied."[13] As he was heading out the door, Patterson said the biggest regret in his four years with the Bucks organization was being unable to defend their championship. "Negativism crept into the whole operation," he said. "There wasn't that great spirit there was before, and that included everybody, not just the players. A little bit less from everyone contributed to our being knocked off the pinnacle. I'm sure this was because success had come too soon—winning the championship in the team's third year of operation. It was less electrifying on the part of everyone. If we could find a formula to prolong the enthusiasm after a championship has been achieved, we would have something."[14] The season didn't end in the way that anyone liked. But for the second straight year, the Bucks drew over one million fans for their games during the regular season and enjoyed 22 sellout crowds for their 36 home games at the Milwaukee Arena. And Robertson erased any doubt by assuring everyone that he was going to return for the 1972–73 season.

In light of the Bucks' playoff flameout, Abdul-Jabbar instantly made headlines as he justified the hefty salary he was earning with the Bucks when appearing on the television program *Black Journal* with host Stan Lathan. "I feel that it's all justified. The Bucks are a public corporation, and since I've been on the team, they have made a lot more money than they did before. It's all related to my presence here," he asserted. He further explained that basketball became a business to him from the moment he decided to go to UCLA. When pressed about his life in Milwaukee, Kareem didn't hesitate to describe the differences he'd seen between living in the Midwest compared to the coasts. "As a place to live, Milwaukee is kind of different to relate to. It's Middle America, and I'm from Harlem.

If ever there were two opposite points, this is an example."[15] That summer shaped up to be a transformational one for Abdul-Jabbar. He planned to stay in Milwaukee for part of the summer as he awaited the birth of his first child. On June 22, 1972, his wife gave birth of to a daughter, who was also named Habiba. Hamaas Abdul Khaalis had named Kareem, his wife, and now his daughter. He reasoned that since he had the most complete Muslim training, he should be the one to name Kareem's first child. Kareem accepted.

Co-existing with his wife and now his daughter came with a learning curve for Abdul-Jabbar. Above all else, he prioritized his privacy and the time he needed to be alone. His first year of marriage was a happy one, but he always felt the need to have his own space and his own privacy even in his home. He later reflected, "I'd been a loner, and when it came time to be married, I wasn't used to dealing with someone in what had been my own territory who was going to leave the cap off the toothpaste or keep the shower stall door closed when I wanted it open. More than that, I found that even though as a solo I had often been bored and lonely, there was also a comfort I derived from solitude that I couldn't find in any other way. There was nothing I could do about it—there was nothing I wanted to do about it—at some point I just felt like being by myself."[16] Some weeks after the birth of his daughter, Abdul-Jabbar traveled to the Northeast. He took some classes studying Arabic at Harvard University to bring himself even closer to his religion. While taking those Arabic courses, Abdul-Jabbar was confronted with a harsh reality. The teachings that he strictly observed under Khaalis did not align with what he was reading in the Quran and the basic teachings of Islam. Soon enough, the very practices and customs that were passed down to Abdul-Jabbar through Khaalis were called into question by fellow practicing Muslims that Abdul-Jabbar had gotten to know over the course of that summer.

Kareem learned that what Khaalis had quoted to him as hadiths—verbal traditions that were passed down from the Prophet Muhammad and put into book form—could not be found in any written collection. He grew more disturbed as he encountered other practicing Muslims who declared that what he had been taught bordered on extremism. "I became very uncomfortable," he wrote. "Hamaas had discouraged us from checking out his edicts with other Muslims because he said they were all charlatans, and many of the people whom I had checked out in the Islamic world *were* charlatans. I had become involved in Islam because I sincerely believed in its principles—they matched my own desire for commitment and purity—and the way Hamaas had taught me about the faith and its culture made a lot of sense to me, demonstrated true insight. Now I was finding that Hamaas may have been insightful, but not correct. I

12. The Captain Makes History

was shaken."[17] Abdul-Jabbar eventually confronted Khaalis with his findings, his doubts and concerns. Khaalis lashed out and doubled down on his teachings and practices. Abdul-Jabbar was dismayed by the entire exchange and the fact that Khaalis had even threatened to leave the house in Washington, D.C.—the house that Abdul-Jabbar had purchased for the use of the Hanafi community—if he didn't stop his questioning. After weighing the situation from all angles, Kareem stood down. He gave the house to the Hanafi Movement but felt totally alone within his own community. He sank himself even further into isolation, and later stated, "My faith in Allah remained strong, but my belief in Hamaas had weakened and that caused me pain. I couldn't abandon my questions, I could only stop asking them in public."[18]

That summer saw the Bucks ownership undergo a major shakeup. Fishman sold his share of the Bucks after putting in what appeared to be a successful bid to purchase the Bulls for a reported $4 million. Fishman and his investment group needed 13 of the other 17 owners—or three-fourths of the league's owners—to approve the deal. He'd gotten to that magic number, but the Bulls were never transferred over to his group. The NBA nixed his bid and, in short order, the Bulls were instead sold to Arthur Wirtz. Wirtz owned Chicago Stadium and the NHL's Chicago Blackhawks. Fishman couldn't secure a lease with Wirtz to have the Bulls play at Chicago Stadium, and he filed a lawsuit once he discovered why that was. It took over a decade for the suit to be resolved, and Fishman never managed to get back into NBA ownership from that point onwards. Not long after Fishman's departure, Pavalon resigned as president of Career Academy and continued to retreat from the public eye, despite still holding the title of the Bucks' chairman. Everything had changed in and around the Bucks in significant ways that impacted the way the team operated for the next few years. The debate over their long-term permanent home raged on all throughout this time.

In what was easily their biggest victory that summer, the Bucks secured a four-year contract extension with Abdul-Jabbar that stood as one of the most lucrative deals in all of sports. He signed the contract while in Boston as he continued his studies at Harvard. Given his lack of affinity for Milwaukee and a future in the city, it was a win for an organization that needed long-term stability in its franchise, according to new Bucks president Bill Alverson. "We think the signing is particularly significant for Milwaukee and the Bucks at this time. We are aware of the rumors as to what would happen to the Bucks if Kareem would leave," Alverson announced to reporters.[19] It was a good thing that the Bucks signed Abdul-Jabbar to a new contract, not just for the sake of keeping the greatest player in the franchise, but also as a bargaining chip. As talks over where the Bucks would play intensified over that summer, they felt that they had encountered a reluctance from state representatives to help build a new facility if Abdul-Jabbar were to leave Milwaukee one day. Alverson relished the fact that Abdul-Jabbar signed on for at least four more years and hoped it would quash that reluctance to build a new arena. "We have been countered with skepticism in our efforts to negotiate for an expanded facility. The skepticism has centered around what's going to happen to Kareem in a couple of years," he said.[20] In signing the deal, Bucks officials hoped Abdul-Jabbar would make Milwaukee his year-round home. When Abdul-Jabbar arrived for training camp a month after his contract extension, he made it clear that was not going to be the case. When he was pressed over whether he ever thought of leaving Milwaukee, Abdul-Jabbar was coy. "It's impossible to say," he said. "The time wasn't any way near appropriate for that."[21]

13

Missed Opportunities
(Dr. J and the 1972–73 Season)

The signature that the Bucks waited on throughout the summer of 1972 hadn't played a minute for them. Within the first month of his tenure as Bucks general manager, Embry had two first-round picks at his disposal—with one of those choices coming to Milwaukee in the Greg Smith trade. With the 12th overall pick, Embry knew he could swing for the fences. The Bucks selected Julius Erving, a forward from the University of Massachusetts. Erving had emerged as the defining superstar for the ABA, where he played for the Virginia Squires for the 1971–72 season as a rookie. He had taken advantage of the ABA's hardship rule, which allowed underclassmen to jump to the pros. He signed a seven-year, $500,000 contract with Virginia, with much of that money being backloaded. Though he was named the ABA Rookie of the Year, the Squires fell short of making the 1972 ABA Finals after losing to Rick Barry and the Nets. Because the ABA didn't have a national TV contract, Erving's high-flying artistry and superstardom was still something of an urban legend or tall tale. So how did Embry cross paths with this young, dynamic forward from Long Island?

That happened when Embry was gearing up for his only season playing for the Bucks' expansion year. What began as an invite to a basketball camp in Schroon Lake, New York—where Embry addressed the aspiring players—ended in a chance encounter with Embry playing Erving one-on-one. Embry later wrote, "We were supposed to play to eleven, and right off the bat, he scored the first seven points. I scored a couple of points to make it respectable, but he was the first to eleven. We were going to play the best-of-three, so he said, 'Mr. Embry, you can play regular basketball against me.' I said, 'Okay, but I'll be easy on you.' I still thought I would hurt him. So I am trying to practice my hook, but he was blocking my shots all over the place. He totally dominated me. That was my introduction to Julius Erving."[1] From then on, Embry kept tabs on Erving's career.

When word got out that he was looking to make the jump to the NBA after his rookie year, Embry knew that his draft rights could give the Bucks a way to add a massive talent.

Even knowing the risks and the many legal hoops the Bucks would have to jump through in order to lure Erving away from the ABA, Embry couldn't have possibly foreseen where this saga would go. Days after the completion of the 1972 NBA draft, it was revealed that Erving had signed a $2 million contract with the Atlanta Hawks a day before the Bucks had selected him. Embry was quick to reinforce the rules the NBA had put in place in regard to the power that teams had over a player's draft rights. "As far as the by-laws of the National Basketball Association go, the rights to Julius Erving belong to the Milwaukee Bucks. It's as clear cut as that," he said matter-of-factly.[2] Things had gotten messy, and fast. The ABA–NBA signing war involved three teams across both leagues which had the player rights to Erving; two of them had contracts with him as well. With the leagues seeking to merge all throughout this and the players associations fighting in the federal courts to prevent a monopoly in pro basketball, the solution wasn't going to come very easy. There was a feeling that NBA commissioner Walter Kennedy was losing his negotiating power when it came to the rivalry between the leagues. He made it clear that the Bucks held Erving's NBA rights, but the summer months passed without a resolution to the matter.

Training camp for the 1972–73 NBA season was on the horizon. The Bucks and the Hawks were in contact with one another over Erving and began to negotiate over some sort of compensation between the two sides. Naturally, neither side wanted to give up on having an inside track to the next NBA superstar. The impasse continued until September 12, 1972, when Atlanta judge G. Ernest Tidwell deemed Erving's contract with the Squires void. That freed Erving up to practice with the Hawks and protect them from the ABA in the process. While it still didn't resolve anything as far as the Bucks and the Hawks were concerned, Erving made it very clear by promptly practicing with the Hawks that day that he never intended to go to Milwaukee. It was clear where he wanted to play if he was to come to the NBA. Embry was livid and took Kennedy and the NBA to task for letting this charade continue. "Unless this matter is settled, and unless the constitution and its bylaws, which we followed, are upheld, the league is inviting complete mayhem," he stated after the decision.[3]

Days later on September 20, the NBA board of governors concluded in a 14–2 vote that the Hawks had violated the league's constitution and bylaws by signing Erving to a contract while the Bucks held his draft rights. Score one for Embry and the Bucks. Yet, the Hawks weren't standing down and owner Bill Putnam openly defied the league's ruling. "It's not as bad as it sounds," Putnam said. "The ruling of the Board of Governors was based on the NBA bylaws and constitution. Our position was that the bylaws didn't apply to Erving since he was not a college student and was a professional."[4] Putnam went on to say that the Hawks had offered the Bucks several first-round picks for Erving's draft rights. The Bucks, though, only wanted Erving, not the picks. Admitting that he and the team could have done things differently, Putnam said signing Erving to a secret contract—which Erving himself requested—the day before the draft was a mistake.[5] With the NBA's ruling in their favor, the Bucks had the ability to sound out Erving through his agent. The Hawks defied the ruling by having Erving not only practice with the team but also play preseason games, even as they did not have his player rights. When the league fined the Hawks $25,000 for playing Erving in two exhibition games—the largest fine ever doled out under Kennedy—the Hawks filed an antitrust lawsuit against the league. After so many dizzying twists and turns, federal judge Edward Neaher ordered Erving to go back and play with the Squires in the ABA on October 2, 1972. The case was sent into arbitration based on a clause in Erving's contract with Virginia. Erving was a Squire for that season and was playing professional basketball not just on one court but two, the other being a court of law.

The Bucks entered training camp ahead of the 1972–73 season still clinging to the hope that Erving would join them. Embry's hopes were not dampened by all of the legal drama. The Bucks entered camp with renewed vigor. Abdul-Jabbar expressed his desire for more help surrounding him. When asked if there was more he could do on the court—after two straight MVP seasons and two straight scoring titles—Abdul-Jabbar was matter-of-fact: "I don't think so."[6] There were greater questions surrounding Robertson as he went into his 13th NBA season and the final year of his contract with the Bucks. Naturally, there was speculation over whether this was going to be his final year in the NBA. His decision would be made with the success of the Bucks in mind, rather than his own individual status and health. Robertson shared, "I'd like to see what our chances are. It depends on how the team is going to be. I'm sure they're going to try to get some inside help, so I'll wait and see. The team and myself are really intertwined in my decision."[7] Speaking of help, Costello had an old friend, Hubie Brown, join his coaching staff. The two men had played together at Niagara University during their playing days. While Costello then played a starring role in the NBA, Brown had cut his teeth coming up through the coaching ranks, first across high schools in the Northeast, next as an assistant at the College of William & Mary and then to Duke University before coming to Milwaukee. The 1972–73 season had a way of testing the Bucks' character on and off the court. Before the season even started, they went through the monthslong dance of trying to secure Erving, only to have that all get shot down and things go back to where they stood in the first place. There was the palace intrigue of organizational changes that brought in new faces to lead the Bucks in its next phase as a franchise. It brought another level of scrutiny to an organization that already faced pressure to secure its long-term future in Milwaukee as plans loomed to build an arena for both the Bucks and a potential NHL franchise.

Bill Alverson, the newly promoted president of the Bucks, had already secured a second contract for Abdul-Jabbar and he kept chopping away at trying to keep the team in the city where it belonged. "What people want is for the Bucks to stay here, and we are just busting our butts so that they will. I don't know how to communicate how strongly I feel about this. But I do, I really do," he stated in a profile in the *Milwaukee Journal*.[8] The more that was shared on the inner workings of the Bucks at the time, the more they looked like a business trying to keep the machine running before the well dried up. The fine-tuning the Bucks did paid off when they began preseason play by walloping ABA clubs for the second straight year. But it was all overshadowed by what happened in Denver following their 130–92 win over the ABA's Rockets. In the early morning hours of October 6, 1972, Abdul-Jabbar and Lucius Allen were taken into custody on charges of possession of marijuana. They were thrown into jail for five hours before being released on bail for $200 each. Embry bailed his Bucks stars out of jail after having a long night himself, catching up with Rockets head coach Alex Hannum. He had been woken up by a phone call from a reporter who wanted his opinion of the incident. He went to great lengths to plan for a quiet return back to Milwaukee as the news swept throughout the country. In consultation with Costello and the rest of the team in Denver and those back in Milwaukee, Embry rerouted the team's flight to Chicago. From there, they bused to Milwaukee. Upon getting off the bus at Mitchell Airport, they planned to have a press conference. Three microphones were arranged: one for Embry, one for Abdul-Jabbar and one for Allen. Only Embry was there to face the music, though. When the bus arrived at its destination, Abdul-Jabbar and Allen peeled off and headed straight for their cars. Photojournalists caught the Bucks players striding away from the press conference and, by the looks of it, demonstrating their lack of accountability. Charges were immediately dropped for Abdul-Jabbar, and Allen waited three months for his own charges to follow suit. Nonetheless, this incident was a precursor of the NBA's own war on drugs and the perception that a predominantly Black league would inevitably see many of its stars battle drug and addiction problems. How the public handled the shock of seeing the best player in the league go to jail for drug possession

13. Missed Opportunities (Dr. J and the 1972–73 Season) 123

foreshadowed how the league eventually cracked down on its players and how it all added to the stigma surrounding the makeup of the league itself.

Recalling the ordeal years later, Embry summed up his growing plight since being appointed to his position earlier that year. "Personally, I was desperate for something good to happen to the Bucks. In my short tenure as general manager, we had far too many bad breaks," he said.[9] Eventually, these ordeals shook the Bucks as they resumed their chase for a championship in the regular season. After winning 11 of their first 13 games, the Bucks entered choppy waters when their dominance over the Midwest Division was finally challenged by their I-94 rival, the Bulls, who overtook Milwaukee for first place in the Midwest. It had been over two years since the Bucks hadn't been in first place in their own division. Milwaukee's early-season lethargy had Costello at his wits' end, and the Bucks hadn't reached the quarter-way mark of the year yet. "I hope something jars them," he said. "I'm trying to, but I don't seem to be getting through to them."[10] Eventually, the Bucks started to get the message. For the rest of the season, they spent only nine days out of first place. They took a six-game win streak into the start of December. After another stumble, a seven-game win streak carried them into Christmas and they eventually stood at 28–11 by the end of the month.

But by the end of December, the Bucks were embroiled in yet another controversy. It started when Wali Jones didn't accompany them on a two-game road swing to the Northwest with games against Portland and Seattle. Embry made it clear why Jones was not joining the team: they wanted him to undergo a physical with a team-appointed physician, citing concerns over his playing weight and a lack of stamina. Since coming to Milwaukee a year earlier, Jones had been a standout advocate for the Bucks on and off the court. He was active in the community, where he organized Concerned Athletes in Action, an anti-drug organization that taught youth the perils of drug use. Jones refused to undergo a physical. His playing weight of 170 pounds was the same as it was the previous season. The Bucks promptly placed him on medical suspension without pay until he satisfied their requirements. He relocated to Philadelphia to regroup with his lawyer, who announced that Jones would undergo a physical with a Philadelphia-based doctor. That was not to the Bucks' liking. Over the next month, a standoff ensued. The public saw the lengths Milwaukee was going to in alienating one of their own players, and a very highly paid one at that. Jones officially protested his suspension at the start of the new year. After the NBA commissioner heard the case and acted as an independent judge, the Bucks decided to waive Jones. Jones had two and a half years remaining on his $240,000 contract—which included no-cut and no-trade clauses. Jones's attorney accused the Bucks of defaming his client, especially after he cleared waivers, with no team making a bid for him. It took Jones three years to wind up back in the NBA as a way for him to finish out his 10-year veteran career and gain a pension. The Bucks had resolved the Jones case, but it left them with one less contributor in their pursuit of a championship.

Just days later, a life-threatening situation developed. On January 18, 1973, tragedy struck when a deadly massacre occurred at the house that Abdul-Jabbar had bought in D.C. and donated to the Hanafi community. Seven of Abdul-Jabbar's friends and fellow Muslims were killed at the house, including five children. At the time, it was the worst mass killing in Washington, D.C., history. The police didn't take long to announce that they were looking into members of the Nation of Islam organization and that as many as eight men were being sought for the killings. Abdul-Jabbar learned with the rest of the world that his spiritual leader, Hamaas Abdul Khaalis, had sent as many as 50 letters to the ministers of all the Black Muslim temples. The letters were critical of their leader, Elijah Muhammad, and his teachings and urged the ministers to leave the organization. Khaalis had originally joined the Nation of Islam and became a high-ranking official when it was led by Malcolm X during the 1950s. Like Malcolm X, Khaalis eventually broke away from the organization and became a Sunni Muslim, which set him down the path of starting the Hanafi community. The Black Muslims now viewed Khaalis as a threat. They sent men from the Philadelphia Black Mafia—which was associated with the Nation of Islam—to kill him. When Khaalis was out of the house that fateful Thursday afternoon, the gunmen took some Hanafi community members hostage and waited for his return. Eventually, they grew impatient and turned to killing some of the hostages. Three of Khaalis's sons were murdered, as was his daughter and second wife. Three infants were also drowned in a bathtub and a sink. The assassins were in the process of leaving just as Khaalis and the rest of his family returned home. They managed to escape the premises before Khaalis could retaliate. The incident left Abdul-Jabbar inconsolable and his connection to the tragedy obviously brought the attention of the authorities and the press.

It was quickly settled that there would be round-the-clock protection for the superstar player, on and off the court, at home and road games. Abdul-Jabbar traveled to D.C. to serve as a pallbearer for the funerals that were held in the aftermath of the tragedy. He was excused from playing in that year's NBA All–Star Game in Chicago, which also served as the home of the Black Muslims, but resumed playing as the Bucks picked back up after the All–Star break. Abdul-Jabbar later remembered the feelings he had during that time and especially as the assassins still were at large:

13. Missed Opportunities (Dr. J and the 1972–73 Season)

> Living in fear has a strange effect on you. The minor impulses of a normal life are disrupted by the constant potential for harm. The desire to see what's in the mail, the late-night urge to drive to the deli for a yogurt—they could cost you your life. Once you incorporate that fear into your daily routine, as you must if you really want to protect yourself, you find both your days and your character a lot less pleasant. Under different circumstances this is exactly the kind of penetrating dilemma I would have leaned on Hamaas to help me cope with, but he wasn't there this time, and I didn't find the strength to do anything but retreat into numbness.[11]

The incident had totally shaken Abdul-Jabbar and he became fatalistic. To bring himself some balance, he focused all of his energy on the court, on each game and on the Bucks season, all while having a slew of security follow his every move. The tension had seeped into the locker room. Embry remembered Bucks players telling him that they didn't want to stand next to Abdul-Jabbar in the warmup line or for the national anthem for fear of getting shot. Abdul-Jabbar, though, made it very clear that the murders in Washington, D.C., were not the start of a religious war, as some began to fear. In a profile with *Sports Illustrated* just after the murders, he stated, "Our beliefs direct us to try to keep a pure mind. We are ordered to exert a positive effect on our surroundings. That's why we fly the American flag outside our community and paste flags in the windows. We want to show that we hope to do good here, to work for the improvement of the whole environment and to work within the framework of the Constitution, which guarantees freedom of religion."[12] The incident and the aftermath brought a new layer of exposure to Abdul-Jabbar, his beliefs and Islam as a whole. And not for the better, in the eyes of an American public that didn't discern the differences between the sects within the religion. Abdul-Jabbar brought more of a focus to Islamic culture, just as Muhammad Ali had done before him. With these incidents of violence, though, what prevailed was the broad brush that painted all Muslims as radicals. The general reception to Abdul-Jabbar's faith remained skeptical, even as his faith hadn't faltered. "Being a Muslim is the best thing I could be. I would never take a backward step on that," he declared in an interview with Terry Bledsoe of the *Milwaukee Journal* more than a month after the killings.[13] The burden on Abdul-Jabbar grew even greater and playing basketball was his only refuge. He could no longer rely on his spiritual leader as Khaalis sank into the depths of paranoia. His home life and attempts to co-exist with his wife still had not clicked. Costello worried about the strain that grew bigger on Abdul-Jabbar's shoulders as the season wore on. So did his teammates, with one going so far as saying, "The poor guy goes out there knowing he could get bumped off, and he still scores."[14]

Despite all of the paranoia and anxiety that seeped into Abdul-Jabbar's life as his every move was being followed by armed guards, the Bucks eventually rebounded and went on to win 60 games that year. They were the first team in NBA history to win 60 or more games for three straight seasons. Given all that had gone on—the many off-court incidents,

Oscar Robertson (right) leaps up to block a shot by Pistons forward Curtis Rowe while Jon McGlocklin (left) watches from the baseline in a game during the 1972–73 NBA season. Despite finishing with 60 wins, the Bucks faced a number of challenges that season before being upset in the playoffs (Historic Photo Collection/Milwaukee Public Library).

13. Missed Opportunities (Dr. J and the 1972–73 Season) 127

the injuries that kept them from being fully healthy for most of the year—the adversity that Milwaukee faced certainly didn't derail them from winning their final 14 games of the regular season. Having tied the Lakers for the most wins that season, there was speculation as to whether the Bucks and Lakers would play a one-off game to determine who'd be the top seed in the West. Los Angeles roundly rejected that notion. Instead, a coin toss was held to see who'd be the no. 1 seed. With that coin flip, the Bucks won the rights to have home court advantage. For the third straight year, they opened their playoff run against the Warriors. The biggest difference this time around was that the Warriors had Rick Barry, who had returned to the Bay Area after six seasons in the ABA. Milwaukee had knocked off the Warriors five out of six times during the regular season that year, and they were determined to not let Barry run loose.

Game 1 gave an indication that the Bucks would run away with the series after a 110–90 victory on their home floor. The Bucks entered the proceedings by wearing a whole new set of warm-up suits, as they had done during their championship season. However, Golden State flipped the script from Game 2 onwards. The Warriors left Milwaukee having secured a 95–92 victory as the Bucks failed to complete an ill-fated comeback. Going to San Francisco for Game 3, the Bucks didn't play around, taking a 113–93 win that was more remembered for its extracurriculars and brawls between Bucks and Warriors players than for the game itself. That was the Bucks' last victory of the season, however. With narrow victories going to Golden State for Games 4 and 5, the Bucks were blown out by the Warriors with a 100–86 victory in Game 6 to finish their upset over the Bucks. It was a surreal ending to a season that no one could have predicted. And even midway through the series, tragedy still managed to strike the Bucks' operations. A 13-inch snowstorm descended upon Milwaukee on Monday, April 9, 1973. The NBA refused to postpone Game 5 of the Bucks–Warriors series that was set to be played at the UW Field House in Madison the next day, because of scheduling conflicts at the Milwaukee Arena. As the second-biggest April snowstorm in Milwaukee history descended on the city, Wes Pavalon's father, Maurice, was driving through an alley off of Wisconsin Avenue downtown. When the weight of so much snow sent a fire escape crashing down in the alley and blocked his car, Maurice walked to a nearby parking lot and promptly collapsed. The 62-year-old was pronounced dead on arrival at Milwaukee's Mount Sinai Hospital.[15]

Some of the familiar problems that had taken down the Bucks a year earlier had resurfaced again. An Achilles injury Robertson suffered in the middle of the series nagged at him as the series went on. Abdul-Jabbar met his match in Thurmond, who made him look more ordinary than usual, and he went on to average his fewest points per game (22.8) for a playoff series as a Buck, while shooting just 42.8 percent from the field. Dandridge had gone into the series with a groin injury that had slowed him down in the playoffs and it showed in his final stat line. In six games, Dandridge averaged 13.8 points per game on 42.1 percent shooting from the field, 4.7 rebounds and 1.2 assists. He even averaged his fewest minutes per game (34.0) in any playoff series while playing with the Bucks. The Bucks' brief playoff run was a microcosm of their season overall. Nothing came together when it was the time for it to.

In the immediate aftermath of such a painful ending, it looked like the Bucks were going to undergo swift changes. All key Bucks figures and officials were either pointing their finger at the biggest targets of criticism or apologizing for the Bucks' unexpected collapse. Embry questioned his team's will and he asked why they couldn't put forth an effort like they had done in the playoffs against a team that they had dominated during the regular season. Abdul-Jabbar apologized to his teammates for his performances during the series when the Warriors swallowed up the Bucks whole. Dandridge was promptly the subject of trade rumors while McGlocklin questioned whether the Bucks had lost their hunger and competitive spirit. It was Robertson, though, who was the voice of reason. Despite the fact that his contract was up, he decided that he would play another season in the wake of the Bucks' campaign coming to a premature end. He took a look at the entire picture behind the Bucks' unsettling season and how much had been lost, reflecting, "There were a lot of upsetting things. Very unfortunate things, too many things that interfered with the game on the court. But that's all secondary, because no matter what you say, the game is on the court and that's where we got beat."[16] For his part, though, Dandridge gave in to the trade rumors and believed a change of scenery could benefit both him and the Bucks. "It's just a matter of me waiting around. I don't have any real hassles about being traded. I would have no bitter attitude because I feel I've performed well here," he told reporters when asked about the rumors.[17] The reality was that Embry had no real desire to trade Dandridge. Dandridge learned himself that the rest of the NBA was cool to the idea of trading anything significant for him as had been speculated. Dandridge walked into Embry's office once trade talks had perked up that offseason and heard things that he didn't want to hear. Embry later recalled, "I put on the speaker phone and called the teams [Dandridge] had listed as his preferences. Bobby did not like what he heard. 'I love Dandridge,' we were told over and over, 'but I don't need another malcontent.'"[18] Needless to say, that helped clear the air.

Some perspective eventually crept back into the proceedings once the situation washed over the Bucks. Embry didn't necessarily seek out major changes with external additions. What he wanted more than anything was changes internally: for the Bucks to find what they'd been looking for, what had once propelled them to a championship and what had remained elusive ever since. At the same time, despite not having a top pick, the draft offered a way to make a splash that could bolster their roster. With the 16th overall pick in the 1973 NBA draft, the Bucks selected Swen Nater out of UCLA. The Bucks had had success with another big man out of UCLA, but Nater was a much different test case. He came to the game very late and hadn't even played during his days at Woodrow Wilson High School in Long Beach. He went to Cypress College—a junior college in California—and his play as a sophomore eventually earned him a scholarship at UCLA. Nater was Bill Walton's understudy and he scored 287 points over his two seasons with the Bruins. He then became the first player to be picked in the draft without ever having started a game in college. If this sounds like a complete shot in the dark, it was far from it. Nater had been selected in the ABA draft the previous year and another bidding war bubbled up between the Bucks and the Virginia Squires, the same team that had Erving. The Squires had the inside track in negotiations with Nater as Milwaukee slow-played negotiations with him. Trade rumors broke of the Bucks looking to flip the Dutch big man to the Rockets for Calvin Murphy, and that left Nater even more wary of their true intentions. Nater was looking for the most money and the Bucks had offered him $50,000. The Squires had offered Nater $300,000 over three years, with payments spread over seven years. Nater took the Squires up on their offer. It was clear the Bucks couldn't even compete with mid-tier ABA clubs financially. For the third straight year, the Bucks saw their top draft choice lured away by the ABA. It appeared as though the Bucks were going into the offseason with no major changes on the horizon.

After an incredibly trying year, Abdul-Jabbar spent the summer of 1973 visiting the Middle East as well as Thailand and Malaysia. He designed the trip to bring him closer to his religion and his Muslim peers. Doing his best to speak Arabic all throughout his travels, he tried not to see himself as the typical American tourist. He visited countries where Muslim culture was dominant and was exhilarated to feel as though he was among the majority. When he arrived back in the States, and back in Milwaukee, everything related to his faith, his fellowship and his marriage had taken its toll on Abdul-Jabbar. "Our life in Milwaukee was entirely predictable. We rarely went out, rarely had people over, spent most of our time listening to music or reading the Quran. The interests that had brought us together had dwindled. Soon, it was clear to me that the main reason we were married was that we were Muslims. Hamaas had been the man who arranged this marriage, and I was out of step with him, and out of love with her," he later recalled.[19] Abdul-Jabbar had found his own moral center after determining that Khaalis no longer served that role for him. He recognized his own failings in sustaining Habiba. When winter rolled around, the two agreed to separate and divorce. Habiba took their daughter back to Washington, D.C., with Abdul-Jabbar occasionally visiting. He likened it to "erasing a mistake."[20] Abdul-Jabbar reverted back to living on his own.

The good news was that after months and years of speculation, the Bucks finally had a long-term home. They didn't even have to move out of the place they'd been playing in, either. On June 13, 1973, the Bucks and the city of Milwaukee finally came to an agreement on a five-year lease for the Milwaukee Arena, with an option for an additional five years. After years of hand-wringing and months of openly courting an arrangement for a new facility on the State Fair Park grounds, the contract gave the Bucks much more security, more desirable dates and eliminated the possibility that they'd have to play playoff games anywhere else but Milwaukee. Their rent for each home game got cut in half, going from $4,050 for the 1972–73 season to $2,000 for the first five seasons of their new lease.[21] They were also due to take over the arena's concessions operations and move their home offices within the premises. All along, the mayor had desired for the Bucks to stay downtown. The months of the Bucks being lured to be the primary tenants of a brand new coliseum on the State Fair Park grounds forced the city to make it more than worth their while to stay rooted in downtown and even forced Maier to intervene at long last. He announced, "Milwaukee is and continues to be major league in every way.... I think there has been a great deal of civic spirited compromise on both sides. The board itself has been very cautious about this whole proposition, but not cautious to the point that our dear basketball team was prone to leave us."[22] After all this time, the Milwaukee Arena would now be referred to as the "Home of the Bucks," as contractually agreed upon. It was only then that the Bucks thought of the Arena as their permanent home.

14

One Last Run
(The 1973–74 Season)

The summer months passed with all fronts largely quiet surrounding the Bucks. Robertson spent the entire offseason getting in the best playing shape possible. He cut down his weight to 217 pounds and signed a one-year, $250,000 contract on the eve of training camp. He made it clear to Embry that this was going to be his last season. He reminded the Bucks general manager that the team had to look for his replacement during and after the season. For the sake of making a run at a title, Robertson and Costello insisted that the 34-year-old Robertson couldn't be overextended over the course of the regular season as he had been the last two seasons. All Bucks reported to training camp, except for Dandridge as he sought a raise in his contract. He missed the start of camp with unexcused absences and subsequently was fined before signing a new contract with the team. Expectations were riding high going into the 1973–74 season, and Dandridge's late arrival to camp didn't dim his optimism. In his mind, it wasn't enough anymore to win 60 games. He didn't see why the Bucks couldn't get back to the top of the mountain. Abdul-Jabbar, when asked about his expectations for the coming season, was blunt: "We've got to be better. We can't be any worse than we were last year."[1]

Milwaukee showed their renewed vigor once the season got underway. The Bucks won 14 of their first 15 games in the regular season. After a three-game losing skid, they rattled off a 10-game win streak and firmly planted themselves as the top seed in the West before December began. After endlessly tweaking his starting lineup for years, Costello put his five most talented players in to start games. Allen had finally come into his own as a speedy, driving guard who helped ease the pressure that was being put on Abdul-Jabbar and Robertson, easing the ball handling burden for Robertson in particular. The Bucks shored up their depth with shrewd moves on the margin by bringing in Ron "Fritz" Williams over the offseason and picking up Cornell Warner in the first stretch of the year. These were the kind of moves that had helped buoy the Bucks when they were making their first push to the finals and a championship. Why couldn't they catch lightning in a bottle once again?

Costello was credited by his players for softening his strict disciplinarian approach, which had only gotten harsher after the Bucks won the title. Costello begrudgingly accepted the rare losses as learning lessons for his squad during the Bucks' blazing start to the year. "It's tough to be tough these days. I don't think even Vince Lombardi could be the same way today as he was when he was coaching. The players are different. Larry bends now, and that's good," Robertson observed of Costello early on that season.[2] The Bucks kept winning. They had to in order to keep their control of the division. The Bulls emerged as a serious threat for the Midwest Division and in the West once again. Even the Pistons were finally on the come up, with Bob Lanier as the man in the middle and overcoming its under .500 seasons. The Bucks had no choice but to play their best ball all season long. Their experience and continuity came to the fore throughout the year. Yes, they were defined by the star presences of Abdul-Jabbar and Robertson. It was as a unit, though, that they had been through the highest of highs and experienced profound disappointment over the last two years. Dandridge believed the collective attitude of the 1973–74 team was the best he had seen in his years in the NBA. Perhaps that was due to Abdul-Jabbar becoming more connected to his teammates just as his marriage dissolved. He saw it as a way to enjoy life in the NBA and was no longer trying to immerse himself in isolation. If nothing else, he viewed Milwaukee as just another road town where he could loosen up. Even if he felt he had no home, it didn't stop him from trying to have fun.

This was the fourth full year the Bucks' core had been together and it certainly showed in how they played off of one another. It was Costello's sixth season at the helm and he and the Bucks celebrated his 300th victory on December 26, 1973, with a 123–110 win over the Cavaliers. He became the tenth head coach in NBA history to reach such a mark. Bucks public relations director John Steinmiller lettered the cake himself before it was wheeled out after the game. The wives of married Bucks players banded together just as their husbands did. They had even formed a charity organization called the Milwaukee Bucks' Wives Association which organized events and took up causes including infant illnesses and diseases.

Everything ran smoothly for the Bucks until Robertson went into Milwaukee's Lutheran Hospital with an ailing back on December 29, 1973. He was in traction and the doctors had to literally stretch him to soothe his flaring sciatic nerve. He was expected to miss 10 days, but he went on to miss 11 straight games. The Bucks went 8–3 during that stretch. It was during that layoff that Robertson was approached by the organization with

14. One Last Run (The 1973–74 Season) 133

the idea of holding an Oscar Robertson Day. Robertson had told Embry he saw that year as his last, and now he saw that the entire organization had taken his words to heart. "Suddenly, it was apparent that the Bucks weren't planning on me coming back either. Whether I was planning to leave or not, I wanted the Bucks to be honest with the fans," Robertson remembered years later.[3] If this was going to be a retirement party—as Robertson thought it was—they chose their final game of the season, versus the Kansas City–Omaha Kings on March 26, 1974, for when it would be held.

The Bucks started to lose their strong grip as the best team in the league after the All-Star break. When they didn't have it on a given night, they lost big. They jumped from wins to losses so easily that they couldn't put it together consistently in one way or another. Costello still kept his eyes on the ultimate prize. Embry noted that Costello became obsessed with beating the Bulls. Costello regularly traveled down to Chicago to watch and scout Bulls games, whether by himself, with Embry or with Hubie Brown. The Bulls increasingly nipped at the Bucks' heels as they started to slip from their lofty place in the standings. Injuries piled up for the Bucks down the stretch that season. For as much as he tried to contribute, Robertson's bad back hampered his play and his role became entirely dependent on how he managed physically in heavy minutes. Dandridge was in and out of the lineup and Abdul-Jabbar was the one trying to keep things whole, just as he was growing used to do.

No loss, though, was more monumental for the Bucks than that of Lucius Allen. With seven games to go, the Bucks went up against the Pistons on March 15, 1974. That game mattered plenty in the standings and in their fight for a division title. The Bucks were in the middle of an ill-fated comeback effort late in the fourth quarter in a game that the Pistons took by a 93–89 edge. Allen made an attempt to block a shot thrown up by Pistons guard Dave Bing with nearly two minutes remaining in the game. He landed out of bounds under the Pistons' basket as he wiped out on a pile of Pistons warmup jackets that were mistakenly left there by a ball boy. Abdul-Jabbar saw Allen's heel catch the cloth of a warmup jacket and Allen crumple to the floor, looking like he was doing the splits. The result was a torn MCL that forced Allen to miss the rest of the regular season and the upcoming playoff run. It was a crushing blow for Allen, who was in the middle of a career year, averaging 17.6 points per game and hitting nearly 50 percent of his shots from the field. He found his niche playing as a clever cog off of Robertson and served as a speedy threat for the Bucks. Robertson lamented Allen's loss and what it meant for the Bucks' attack against the backcourt pressure they were sure to face in the postseason. Allen himself went so far as to say it was a matter of negligence on the Pistons' part. "I felt that negligence was involved. Negligence on someone's part—the Pistons' management, the officials, someone. And I'm very teed off because it hurt our chances in what I thought was our year. Now, we can go into the playoffs, and I can't be a part of it," he sternly said.[4] The Bucks were still able to wrap up the division title a few nights later with a win over the Warriors. Abdul-Jabbar was named the league's Most Valuable Player, taking home that honor for the third time in four seasons. The Bucks entered the postseason with the best record at 59–23, though they fell short of winning 60 games for the fourth straight year.

The day finally came for Robertson. One game remained in the Bucks' regular season and the enduring meaning that came out of it was highlighting an incredible talent and his entire basketball career, from high school to college and all the way to the NBA. Robertson had plenty of friends, family and teammates in attendance: three of his most influential coaches, local politicians such as Wisconsin governor Patrick Lucey and Maier. The Milwaukee mayor declared Tuesday, March 26, 1974, to be "Oscar Robertson Day." Over the course of a 118–98 victory over the Kings, Robertson received four standing ovations, one when he was introduced as part of the Bucks' starting lineup, one when he took the floor for the halftime ceremony and before and after his acceptance speech. No one remembered the fact that he finished with 14 points on 10 shots and nine assists. What everyone remembered and spoke of was the way Robertson's greatness, courage and generosity had shone through everything he did on and off the court. The Bucks announced the start of an annual scholarship in his name to the University of Wisconsin-Milwaukee and a fellowship to aid Nigeria's basketball program. Robertson's friends, coaches and teammates all remarked on how special he was to them, to fans and to cities like Cincinnati and Milwaukee. He received a motorcycle, sculptures, a movie projector, a money clip and a humidor. To Robertson, though, nothing mattered more than the connection he had made with everyone who took part in the ceremony. "The most rewarding thing is to have your friends with you on a day like this," he later wrote. "That's better than any material thing.... Basketball has been my life. I have enjoyed it and I hope I've given you fans a lot of enjoyment as well. My high school coach, Ray Crowe, taught me that no matter what you do today, there's always a game tomorrow, and I've always tried to abide by that."[5] All in all, the ceremony was a grand send-off for one of the game's greatest players—just as Robertson expected. It was around this time, though, that Robertson was perhaps having a change of heart. He said after the game that he would know whether he'd retire by the beginning of the summer. Costello thought differently when asked after the game about Robertson's playing future. "The way [Oscar's] playing now, he could play another five years," he said.[6]

A familiar foe waited for the Bucks to start their playoff run. The

14. One Last Run (The 1973–74 Season)

Lakers had lost Chamberlain in the offseason upon his retirement. While they won the Pacific Division with a 47–35 record, it was far from an easy season. West threatened to retire at multiple points as he was limited to just 31 appearances during the regular season. West and Lakers coach Bill Sharman openly talked about the Bucks being the best team in the NBA that year and felt that the Lakers' chances of getting through the Bucks were remote at best. They were reminded of that opinion when the Bucks tore through the Lakers and won the series in five games. Next up was the Bulls. The Bulls had outlasted the Pistons in seven games, winning Game 7 by a 96–94 margin. Costello's obsession with beating Chicago had not subsided and losing to them was simply not an option. Nine days had passed since the Bucks wrapped up their series with the Lakers. On April 16, 1974—Abdul-Jabbar's 27th birthday—the Bucks opened their series with the Bulls with a 101–85 victory. They escaped with a 113–111 win in Chicago for Game 2 to put the series at 2–0 and were led by Abdul-Jabbar's 44 points. Playing Game 3 back on their home floor, the Bucks pummeled the Bulls on their way to a 113–90 win. Finally, frustration set in for the Bulls. Bulls players barked at the referees all night. Coach Dick Motta got into a shouting match with legendary referee Earl Strom and threw his coat at him. He earned his ejection, and so did Benny the Bull, Chicago's mascot. Benny made the trip up to Milwaukee, backed up his coach, and joined him in the locker room. Never before had a mascot been thrown out of an NBA game and likely no mascot has been tossed since. Chicago was demoralized and on their last legs when Milwaukee finished off the Bulls in Game 4 by winning 115–99 in Chicago Stadium in a series sweep. Costello walked into the locker room and was greeted by Embry, who promptly bearhugged his coach. Bucks players were beaming with confidence.

Almost three years since winning the NBA title in 1971, the Bucks were back in the NBA Finals. The team was once thought to be the next NBA dynasty, but a number of detours had taken them off that path, many of which they couldn't foresee. They returned to the finals older and a little more weary. But they could still kick it into gear and appear as the devastating force that left many wondering if there were any championships left to be had for the rest of the NBA. It was only fitting that the Bucks went up against the prototypical NBA dynasty, the Celtics. All roads had led to the finals for the two best teams in the NBA, who would battle against one another for the big prize. They both tore through their opponents in the playoffs and had split the season series with one another during the regular season. Milwaukee had home court advantage, but Boston could say they were entering the series at full strength. The Celtics were back in the finals for the first time since 1969 and it was their first trip without Russell anchoring them from the middle. Russell's retirement had made way for Abdul-Jabbar to be the new face of the league, at the center of everything in Milwaukee and, presumably, the entire NBA. These were the same Celtics that prevented Robertson from making it out of the Eastern Conference while he was with the Royals. The same Celtics that Costello downed while with the 76ers in 1967, putting an end to their streak of eight consecutive NBA championships. The same Celtics that Embry played for and won a title with in 1968. There were a lot of personal motivations and experiences going into a showdown with such a storied franchise.

It didn't take long for Boston to nullify the Bucks' home court advantage. The Celtics came through the Milwaukee Arena on a Sunday afternoon. They played with a fury that Milwaukee couldn't match. Boston ramped up their pressing defense from the jump and put even more heat on the Bucks' ball handlers. They raced out to a 35-point first quarter, leading the Bucks by 16 points, and never looked back after the first frame. The Celtics beat the Bucks 98–83 to take Game 1 and set the tone of the series. Costello immediately confided that he was thinking of lineup changes following the loss. He searched for any way to combat the Celtics' fast break and their speed from all five spots on the floor. He sought to make the series one that was defined by half-court basketball. Precision and execution was the key to Milwaukee. The Bucks missed Allen and if that fact wasn't brought home before, it certainly was over the course of the series. To make matters worse, the Bucks' backcourt faced another hit with McGlocklin being hampered by a calf injury that subdued his effectiveness for the rest of the series. Their back was against the wall, but just like they had done pretty much all season long, the Bucks found a way to respond in Game 2.

It took an overtime period for the Bucks to get it over the finish line. After nearly letting a 14-point lead at halftime slip through their fingers by the end of regulation, Milwaukee evened the series with a 105–96 victory. The deciding nine points scored came courtesy of obscure heroes such as Warner and Williams. Life was still hard for Abdul-Jabbar, who operated below his standard efficiency amid the Celtics' pressurized defense. The Bucks coughed up the ball with the Celtics hounding them up and down the floor and running like a string. Robertson did his best to command the team and he was seeing the floor for nearly every second of every game. Dandridge alternated between efficiency and being ineffective, but his speed was still useful in breaking the Celtics' pressure. The chess match evolved in turn after turn and it was now Boston's time to counter.

The Celtics played host for the first time in the series in Game 3 and raced off to another hot start that left the Bucks reeling. A 32–13 advantage at the end of the first quarter separated the two clubs, and Boston eased

14. One Last Run (The 1973–74 Season)   137

into a comfortable 95–83 win to put the series up to a 2–1 lead for them. They made flummoxing the Bucks look routine as they finished with 27 turnovers for the game. The Celtics pounced on every pass or mishandle from Bucks ball handlers, making them look old and slow. Costello went back to the drawing board for Game 4. No series better showed his tactical acumen and his basketball genius than this one. He had far fewer weapons at his disposal as injuries mounted throughout the series. Yet, Costello found a way to adjust and did so when it was the right time. For Game 4, he turned to Mickey Davis, who had come to the Bucks in the 1972 draft, and inserted him into the starting lineup.

With Davis playing with the starters, the Bucks injected some much-needed shooting and ball handling to ease some of the pressure from the Celtics. The change was enough for the Bucks to hit enough shots and make the Celtics think twice about doubling Abdul-Jabbar in the post or applying full court pressure on Robertson. Davis was a spark plug, finishing with 15 points on 5-of-9 shooting. McGlocklin finished with 10 points off the bench. The Bucks got all of the help they needed to win 97–89 and tie the series at two games apiece. It was now a best-of-three series and the Bucks knew two of the remaining games would be held on their home floor if it went full tilt. Game 5 in Milwaukee was not pretty for the Bucks, and it certainly wasn't in the third quarter. They got vintage performances from Abdul-Jabbar—37 points, 11 rebounds, and six assists—and Robertson—23 points on 13 shots. They entered halftime down 45–44. Seven minutes into the third frame, the Bucks fell into an 18-point deficit that proved to be insurmountable.

Walking off the Arena floor after a 96–87 loss, they faced a do-or-die scenario going into Boston for Game 6. Save for Game 2, it was the road team who reigned supreme in this series. If there was ever a series in NBA history that pointed to the futility of home court advantage, it was this one. Yet, the allure and history of the Boston Garden and the intimidation of knowing your season was on the line and a win in the Boston Garden was needed in order to live another day could faze even the most experienced and professional of players. Costello was not about to let this opportunity slip through the Bucks' fingers, though. He called his shot as the Bucks readied themselves for Game 6. "We're going to win," he told reporters. "This has been our goal—to win the title. We'll be back in the Arena Sunday."[7] The Bucks came out with no fear of the Garden mystique or worry about how the Celtics had stymied them throughout the entire series. They hit shots and ran away with Game 6 through the first two quarters. They went into halftime with a 47–40 lead. No lead was ever safe from this Celtics team, though. Their ability to claw their way back into games was the biggest thorn in the Bucks' side. The chess match aspect of the series was never more apparent than at this point. The Celtics pressured the Bucks into mistake after mistake, leaving the Bucks with another whopping 27 turnovers for the night. When the Bucks failed in execution or saw the well go dry, the Celtics almost always had an answer. The Bucks' grasp on the lead dwindled down the stretch. With 1:52 left in the final quarter of regulation, the Bucks had stalled at 86 points and a four-point lead. The Celtics answered with shots from John Havlicek and Dave Cowens to tie the game at 86 each with a minute left. It was helter-skelter from then on and no one mustered up a shot to decide the game. The buzzer sounded and here came overtime.

The entire NBA season had culminated in a game that featured two teams trading blow after blow. It had been a long year and a long series, and it all caught up with the Bucks and the Celtics. The first overtime period featured eight points scored between the two teams over five minutes. The Bucks had a chance to put it away after being up 90–88 with 24 seconds remaining. But as was the case all series long, the unexpected happened. An errant pass hit the tips of Dandridge's fingers and in the ensuing scramble the ball bounced Boston's way. Havlicek had the chance to be the Celtics' hero and put the game into another overtime. He followed up a 15-footer that clanked the front rim with a second chance bucket to tie the game at 90 with five seconds remaining.

Both the Bucks and the Celtics still had something left in the tank in the second overtime. For the Bucks, the motivation was to force a Game 7. The Celtics knew glory awaited them with a win and a celebration to follow on their hallowed floor. The lead flipped an incredible 10 times in the final three minutes and 23 seconds of double overtime. First, Abdul-Jabbar traded buckets with Havlicek. Then, Robertson traded shots with Jo Jo White. Robertson then traded scores with Havlicek. The clock ticked down to the final 90 seconds. Cowens fouled out and the Celtics replaced him with Henry Finkel. 99-98, Celtics lead. Turnovers galore occurred before Davis broke the gridlock with an arching baseline jumper to put the Bucks up 100–99 with 24 seconds left to go. The Celtics came down the floor and didn't call a timeout. They trusted Havlicek with the ball, as he had all the answers that night. He put up an arching baseline jumper of his own on the other end of the floor. The Celtics went back up with the score standing at 101–100 with 7 seconds remaining. The place was rocking. The Bucks called a timeout. No one could ever accuse Costello of being uninventive. He had entire playbooks and scribbled-up yellow legal pads ready for this kind of moment. Just as he had done in any other timeout situation, he diagrammed a play. Robertson was the inbounder and Abdul-Jabbar—with 32 points in all—would set the screen at the free throw line for a streaking McGlocklin. Costello designed the play so either McGlocklin would have

14. One Last Run (The 1973–74 Season) 139

the daylight to fire away an open jumper or a rolling Abdul-Jabbar would have an open lane all the way to the basket.

Costello was a basketball genius in every sense of the word. But not one of his players heard who the play was for or where the ball was going when they broke from the huddle. The play began with Robertson holding the ball and McGlocklin covered by his man. The Big O improvised. He saw Abdul-Jabbar unchecked at the elbow and with Finkel draped behind him. Abdul-Jabbar got the inbound, spun around and grasped the ball above his head. He began driving toward the baseline and, to hear him tell it, left the Bucks and the entire city of Milwaukee in amazement: "There were only seconds left in the season, but I had my *chi* focused and had no worry. I felt as if everything was moving in slow motion and all power was mine. There was no sound, not even a real sense of bodies. My head was clear. I don't think I've ever felt quite so totally, comfortably alone. Henry Finkel was guarding me…, and I just dribbled to the baseline, turned, and put up the hook. It went right in."[8]

Abdul-Jabbar delivered with his signature "skyhook" shot—a Doucette original coinage—to put the Bucks up 102–101 with three seconds remaining. No longer did the Celtics have an answer. Instead of the Boston fans and players mobbing each other on their home floor to celebrate and drink to the feats of a title run, they saw Bucks players mob Abdul-Jabbar and each other. The series was going to a Game 7 and back to where it all started—Milwaukee. After the win, Costello was asked how he could sit through a game like that. He exclaimed, "Sit through it? Hell, I jumped through it!"[9] It had been a long time since the Bucks could celebrate like this. Probably not since they had won it all in 1971. This was supposed to be routine to them. With players as good as Abdul-Jabbar, Robertson and Dandridge, they were supposed to feel this way all of the time. But things hadn't gone to plan. The talk of a Bucks dynasty that would take over the NBA never came to pass. This was a Bucks team that had taken a left turn from dynastic status and had gone to hell and back. They had plenty more miles under their belt and had grown much older than they had been when they made their first trip to the finals. This overwhelming machine had to weather all of the punches the Celtics were throwing at them in order to witness Abdul-Jabbar's moment of brilliance to bring this series to a Game 7.

You couldn't fault any of the Bucks players for being tired, especially the ones who were powering through whatever injury, knocks or bruises they were dealing with at the time. Three hundred and three minutes of basketball played over six games. Three overtime periods. There was no rest for the weary and Abdul-Jabbar couldn't find any after Game 6. He later shared that he couldn't fall asleep after the comeback win: "I often have insomnia after games, sometimes even see the dawn. That night all

I could do was lie in bed and replay those last seconds. Total adrenaline OD. I got on the plane to return to Milwaukee the next day, and I had not slept."[10] Game 6 wrapped up in Boston during the wee hours of the morning on Saturday, May 11. Game 7 tipped off at 1:40 p.m. Central Time on Sunday, May 12, at the Milwaukee Arena. It was the final leg in a long and hard-fought journey. Whoever wound up victorious would finally get the rest and relaxation they deserved, knowing the job was finished.

The Celtics went into Milwaukee that fateful May day knowing they had one ace up their sleeve. All series long, the Celtics had defended Abdul-Jabbar straight up as they opted for one-on-one defense. Celtics head coach Tommy Heinsohn was asked about it plenty. Cowens had done more than a solid game's work. Abdul-Jabbar put up his points, but he was working for his open shots. For Games 1 through 6, doubling Abdul-Jabbar was not an option and only reserved for special situations like the impromptu scramble and skyhook at the end of Game 6. Game 7 was a different occasion, however. Heinsohn knew there was glory on the line. He didn't believe the Celtics could do it all game long, but shocking the Bucks' system in the opening moments by throwing multiple bodies toward Abdul-Jabbar could be enough to get the strong start they needed.

The game tipped off and lo and behold, Abdul-Jabbar saw crowds of Celtics defenders. It largely made no difference to Kareem. He found daylight to put down shots and sliced through the defense to find the open man. He couldn't do it alone, however. The Celtics held a 22–20 lead after the end of the first quarter. The Bucks ran themselves ragged trying to get the ball into the post for Abdul-Jabbar and chewed up the clock to find a solid shot for anyone not named Abdul-Jabbar. Things began to break down. The Celtics had a seemingly endless amount of gas in the tank. They remained resolute on defense and their fast break was overwhelming for the old, tired and injured Bucks. They carried a 53–40 lead into halftime. Milwaukee made their run in the middle of the third quarter. They maintained a string of defensive stops and found their mojo playing their way— the Bucks way, feeding Abdul-Jabbar to bring their deficit down to single digits. Those single digits ticked down to a one-possession game early in the fourth quarter as the Celtics held a 71–68 lead with 11 minutes remaining. Celtic pride kicked in. They brought the doors down at the Arena. The Bucks clanked every part of the rim on numerous trips down the floor and they couldn't withstand the Celtics' fast break or the brilliance of Havlicek, Cowens and others. The Bucks were on their last legs and were on the point of being put out of their misery. They had come this far, shorthanded and all, but the Celtics were the better team and they had the depth of stars to carry them to a championship. Costello pulled his Bucks starters with two minutes remaining and his team down 98–79. It was the last time that

14. One Last Run (The 1973–74 Season)

Robertson was on an NBA floor as an active player. He had talked about waiting to make his decision about retiring until the early months of summer, but he was listening to his body and what the Bucks had been telling him that season. The final buzzer sounded. The scoreboard read: Celtics 102, Bucks 87.

The Celtics players mobbed each other instantly and shuffled into the locker room. They uncorked the best champagne they'd ever taste, the same champagne the Bucks had bought for themselves if they had won. The Bucks players saw the winners soak it all in as they walked off the floor. Many left with the agony of defeat showing on their face. They felt resigned to their fate immediately. They thanked the fans for all of their vocal support that day and felt the weight of letting them down with history on the line. Robertson cast his ire at the officials and questioned the foul calls that plagued the Bucks that day. The same went for the likes of Dandridge and Curtis Perry. Some—like Davis—blamed himself for being targeted by the Celtics' offense and vowed to play better defense next time around. McGlocklin, however, took his anger out on the circumstances. He knew the Celtics had played harder, with more intensity and urgency. He felt the Bucks just didn't answer the call. Abdul-Jabbar surely accepted his fate, saying, "Victory and defeat are in the hands of the creator. There are times when we've played worse and won, and there are times when we have played better and lost. I am a Muslim and I accept whatever happens. Most Westerners call it fatalism."[11]

These were all Bucks who had made it this far before and some who had climbed to the top of the mountain. But take someone like Warner, for example. He was cast off by the lowly Cavaliers early in the season before the Bucks picked him up. He played the role of an unlikely hero in Game 2 of the finals and put in a valiant effort of heart and hustle throughout the entire series. Here in the face of defeat and after having gone from the worst team in the East to the best team in the West, Warner couldn't believe that his luck had run out. "This whole thing just hurts. I've never been this close to anything like this. And then, to see it slip away, a chance of a lifetime, it's just not an easy thing to take," he shared to reporters in a sullen Bucks locker room.[12] Sure, the Bucks players may have each gotten $15,714 for their troubles for having gone that far. But all of the money of the world couldn't equal the feeling of being called an NBA champion once again.

15

Exit Strategies

Warner's words in the locker room after the end of Game 7 could have applied to the Bucks as a franchise approaching a crossroads. The old phrase "there's always next year" no longer applied to the Bucks—not just to play for an NBA championship, but to make it to the finals in the first place. The winds of change were in the air over the summer of 1974. An expansion draft had already taken Perry away from Milwaukee to join the upstart New Orleans Jazz. Costello lost his right-hand man in Brown, who got his chance to be a head coach with the ABA's Kentucky Colonels.

The summer months passed without any update as to whether Robertson was calling it a day, though. All along, Robertson desired to retire, but he stayed in shape throughout the offseason. When he said he wasn't sure whether he'd actually retire or not at season's end, the Bucks were forced to protect him in the expansion draft. The matter of whether Robertson would continue playing in the NBA and do so in Milwaukee wasn't brought up until later in the summer. Eventually, Robertson committed to playing what would have been his 15th NBA season. A meeting between him, Embry and Alverson was held over a new contract. Robertson wanted to be signed to the same contract that he had previously with the Bucks, at $250,000 a year or more and with no-cut and no-trade clauses. If the two sides couldn't agree to a deal by August 1, 1974, he'd be a free agent since he would be out of contract.

Embry had braced for Oscar's exit by drafting a couple of guards that summer in the 1974 NBA draft, and his stomach went into knots when he learned that Robertson wanted to return. The Bucks wanted Robertson back, but it was not unconditional. They wouldn't commit to those same clauses in his contract, protecting him from future expansion drafts, that Robertson had worked hard to earn and used to his advantage to come to Milwaukee in the first place. The Bucks did not formally offer him a new contract by August 1, making Robertson a free agent for the very first time. There was no going back to the negotiating table for Robertson and the Bucks. "When you've played and worked a long time in sports, you get accustomed to people and their dealings. The meeting ended. August first came and went. I officially became a free agent. From my end, that was pretty much the end of things between the Milwaukee Bucks and me. While I wished them nothing but success, the moment they relinquished their rights to me, I stopped being interested in what they did," Robertson later reflected on his unceremonious departure.[1] Word slowly trickled out by the end of August as the *Milwaukee Journal* reported that Robertson had emerged as a free agent. Speculation immediately arose as to whether he'd continue his playing career in the ABA, but he never entertained the idea of jumping to that league. Instead, Robertson hung up his Chuck Taylor shoes for the microphone. He agreed to be the color analyst for the *NBA on CBS* telecasts, alongside Brent Musburger. The secret negotiations that brought him on board to the broadcast took the public by surprise. For Robertson, this was the end of a 14-year NBA career. There was no bending with him. When he felt he was no longer wanted, he found his way out. When it came to negotiating with Oscar Robertson, you met his way fully and conceded to his demands. The NBA learned that as the antitrust suit dragged on and continued to block a merger with the ABA.

The Bucks made the calculated risk of not giving fully in to Robertson. Yes, he was no longer the dominating force that had made him possibly the most complete guard to ever play in the NBA. But even in his physical decline, he still proved to be irreplaceable for a Bucks team that hadn't lined up a succession plan. The warm feelings that emanated from Oscar Robertson Day had cooled and hardened. Instead, a cold, hard business decision separated Robertson and the Bucks for good. All of his points, assists and minutes for the Royals still stand atop of the franchise's record books, even though the franchise didn't stay in Cincinnati, the city where Robertson set all of those records. The Royals moved to Kansas City–Omaha, where they became the Kings, then simply went by Kansas City, before moving in 1985 to Sacramento, where they have remained ever since. Robertson's no. 14 hangs in the rafters of the Golden 1 Center where the Kings play, but it feels foreign there. It's Milwaukee that will be recognized as Robertson's NBA home for as long as the Bucks remain there. The Bucks retired Robertson's no. 1 jersey for the home opener of their 1974–75 season, making him the first player in the franchise's history to have his number retired. He chose Milwaukee while on a mission to secure a championship. If nothing else, he accomplished that mission, for himself and on behalf of the city of Milwaukee.

Robertson's appointment to the broadcasting booth rankled some owners around the league. To them, Robertson was an adversary of the NBA as he challenged them in court on behalf of all NBA players, blocking a merger with the ABA. Now, he was the broadcasting face of the NBA.

Robertson never had the patience needed to grow into his new role or fulfill his aspirations of becoming a polished announcer. Criticism of his performance on the air was sharp inside and outside of the league. He and a rookie Musburger never fully clicked in their on-air chemistry. From the moment his first season in the booth was over, Robertson knew he was not getting a second chance. "If I hadn't had secret negotiations with and through the network, I wouldn't have been hired in the first place," he later wrote. "But once I was on board, the powers that be were upset. While they couldn't fire me or directly pull me off the air during the season, after the season was over was a different matter."[2] The very reason Robertson was so untrusting of authority—especially authority in the NBA—was that his skepticism was always vindicated. The stigma of having challenged the NBA and its owners blocked Robertson from ever having a post-playing career in the NBA. The one-year experiment in the booth came and went. He was never given a chance to coach or run a team like many, if not all, of his peers. Whether he ever had the desire was irrelevant. Ultimately, Robertson's legacy can be seen in the way he fought for the rights of NBA players during those unsettled days. The Oscar Robertson Rule was established when the NBA finally agreed to settle with the players' union on February 3, 1976. Robertson still played an active role as the head of the retired players union. The agreement saw an end to the reserve clause, made underclassmen and high school players free to enter the draft and instituted true free agency. The ABA officially merged with the NBA in the summer of 1976, bringing in four teams from what remained in the dying league: the Indiana Pacers, the Denver Nuggets, the San Antonio Spurs and the New York Nets. After six years of court battles and legal fees worth north of $50 million being spent on both sides, pro basketball finally had its house in order. There was no agent of change who sacrificed more and was given less than he deserved than Oscar Robertson.

16

You're Now Leaving Kareem City

The Bucks sought some stability and they signed a new, multi-year contract with the only head coach they had ever known. A month before the start of the 1974–75 season, the Bucks made it official that Costello would be in Milwaukee for at least two more years. At the time of the agreement, Costello had a 333–161 coaching record and his 67.3 winning percentage was the highest in league history. Yes, the bulk of that success had come with Abdul-Jabbar and Robertson, something that Costello's detractors often cited. But winning all of those games—some of them the biggest in Bucks history, even to this day—came with Costello maximizing everything he had to work with. He had some of the greatest players the game had seen. He helped journeymen and castoffs from other teams become unlikely success stories in Milwaukee. He demanded the best out of his players, whether in games or in those long practice sessions. You had to know the playbook and all of the many plays within those pages. For all of the hard work he expected from his players, Costello was the eternal optimist. He went into that first season without Robertson with the same title aspirations that the Bucks had before. You couldn't blame Costello, especially after having been one game away from a championship the previous year. He'd learn just how committed the Bucks were to him over the duration of that contract. Things were changing and fast.

Abdul-Jabbar entered his sixth NBA season with a new lease on life. For the first time while in Milwaukee, he stayed in the city for the summer. He rigorously kept in shape, running 12 miles each day. He played tennis, ran cross-country and swam regularly. He didn't do much work on the basketball court, but stayed sharp in his conditioning. He did all of the things that he had shunned ever since arriving in Milwaukee and showed a desire to embrace the celebrity lifestyle that he had previously sworn off. One couldn't escape the impression that perhaps—at long last—Abdul-Jabbar's hard exterior was softening, that he was more willing to let in those outsiders that had wanted something from him at every turn. There was another reason why Abdul-Jabbar embraced all that Milwaukee had to offer: he wanted to leave Milwaukee after the 1974–75 season.

This was always where it was going to go for Abdul-Jabbar and the Bucks. It wasn't until he decided he wanted to leave Milwaukee that he was at peace with the city that gave him his start in pro basketball. He had chosen the Bucks over the Nets and the ABA. As he explained it, it was a professional compromise to come to Milwaukee in the first place. The question of why the 1974–75 season was Abdul-Jabbar's last in Milwaukee is a curious one and there has never been a straight answer. Perhaps Robertson's retirement spurred it on. Seeing his equal leave put a greater burden on Abdul-Jabbar to elevate the Bucks and keep the train on its course. The Bucks had proven that they couldn't get someone of note through the draft to help Abdul-Jabbar before and there was little hope of that changing moving forward.

When Abdul-Jabbar had made up his mind, he paid a visit to Pavalon at his farm in West Bend. The two were fishing when Abdul-Jabbar broke the news to him. Pavalon was still chairman of the board by title, but it was merely a figurehead position at this point. He and Abdul-Jabbar always remained in touch and were close. By all accounts, Abdul-Jabbar's wish to leave Milwaukee devastated Pavalon. This was the same Pavalon who had said that money was no issue in securing Abdul-Jabbar as he was entering the pros, that whatever million-dollar offer the ABA was putting together as a league couldn't match what the city of Milwaukee and the entire state of Wisconsin offered to a young phenom like Abdul-Jabbar. Embry remembered the day vividly. October 3, 1974. He got a call from Sam Gilbert—the same UCLA booster and advisor to Abdul-Jabbar who had negotiated his first NBA contract. Gilbert and Abdul-Jabbar wanted to meet with Embry, Alverson and Pavalon after an afternoon practice between preseason games. While Embry believed that Abdul-Jabbar wanted to renegotiate his contract, a call from Pavalon let him in on the big secret. Embry's first reaction to Abdul-Jabbar wanting to leave Milwaukee was to try to change his mind.

Embry reserved the biggest suite at the Sheraton West Hotel in nearby Brookfield for the meeting with Abdul-Jabbar and Bucks management. He went the full nine yards, going so far as contacting the food and beverage manager at the hotel. The suite was stocked with expensive red wine, Chateaubriand and all of Kareem's favorite foods. Abdul-Jabbar arrived at the suite at exactly 7 p.m. Eventually, he opened up as to why he wanted to leave Milwaukee. Holding nothing back, he said to Embry, "I am unhappy in Milwaukee, and I want to be traded when the season is over. I am not culturally satisfied here. I'd like to go to New York, Washington, or Los

Angeles. I am telling you now so you can get something for me, rather than sitting out my option year and then signing with one of those teams or the Nets of the ABA."[1]

The leverage that Abdul-Jabbar had in his pocket—in case the Bucks wouldn't honor his wish to be traded—was that he had two years remaining on his contract, with the final year being an option year. Abdul-Jabbar made the calculated gamble that sitting out his option year and going into free agency would be the fail-safe option for him in fulfilling his destiny of playing in a bigger city. Embry wanted to know why Abdul-Jabbar wanted out. He recalled asking if it was a matter of wanting more money, getting a new coach or getting better teammates. It was the start of the Bucks making all sorts of promises in order to appease Abdul-Jabbar into staying in Milwaukee—stuff like buying him the lavish Oriental rugs that he liked to collect. Probably the most outlandish scenario proposed was Bucks management offering to buy Abdul-Jabbar a house in New York where he could live part-time and commute to games. The big man made it clear that was not going to work and he was not going to change his mind. By the end of the three-hour meeting that night in Brookfield, the Bucks brass agreed that they'd look into trading him. Washington had fallen out of consideration, given the murders that took place there at the Hanafi house. That left just New York and Los Angeles as the teams that Abdul-Jabbar wished to go to. All five people in the room agreed to keep this between themselves as a way of maintaining the Bucks' leverage in trade talks. When Embry left the hotel that night, it was with mixed emotions. He later recalled, "I kept thinking that if I did not have bad luck, I would not have any luck at all. Then I thought this might bring a solid foundation that we could build on. After all, it was difficult to draft quality players when we had the Number 18 pick every season. I did not have any idea the kind of year we would have without Oscar and with this hanging over our heads.... The franchise was about to change. Only five of us knew it."[2]

Going into his sixth season in Milwaukee, nothing sustained Abdul-Jabbar anymore in the city. He'd gone through many personal hardships to this point. He lost his connection to his parents after immersing himself in his religion. He became estranged from his spiritual leader and some of his closest friends in the Muslim community had been murdered. Yes, he became a father, but he already was divorced from his wife. Abdul-Jabbar had been through it all. From the moment he no longer withdrew into himself and was buoyed by what was going on all around him, the countdown began to when he'd want out of Milwaukee. Abdul-Jabbar forged a new path and it was on the Bucks to accept the professional compromise that he had extended to them. That season, the Bucks and their many key decision makers had to live with the fact that Abdul-Jabbar no longer wanted to be there. He was the principal reason why the franchise had been formed when it was. Abdul-Jabbar was the one they had eyed from the beginning. Pavalon and Fishman were more than willing to go through their fair share of lumps as an expansion franchise if it meant that Abdul-Jabbar played out his NBA career in Milwaukee. Some board members didn't want to accept that Abdul-Jabbar wanted to leave Milwaukee. Things were in motion behind the scenes that led to changes beyond the fact that Abdul-Jabbar wanted to be traded. His trade request didn't just splinter the Bucks players. It was splintering the operation at the very top. Factions began to form. A struggle for control of the team simmered for months and even years. No player or coach was granted mercy.

Mere days after that meeting in Brookfield, the Bucks played a preseason contest in Buffalo with the Celtics, the team that ended their season just months before and celebrated a championship on the Bucks' home floor at the Milwaukee Arena. Needless to say, the Bucks were motivated to believe they could still hang with the defending champs, Oscar or no Oscar. No one would remember that the Bucks beat the Celtics 112–98 in a meaningless preseason game on October 5, 1974. What everyone remembered was what happened early in the fourth quarter. Battling for a rebound, Abdul-Jabbar and Don Nelson tousled about and Nelson inadvertently poked Abdul-Jabbar in his right eye. The poke left Abdul-Jabbar staggering on the court as he held his face in his hand. Frustration and anger quickly set in and Abdul-Jabbar took it out on the stanchion. He connected on a blow that broke his right hand. The initial diagnosis was that Abdul-Jabbar would miss anywhere from the first three to six weeks of the regular season. He later referred to the incident as being the stupidest he ever felt in his life.

The regular season hadn't tipped off and things were already in flux for the Bucks. There'd be no Kareem and no Oscar to guide them as the start of the season was in view. The Bucks were getting an early experience of how life could be without Abdul-Jabbar. Making matters worse, they had no center on their roster to take his place. They had played in the league's most competitive division just a season before. Being without their best player for an extended stretch of time made the climb up that mountain much more steep. Even with all of that known, the *New York Times* still predicted the Bucks would win that year's championship.[3]

The Bucks didn't look anything like a championship team when the season tipped off. Not by a long shot. Through the first month of the season, they won one game out of 14 tries. One game. Not many players on the roster had felt the sting of defeat on such an extended level during their time in Milwaukee. Now they were overwhelmed by it. It didn't take long for the tearing down to begin. The Bucks hastily traded away a

16. You're Now Leaving Kareem City

now healthy Lucius Allen to the Lakers for Jim Price, citing the need for a true point guard. Allen had made his mark on those Bucks teams that earned 60 or more wins every year. He had been to the finals twice and won that glorious championship in '71. Just like that, he was cast off like all of it had meant nothing. Allen fit the running mantra that Costello had wanted to go back to. But with the Bucks sliding out of the gates and Kareem still on the mend, circumstances forced the Bucks' hand. Dealing away Allen also meant removing someone that Kareem had connected with, dating back to their time at UCLA. Embry observed how trading away Allen worried some Bucks board members who had clung to the thought that Abdul-Jabbar would change his mind about leaving Milwaukee.

Throughout this stretch, Kareem was seen as the lifeline the Bucks could fall back on to help them climb out of this mess. The hole grew deeper and updates about when he'd be able to remove his cast and the goggles he'd start wearing upon his return served as a much-needed salve for Bucks fans. The same went for the players when they knew that Abdul-Jabbar was nearing his return to action. The Bucks stopped their losing streak at 11 games. When Abdul-Jabbar returned to the starting lineup on November 23, 1974, in a game against the Knicks, they had to make up a lot of ground. The *Milwaukee Journal* estimated that for the Bucks to hit the benchmark of 50 wins that was needed to win their division, they had to win more than two-thirds of their remaining 65 games.[4] It seems ridiculous to think that even having Abdul-Jabbar back in the lineup could make that scenario a reality. The Bucks weren't used to anything but winning at the highest level with Abdul-Jabbar in the mix. But how would he fare upon making his return from the longest absence of his basketball life? He certainly welcomed the challenge. With Kareem back and finding his wind again, it was expected that the rest of the Bucks would follow suit. They had won five of the first six games he'd played that season, but they never got on that winning roll that was so routine over the last five years. The faces changed around Kareem before and after he returned. So did the Bucks' playbook as Costello tinkered with new plays and sets that were designed to make things easier for the Bucks and their best players. Dandridge compared having to learn Costello's revamped playbook to being in math class. It didn't take long for him to see when his teammates were struggling to grasp new plays and were destined for Costello's doghouse.

Finding the path toward success wasn't easy by any means for the Bucks. Kareem was on a different course from everyone else on the roster. As great as he was, he had to be afforded the time to get back to full strength. But the Bucks just didn't have the patience, nor the time, to give him that chance. It was all about winning, winning, winning. Missing the playoffs wasn't an option. It was a situation that could spell doom for a Bucks team that could hear the clock ticking. It wasn't all doom and gloom for Abdul-Jabbar, though. During that season, he branched out into a completely different field than he had ever known. On December 7, 1974, he showed up at the studios of WNUW-FM and hosted the first episode of a three-hour jazz show titled *Cantaloupe Island*. The program was named after the song by Herbie Hancock, one of Abdul-Jabbar's favorites. He had gotten in touch with the station director through Doucette. For Abdul-Jabbar, it was a chance to show off his stuff and broadcast some of his favorite jazz music and the records he had collected. Addressing his listeners at the top of the program, Abdul-Jabbar declared in his soft and dulcet tones, "The music is for everybody, not any special interest group. Just nice vibrations."[5] He played hits by Miles Davis, John Coltrane, Eddie Harris, and Cannonball Adderley. When it was time to close out the program, Abdul-Jabbar mistakenly flubbed his own name. Listeners lit up the phone lines throughout the program and the station manager said they enjoyed having Abdul-Jabbar come out of his shell. Kareem was due to broadcast the show live when the Bucks were home and to tape it in advance when the Bucks would be on the road. Just a few days later, though, he announced that his program was a one-off. "It takes too much energy away from basketball to do the show," he said. "It sure was fun and I thought I did a good job, but basketball is more important. I feel sorry for the people at the station who were so nice to me and all my fans who called to say what a good show it was."[6]

When the calendar turned over to 1975, the Bucks had a 14–19 record. They were 10–6 since Kareem made his long-awaited return and carried a five-game winning streak into the first few days of the new year. They climbed out of last place in the West, but continued chasing the Pistons and the Bulls in the division. They were climbing back into the thick of things. On January 16, 1975, they reached .500 at 21–21. A 122–108 win over the Trail Blazers put the Bucks over .500. The next five days were the only time the Bucks could boast they had a winning record at any point that season. The alarm bells sounded for Milwaukee as they promptly went into a slide after having gotten their heads above water. After a 117–101 loss to the Hawks that put them back below .500, questions over the Bucks' morale and chemistry were a topic of conversation. The roster was split between the players who had championship experience and those who hopped around to simply make it in the NBA or the pro game overall. Costello was trying to find any kind of sustainable winning formula to turn the Bucks' fortunes around. Everything came into question: the starting lineup, the substitution patterns, the playbook. Criticism was directed at the team's players and why they weren't clicking with each other. Dandridge was the team captain and he told things exactly like they were. The Bucks' only consistency was their inconsistency, and time was running out to find the answers for clinching an unlikely playoff berth.

Rumors began to circulate. Embry found out that some of the board members wanted to remove Costello as head coach—regardless of whatever was to happen with Abdul-Jabbar. The ABA set their sights on Abdul-Jabbar once again, even as many of their successful clubs were in the red financially. That didn't matter to John W. Brown, the owner of the Colonels, who threatened to poach Abdul-Jabbar from the Bucks and the NBA. "I think the league ought to sign Abdul-Jabbar when his option runs out, and we're certainly going to make a try at it. We're going to approach his representative and see what it would take to get him," he said.[7] As if they didn't have enough on their plate as it was, the Bucks lost one of their three All–Stars to injury for the rest of the season. They had acquired Price to give them some stability at the point guard position and within their backcourt. With 25 games to go, he underwent surgery to heal torn cartilage in his knee that forced him out for the rest of the season. The slide continued from there. The margin for error was so thin that the Bucks couldn't afford any loss over the final few weeks of the season if they were to climb back into the playoff race. They spent all the rest of the season chasing the competition and hoping to get out of the basement. They managed it for small stretches, but it never took.

Throughout all of the Bucks' futile efforts during that 1974–75 season, no word leaked out that Abdul-Jabbar would likely not be in Milwaukee for long. It wasn't until a Knicks radio announcer, Marv Albert, broke the story to New York radio listeners that fans knew Kareem Abdul-Jabbar wanted to leave the Bucks and Milwaukee after the season. "I've been reliably informed that Kareem Abdul-Jabbar has told the Bucks that he wants to play next year in New York or Los Angeles," Albert said. "He still has one year remaining on his contract, plus an option for another year, but he asked to be let out of it. He says he will only play in New York or Los Angeles. He is hoping his obvious dissatisfaction in Milwaukee will force a trade." Albert went on to say that Abdul-Jabbar didn't have his heart set on playing for the Knicks in New York. He'd welcome playing for the Nets in the ABA, but switching leagues required more hurdles to jump through. Albert closed by saying that the Bucks were on the spot: "They may be forced because an unhappy Kareem won't do them much good, and if they're to make the trade, now would be the time to pick up heavy value."[8] Finally, the secret was let out. It wasn't hard to put two and two together and see why it was surfacing then and there, especially when the source was a Knicks announcer. Word traveled fast. Reports outside of Milwaukee cited Abdul-Jabbar's past comments about the city and the team dropping off in success that season. Sources wrote that Abdul-Jabbar had requested to be traded prior to the start of the current season.

Embry offered no comment on the report and Abdul-Jabbar initially followed suit. Alverson said he'd heard similar rumors before Abdul-Jabbar signed his second contract with the Bucks preceding the 1972–73 season. He was scornful about the fact that New York sports officials believed the best athletes belonged in New York. "Nothing, just nothing, hacks me off more than that," he said.[9] Just a day later, though, Abdul-Jabbar couldn't keep quiet about his trade request any longer. He revealed it all after the Bucks' 105–104 loss to the Lakers, saying, "I don't have any family or friends here. The things I relate to don't happen to be in this city to any meaningful degree. Culturally, what I'm about and what Milwaukee is about are not compatible. Milwaukee is just not the kind of city I'm about. I'm not knocking it or the people. It's just that socially and culturally, I don't fit in Milwaukee." Abdul-Jabbar had said similar things about Milwaukee in the past, in even harsher terms. But he was sensitive to the fact that he could be seen as knocking the people that lived and worked in the city and he didn't want to make it look like the city was unworthy of having him there. He was happy about his time with the Bucks. His relationship with the Bucks was sound and he saw the talent the team had, despite its rough year. As for the timing of when his request had leaked, he couldn't put a finger on why.

Bucks officials were pressed as to why Abdul-Jabbar wanted out and how often he'd expressed his dissatisfaction to being in Milwaukee over his six years there. Per Alverson, Kareem had an open forum to express his frustrations about anything, as did all the players. "I don't think it's a matter of money," he said, "but more a matter of lifestyle.... Kareem has told me several times that he's unhappy, that something is bugging him. What it was depends on what point in time you're talking about. Sometimes, it has been personal matters, the city, a small arena. A lot of things over a period of years." Alverson was asked whether Costello had factored in Abdul-Jabbar's decision to be traded. He delicately explained, "If you ask me if Kareem has ever expressed dissatisfaction with Larry, the answer is yes. But if you ask me whether that would be a deciding factor in his staying, I just don't know."[10] Trying his best to quell the controversy, he said that the Bucks were not actively looking to trade the big man and had no plans to trade him—to New York, to Los Angeles, to wherever. "It's not hot news or anything new," said Alverson. "We have known the way he felt since he came into the league. It has been a standoff for six years and I'm not about to give up now. Kareem hasn't been happy in Milwaukee because he has no social life here. When he signed his second contract with us, and got married, I thought he might have found happiness."[11] There was a growing sigh of relief among Bucks players that Abdul-Jabbar's feelings about Milwaukee had been made as clear as they could be. Dandridge was far from surprised to hear that Abdul-Jabbar wanted to move on. McGlocklin said that Abdul-Jabbar had made his feelings known about wishing to play in L.A. or New York from the moment he entered the league. For Embry, the fact that Abdul-Jabbar had spoken of his trade request publicly made it easier for him to sell the board of directors on the idea that they should move him over the summer. He later reflected, "I convinced our board I could make a deal that would give us a solid foundation. I added that Kareem had given us six terrific years and a championship and that out of respect for him, we should try to grant his wish."[12] Talk surfaced of what trading away Kareem would mean to a young franchise like the Bucks. He was already a three-time Most Valuable Player, and the Bucks were a draw by virtue of having him there. How the Bucks could manage to exist without Abdul-Jabbar was not just on the minds of fans, but Bucks executives as well. When the prospect arose that the Bucks might miss the playoffs that year, the head of CBS programming was dismayed that they would be missing out on a basketball-hungry market like Milwaukee.[13]

As the Bucks fell further out of the playoff race, there was nothing else to talk about other than Abdul-Jabbar's future in Milwaukee and what the Bucks could possibly get for someone as valuable as he was. The Bucks guaranteed their first losing season since their expansion campaign with a 92–87 loss to the Suns on March 25, 1975. A week and a half later, they were eliminated from the playoff race with two games left to go in the regular season. Falling from expectations of competing for a championship to missing out on the postseason entirely—even with all of their injuries and inconsistencies—was hard to fathom for everyone in Milwaukee and within the organization. Fingers were pointed in every direction. At the players, who were perceived to be growing weary of Costello's drilling and didn't coalesce together. At Costello, who was perceived to have fallen further into his workaholic habits and couldn't pull the right strings at the right time. At the organization, because it hadn't built a roster worthy of a playoff team and was under fire for not keeping Kareem happy. The poor start to the season proved to be insurmountable even for a team that had Abdul-Jabbar appearing in 65 games that year and averaging 30 points on 51.3 percent shooting from the field, 14 rebounds, 4.1 assists and 3.3 blocks in 42.3 minutes per game.

Whatever the reasons for casting blame one way or another, it didn't change the downward course that the Bucks had followed. Their 1974–75 season was a microcosm of the dysfunction that surrounded them. There were many voices pulling the franchise in all sorts of directions. Most of all, Kareem's decision was pulling them toward the biggest change of all. The Bucks' final game of the season saw them hosting the playoff-bound Bulls, who won the division that year. Milwaukee was used to playing in meaningless games at this time every year, with Costello electing to either pull his starters from heavy minutes or sit them entirely, all in the name of gearing up for what they hoped would be a long playoff run. Now the Bucks were on the other side of a meaningless game—one where they had nothing to play for and weren't readying themselves for the playoffs. The Bucks' slide out of playoff contention had done nothing to keep their fans from showing up in support of the team. In their final game of the regular season, the Milwaukee Arena saw 10,938 people in attendance. That made for the Bucks' 24th sellout in their 38 home games that year and averaged 10,611 fans per game over the entire year—the best mark in their six years as a franchise. That game on April 6, 1975, wasn't all that memorable beyond that. Abdul-Jabbar finished with 34 points, 10 rebounds, five blocks and four assists. The Bucks had four other players in double figures besides Abdul-Jabbar. They lost to the Bulls 112–100. The Bulls players remarked after the game that it seemed like some Bucks players didn't want to play. The final buzzer sounded on the Bucks' season at 9:58 p.m. Central Time that night. Just three minutes later, at 10:01, Abdul-Jabbar changed into his street clothes and walked out of the locker room for the final time as a member of the Milwaukee Bucks.[14]

The offseason finally arrived and everything was on the table for the Bucks. Alverson made it clear in an exit interview that he couldn't guarantee that Costello would be back and that they hadn't made any effort to trade away Abdul-Jabbar, despite his trade request.[15] Every decision had to be made as a committee or had to reflect a consensus, given the volatile state of the board of directors. Embry, though, welcomed the challenge of setting sail in these choppy waters and charting the next decade for the Bucks. He believed that it was on him to move Abdul-Jabbar to where he desired to go and to help the Bucks find the best deal they could. He was not about to be held hostage by their superstar because he wanted out of Milwaukee. It was possible that both parties could come away with exactly what they wanted. Embry took a room in the Marc Plaza Hotel downtown to be away from his office and telephones. This was going to be his decision to make and for him to make alone. He set down a guideline for the kind of return he wanted in exchange for Abdul-Jabbar. He wanted young, talented players who would develop over the next couple of years. Anticipating the level of losing that would come with having a rebuilt roster, he wanted high-character guys who would buy into what they were building. That meant buying into the situation, the team's future and their surroundings. More importantly, it meant buying into Milwaukee.

16. You're Now Leaving Kareem City

Embry sought to interview draft prospects—something he had never done before. The Bucks were accustomed to picking so low in drafts that they hadn't bothered to interview before. No longer did Embry take players for granted.

For the first time in his years as the Bucks' general manager, Embry sought to build the team of his vision. He would no longer serve the stars he inherited and even helped bring to Milwaukee. His superstar had one foot out the door and Embry was not going to let this chance go to waste. How the Bucks moved forward in trade discussions for Abdul-Jabbar would have ripple effects in the years to come. It was no surprise who the first team was that came calling as soon as it was possible. The Knicks didn't hide their wish to land the superstar center, and they knew that they played in one of the few destinations where Abdul-Jabbar wanted to live. Abdul-Jabbar had not been shy over the years in sharing what it would be like to play for his hometown team. Knicks decision makers flew out to Milwaukee to talk a deal. They offered up All-Star players like Walt Frazier and Willis Reed. They offered up their first-round pick—the ninth overall selection in that year's draft. Embry rejected the deal on the spot. He said that it didn't fit the criteria of players and the picks he wanted. The Knicks didn't take no for an answer. They offered up cash in order to sweeten the pot in hopes of moving Embry from his stance. After their offer climbed to a million dollars, Embry and Alverson shut down discussions. Alverson was disgusted by the Knicks' tactics during negotiations. "Who do you think we are? Some hicks from Milwaukee? Well, we are not," he shouted back at the Knicks decision makers. Embry was more matter-of-fact about ending the meeting, later saying, "Money could not score or rebound, and we did not want the players they were offering."[16] Embry was intrigued by the Hawks, as they had young players whom he felt could jump-start the Bucks' rebuild. But they weren't on Abdul-Jabbar's wish list, so Embry didn't look all that long.

Embry connected with the Lakers and he and Alverson met Lakers officials at the Denver airport to talk a deal. They went into those talks prepared to return back to Milwaukee that night, no matter what the outcome was. Embry liked the Lakers' recent draft picks, Junior Bridgeman and Dave Meyers. He knew the Bucks needed a center to replace Kareem and he thought Elmore Smith was a capable option. He also liked the stylings of a smooth shooting guard by the name of Brian Winters. That was more than a solid base to work with and talk a deal with the Lakers. Embry made it clear he wanted Bridgeman, Meyers, Smith and Winters. Pete Newell, the Lakers' general manager at the time, scoffed at such a trade package. Newell didn't see the point in negotiating over players, knowing that Abdul-Jabbar didn't want to be in Milwaukee anymore. He knew that if given an opportunity to jump ship, Abdul-Jabbar would take it. Embry wasn't having any of it. He said he and Alverson had come to talk a deal and if Newell wasn't going to, they were going to go back home to Milwaukee. Eventually, the Lakers' brain trust convened and softened their stance. They were willing to trade Bridgeman, Meyers and Smith. But no Winters. Embry didn't back down, and the Lakers' offer to include Gail Goodrich did not budge him. Embry had heard plenty about Winters and he saw the potential in the sharpshooter out of South Carolina. The Lakers picked him 12th overall in the previous draft and he had put together a solid rookie season, 11.7 points per game on 44.3 percent shooting in 22.3 minutes a game. Embry knew he was the key to the deal and the Lakers did too.

There they were in the Denver airport. Hour after hour passed. The Bucks and Lakers brass took breaks to phone their respective offices and pass along updates. The stalemate continued into the afternoon and into the evening. Newell occasionally played the card that Abdul-Jabbar was more than willing to leave for the ABA and that the Bucks would end up getting nothing to show for him. Eventually, Embry responded to Newell's posturing, saying, "Pete, if he goes to the ABA, you won't have him either. You don't want that to happen, do you?"[17] Embry negotiated as if he had all the leverage in the world. He was the one who had acquiesced to the trade request made by the greatest player the Bucks had ever known, yet he was holding all the cards. He took a hardline stance, both in the kind of players he wanted and the picks the Bucks needed to build out their roster. Embry was already a shrewd negotiator. Now, he had the freedom to act as he wanted and execute the kind of deal he thought could stabilize a Bucks franchise that was mired in dysfunction. The stalemate continued into the night and eventually Embry and Alverson booked a red-eye flight back to Chicago. Right before they left, one of the Lakers' contingent, a lawyer named Alan Rothenberg, joined them on the flight. Rothenberg was coming to Chicago to close the deal. Embry caught up on as much sleep as he could on the flight. Before he and Alverson parted ways with Rothenberg, he gave him one final reminder as they waited for their rental car. "No Winters, no deal," Embry said as he closed the door to the car.[18]

Not even two hours later, a sleeping Embry was woken up by his wife, who had received a call from Alverson. Rothenberg had traveled up to Milwaukee to finish the job. Embry later learned that Lakers owner Jack Kent Cooke had ordered Newell and Rothenberg not to come back to Los Angeles until they had a deal. It wasn't long before Winters was a part of the package that got the deal over the finish line. The two sides crossed the t's and dotted the i's. On Monday, June 16, 1975, it was announced that the Lakers had made their latest and biggest deal. They had acquired

Abdul-Jabbar—along with Walt Wesley—for Bridgeman, Meyers, Smith and Winters. Abdul-Jabbar welcomed the chance to return to Los Angeles. But a strange feeling had come over him during his final few months in Milwaukee, knowing that he was likely bound for a bigger city. Recalling when he heard that his time with the Bucks was coming to an end, Abdul-Jabbar wrote,

> It was strange, though. By the time I was about to leave Milwaukee I had finally developed an appreciation of its people. The team owners treated me with respect and paid me well, and the fans turned out to be great. They are the salt of the earth; they show up when you're winning, they show up when you're losing. They come early, stay late, and let you know what's happening while they're there. When I first arrived the fans weren't very knowledgeable about basketball itself, but as the Bucks played it for them they developed rapidly, and by the time I left they were on top of the game. They were a different kind of people than any I'd met before, but I came to know them as generous and good. In New York the fans boo anybody on the opposing team; in Milwaukee they cheer anyone they appreciate. I ended up, much to my surprise, liking Milwaukee. It's too cold for me, but it's too cold for the people who live there too.[19]

There was a feeling of finality in the air. The Bucks made the best of a bad situation, according to the NBA and Milwaukee pundits. The playbook on what to do when your superstar wants out of the city your franchise plays in hadn't yet been written in those days. The Bucks were restoring hope in a fanbase that saw its original and greatest hope leave the city, a city he never fully embraced from the start. This wasn't nearly the same as seeing the Braves leave town. The show would still go on for the Bucks in Milwaukee. What his leaving spoke to more—and what Milwaukee still is struggling to rectify today—is the plight of a young, successful Black man trying to find a sense of community and belonging in a city that hasn't made advancements for people of color. Leslie Johnson Clevert, in the *Milwaukee Journal*, gave voice to the factors that surely played a part in Abdul-Jabbar's decision to leave. "There are probably very few people in Milwaukee with interests and goals similar to Abdul-Jabbar's or the financial capacity to achieve them. There is absolutely no social life here for a young, wealthy black man. Also, [Abdul]-Jabbar, a deeply religious man, must have had difficulty finding anyone here of his faith, and there is no mosque to attend," she wrote nearly a month after Abdul-Jabbar had been traded to Los Angeles.[20] It never was just about basketball. Milwaukee was seeing an exodus of people, jobs and industry just as the Bucks had ascended to the top of the NBA. Abdul-Jabbar just happened to be the most famous emigrant of them all in a city that has always been sensitive about its reputation to outsiders and has sought ways to make it appealing for people to live and work there.

One thing that Abdul-Jabbar took solace in is that he knew he was appreciated. When he played his first game in Milwaukee as a Los Angeles Laker, from the moment he stepped onto the court from the visitors' locker room he was showered with ovations and cheers by Bucks fans who never lost their appreciation. And at the very least, that's all he ever really needed from them.

When the NBA awarded the 1977 All-Star Game to Milwaukee just a month after the Bucks lost to the Celtics in the 1974 NBA Finals, it was presumed that Abdul-Jabbar would represent the Bucks in the league's biggest showcase of its stars. Milwaukee was a model franchise and Abdul-Jabbar was most responsible for catapulting the Bucks to the top of the league and helping them become a drawing power. But when that All-Star Weekend was held in early February of 1977, the Bucks were nearly unrecognizable. Gone, obviously, was Abdul-Jabbar, along with Robertson and Costello, and Dandridge would follow soon after the end of the season. It marked the first time the Bucks did not have an All-Star since coming into the NBA.

This was the first All-Star Game since the ABA and NBA had merged. The Bucks were in the middle of their worst season since their expansion year. They were 17–42 by the time All-Star Weekend rolled around. Hosting this marquee event was the saving grace for all of the instability and changes that had embroiled the Bucks over the last couple of years and a major transition of power within the board of directors. New Bucks chairman Jim Fitzgerald took it upon himself to ensure that everyone who descended upon Milwaukee would leave impressed. The game tipped off at 12:45 p.m. Sunday afternoon on CBS. The network was in the middle of a good year televising NBA games and it hoped that holding the All-Star Game in the afternoon would bring in plenty of eyeballs during a good time slot. It was also the first year in which the NBA held its first Slam Dunk Contest, adopting it from the ABA just a year after it famously debuted at that league's final All-Star Game. All 10,938 seats were filled in the Arena for the game. Some Milwaukee fans tailgated in nearby parking lots before the game, grilling up bratwursts and burgers on what was a balmy 35-degree day in February. The game itself was well-received and it went down to the wire as the West clinched a 125–124 win over the East. Even in defeat, Julius Erving was named MVP of the game—a decision that drew a heavy mix of boos from the Milwaukee faithful. The highlight of the game arguably came before it even began for all the Milwaukeeans in attendance. Abdul-Jabbar arrived in Milwaukee that weekend on a quick turnaround after having played in Denver on a Friday night. In the process, he forgot to pack his Lakers warmup jacket, or at least that was how he explained it after the game. When it was his turn to be introduced

16. You're Now Leaving Kareem City

to the Milwaukee fans, he strolled onto the court wearing a Bucks warmup jacket that was given to him by the Bucks' athletic trainer. It brought all those fans in the Arena to their feet as they gave their former superstar and sports hero a rousing standing ovation, just as they had done for his six seasons there. He was the only All–Star to receive such a reaction that day.

It wasn't until years later that Abdul-Jabbar finally articulated what playing for the Bucks and being in Milwaukee ended up meaning to him. His final season in 1988–89 brought out all of the praise and adulations that was befitting for one of the game's greatest players. Wherever he and the Lakers traveled throughout the season as they looked to defend their championship title and help the big man go out on top, Abdul-Jabbar was showered with gifts. Not just for his 20 years of NBA service, but for a basketball career that had been talked about and hyped from his teenage days when he went by the name of Lew Alcindor and was a budding star for Power Memorial Academy in New York. Where Abdul-Jabbar played would be of great interest to basketball observers and fans of the sport as he climbed from high school to the college ranks with his decision to play for UCLA under legendary coach John Wooden. Abdul-Jabbar's presence on your team—even as he was only beginning to discover the extent of his powers—meant winning. And being among the teams that made up that exclusive club meant being in a class of your own.

The Milwaukee Bucks knew that better than anyone. The promise of Abdul-Jabbar was openly talked about days after Milwaukee earned the rights to an expansion NBA team on January 22, 1968. Their first season would be finished by the time Abdul-Jabbar was entering the pro ranks, where he was wooed by multimillion-dollar offers, ownership shares of ABA teams and more. A coin flip stood in the way of the Bucks winning his NBA draft rights, followed by a fight to secure his signature as the ABA eventually fumbled the bag and lost the chance to truly challenge the NBA in an economic sense. In their first year—before Abdul-Jabbar arrived—the Bucks won 27 games. The next season, now with Abdul-Jabbar as the man in the middle, they won 56 games. The next season, the Bucks acquired Oscar Robertson, won 66 games and dominated their way to that year's NBA championship. Abdul-Jabbar was anointed with the nickname "The Franchise," by Bucks announcer Eddie Doucette not long after landing in Milwaukee, and with good reason. By coming to Milwaukee, Abdul-Jabbar made the Bucks a significant draw within the NBA. Not only did their fortunes on the court change once Abdul-Jabbar settled into the NBA during his rookie years, their fortunes off the court changed too. His presence meant being in the mix for nationally televised games on ABC, in those nascent days of three television networks. The Bucks were one of the league's hottest tickets. Not just at home in Milwaukee Arena, but on the road, too. Abdul-Jabbar meant big business for everyone, but for his first six NBA seasons, it was the Bucks who benefited the most. His presence assured them of their place in the league and the world of pro basketball. Those benefits ran out the moment Abdul-Jabbar privately requested a trade in the weeks leading up to the 1974–75 season.

So, there he was, making his final visit as a player to the city where he first played in the NBA and stood as the league's all-time scoring leader. It was December 11, 1988. The Bucks were just 8–8 to start the 1988–89 season and had just opened the Bradley Center, the brand new arena that was constructed to ensure the team's survival in Milwaukee. In many ways, it should have been the house that Abdul-Jabbar built, but the Bucks' efforts to build a new arena from the moment they entered the NBA never came to pass until then. For all its drawbacks, the Milwaukee Arena had to do for their first 20 seasons in the NBA. It took the philanthropic efforts of Jane Bradley Pettit and her second husband, Lloyd, and their pledge of $90 million to build a new facility and Herb Kohl buying the team from outgoing owner Jim Fitzgerald in March of 1985. The Bucks had endured in the years that followed Abdul-Jabbar's departure and, to their credit, punched above their weight. Whereas Abdul-Jabbar was competing for championships and played a part in the Lakers' dynastic run throughout the 1980s, the Bucks were a steadying force at the top of the Eastern Conference throughout the decade. For as good as they were under head coach Don Nelson and with players like Marques Johnson, Sidney Moncrief, Terry Cummings and Paul Pressey—to name a few—they could never get past the Philadelphia 76ers and the Boston Celtics in any playoff run.

Abdul-Jabbar's final visit to Milwaukee as a player didn't see him on the court at all. A knee injury prevented him from seeing any action and the only time he stood at the center circle was for the opening ceremony that celebrated his impact in Milwaukee and on the NBA as a whole. There he stood, dressed in street clothes amid all the pomp and circumstance. The Bucks pulled out all the bells and whistles. The venerable Jon McGlocklin served as the emcee and he took great delight in helping unveil a painting by George Pollard commemorating Abdul-Jabbar's infamous "skyhook" in both Bucks and Lakers uniforms. A tribute video featuring the big man's Bucks highlights flashed across the Bradley Center scoreboard. But it was the $13,500 custom Harley-Davidson motorcycle that Kohl and the Bucks gave to Abdul-Jabbar that left the big fella speechless and brought the sold-out crowd at the Bradley Center to their feet, hooting and hollering. After admiring the bike for a minute, Abdul-Jabbar hopped onto the cream and gold Electra Glide Classic, gave an "A-OK" gesture and flashed his beaming smile.

Abdul-Jabbar never presented himself as someone who embraced

16. You're Now Leaving Kareem City

Milwaukee and its community over his six seasons with the Bucks. It took becoming a permanent visitor in his subsequent seasons with the Lakers for him to come to appreciate his time in Milwaukee, his success with the Bucks and the growing pains he went through. Over the years, his feelings for the city of Milwaukee softened and his appreciation of Bucks fans grew. Yes, he wanted out of Milwaukee, and for all of the roster building the Bucks did to make up for what they had lost, Abdul-Jabbar was the needle mover to ensure a championship. There was no getting around that and it hung over a Bucks franchise that couldn't break through to make another NBA Finals appearance for a very long time after the departure of their original superstar. As he approached the microphone, the words Abdul-Jabbar had rehearsed in his head escaped him. Instead, he spoke off the cuff. He thanked the Bucks and their fans for the warm reception and standing ovation he had received, for all of the tributes and gifts made to him, and for coming together to celebrate him in Milwaukee. "This is nothing new. You people have always been like that," Abdul-Jabbar remarked.[21] He further reflected on the changes he underwent while in Milwaukee: "I think of all of the changes I've been through since I came here. I was 22 years old, I had a little more hair. Life was different, Nixon was president—a whole lot of things have changed since then." Abdul-Jabbar paused for a moment as he gathered his thoughts. "But one thing hasn't changed, and that's the appreciation you've always shown me."[22]

The Bradley Center crowd of 18,633 people roared and got to their feet as he emphasized that last sentence. For so long—or at least while he was in Milwaukee—Abdul-Jabbar had kept people out. He didn't want to let in the attention-seekers, whether it be fans or the press. He held on to his privacy, and his devotion to Islam made him even more inscrutable to a public that did not understand his chosen faith—whether he intended that or not. Time passed and the personal turmoil he experienced while in Milwaukee brought him to sunny Los Angeles. As he approached middle age, slowly started to feel his physical and athletic decline, and neared the finish line of his basketball career, it was clear he felt his mortality. His first autobiography—*Giant Steps*, published in 1983—was the first look into Abdul-Jabbar's life and true glimpse behind the curtain. As he braced for what kind of reception his book would receive, he found that it didn't elicit the response he feared. "When that didn't happen, it eliminated some of my suspicions. I was able to relax, and things have gotten better ever since," he said.[23] The promise of his Bucks jersey being retired the following season—Abdul-Jabbar's first after his retirement—was made, but didn't actually come to pass until April 21, 1993, during the Bucks' 25th anniversary season.

By then, whatever distance there was between Abdul-Jabbar, the

Bucks and the city of Milwaukee had shrunk. The guard had long come down for Abdul-Jabbar, and the place where he felt the most ill at ease as a player no longer felt that way to him. "The city let me leave with the same open arms with which it had welcomed me. It was as if the fans knew I didn't really belong there forever, and they let me go with all the appreciation they had always shown for what I did on the court. This made it both easier and harder to step away," Abdul-Jabbar wrote in his second autobiography, which focused on his farewell season.[24] It would be a long time before someone of Abdul-Jabbar's caliber and talent played in Milwaukee again. Luck was involved in order to land him in the first place and by all accounts the Bucks did everything possible to make him happy and satisfied, both on and off the court. Abdul-Jabbar's feelings for Milwaukee were his own and he was within his rights to leave as he did. In the process, though, it cast a stain on the city: that it was not big enough to keep a worldly individual like him happy beyond professional reasons, that it wasn't major league, that it was second-rate. If Milwaukee couldn't keep Kareem Abdul-Jabbar for more than six seasons, the thinking went, there was no way it could find anyone who would be content with what the city had to offer. These were all things that Milwaukeeans had heard before and that Fishman, Pavalon and others had to fight against, outside of Milwaukee and even within it.

Milwaukeeans revered their sports heroes and they took pride in their city being on top of the baseball world in '57 and the basketball world in '71. Fishman and Pavalon may have built the enterprise, but Abdul-Jabbar was the one who made their dream become a reality. And on that cold December night, he completed his own hero's journey. He had helped restore the city's sporting pride with his MVP honors and by winning the championship three years into their team's existence. His no. 33 jersey still hangs from the rafters of Fiserv Forum—the Bucks' current home—as does that 1971 NBA championship banner. On the way up into the arena's concourse stands a 10-foot bobblehead-like figure in his likeness. But the breadth of Abdul-Jabbar's impact on Milwaukee isn't seen beyond the concrete walls of Fiserv Forum. There are no statues or landmarks within the city itself that signify his presence or the impact that he had on the community that he was once reluctantly a part of. In that sense, it's almost like he was never there. But for as long as the Bucks stay and play in Milwaukee, Abdul-Jabbar's greatest legacy to the city will be the fact that he made the Bucks a franchise worth preserving long after he left.

Epilogue
Larry's Last Stand

Costello waited and waited. April turned into May and May turned into June. He was still under a contract for another season, but public remarks on his job status dashed any sense of security that the Bucks' coach could have. The Bucks now had made a landmark trade and Costello stood as one of the remaining links that bridged the Bucks from the beginning to this new, uncertain phase. Amid a superstar leaving the city and rumors of dissension within Bucks management, Costello stood as a sympathetic figure. Could he survive to see out the Bucks' new future? Did he even have a say in the matter? He wasn't in attendance when the Bucks presented the four new faces of the franchise who had the illustrious distinction of being traded for Kareem Abdul-Jabbar. Talk about big shoes to fill. At the press conference that introduced Junior Bridgeman, Dave Meyers, Elmore Smith, and Brian Winters, Alverson stopped short of reassuring reporters that Costello would be back to coach the Bucks. "Larry Costello has a contract and he will continue to coach the Bucks for as long as his contract runs and as long as the board of directors want him," he said.[1] There were too many cooks in the kitchen. The Bucks' board of directors had grown and grown over the years, to the point where there was no unanimity in what direction they sought to take the franchise after dealing away the best player the franchise had ever known. That was, until Embry forged ahead to do the job he was asked to do.

Costello went into the 1975–76 season still as coach of the Bucks. It was his seventh season at the helm, but he acted like it was his first. Save for key exceptions, he was coaching a whole new team and he looked forward to the challenge of rebuilding the Bucks without Abdul-Jabbar. He appreciated the fact that the organization didn't move on from him at such a critical juncture in the franchise. He was being given a chance to build the Bucks from the ground up for the second time now. The second time wasn't quite like the first. Costello ran into problems as the Bucks started

0–5 that year. Dandridge was not happy—as seen by his trying to renegotiate his contract over the offseason and his submitting a trade demand in the face of such a poor start. The key of having everyone buy into what the Bucks were building was already being threatened, and Costello was not having it.

Neither was Jim Fitzgerald. The Bucks prepared for a bumpy road as they rebuilt themselves going into that season. They played as if they were a young team and alternated between the win and loss column for much of the year. A winning streak followed a losing streak. A win was followed up by a loss. They were hurtling toward .500 at best. All the while, Fitzgerald was working behind the scenes. He had been the loudest of the dissenting voices in the room when it came time to plot their path once Abdul-Jabbar wanted out. He was the one who wanted Costello gone. He was, as Embry later referred to it, the head of the Janesville group that made up the Bucks' fractured board of directors (Fitzgerald lived in Janesville, Wis.). Fitzgerald came on board in the fall of 1972 after having built a cable television empire called Total TV and was in need of a cash infusion to expand its operations throughout the state. The Bucks' board was on the cutting edge of advocating for cable television, knowing the massive impact that its broadcasting Bucks games could have on their overall business. Fitzgerald's business and ability to expand the Bucks' footprint with his own cable operation steadily made him more and more of a special commodity on the Bucks' board of directors, and he knew it too. As the Bucks began to deal with Abdul-Jabbar's trade request and subsequent departure, Fitzgerald began acquiring shares of stock in the team from the Bucks' board members—most notably from Pavalon—and preparing to take over Milwaukee Professional Sports & Services, Inc. On January 3, 1976, the top headline in the *Milwaukee Sentinel* read, "BUCKS TAKEOVER IN WORKS."[2]

Far down in that story, it was reported that Fitzgerald was contemplating a change in management and coaches.[3] By that point, he had acquired 25 percent of the 505,705 outstanding shares that were held by Bucks stockholders. He was now the majority shareholder of the company that owned the Bucks. In his public comments he tried to quell the rumor that he was taking over the company by himself, but he did very little to diminish that perception. No longer was Fitzgerald lurking in the background or his name only found buried deep within reports on the Bucks' stockholdings. He was on the verge of becoming the most powerful voice in the room as far as the Bucks' operations were concerned and he had the deep pockets to prove it. Costello grew more uneasy as the Bucks progressed through that season. Yet by some miracle, the team had plodded along but still found themselves in the playoff race. Internal expectations changed beyond just Fitzgerald's taking charge. The people of the press were Costello's biggest defenders and the Bucks fans in Milwaukee were a close second. They came to his defense the more Costello's job security was called into question. The same certainly went for Embry. Embry found that the growing power within Bucks management had been talking to players and gaining input on Costello's coaching and the relationship he had with them. He saw this as contributing to why Costello's footing with the organization was slipping. "Throughout my playing career, and my short time in management, I never thought the players should determine who coached the team," Embry wrote later. "If that was the case, there'd be coaching changes every week."[4]

By the end of the 1975–76 season, the Bucks had punched their ticket to the playoffs by winning their division with a 38–44 record. Costello could not have cared less about winning the division with a losing record. Even so, Fitzgerald made his move. He offered Costello's former right-hand man and Niagara teammate, Hubie Brown, the Bucks' head coaching job. Fitzgerald did so without full approval from the board. Brown had won an ABA championship the year before with the Colonels and he was looking for a life raft. The ABA was falling apart and nearing its end after the merger was finally announced. As much as they tried, the Colonels weren't going to make the jump to the NBA. Brown wanted back in, somehow and someway. Was he about to take his friend's job just to get back in the NBA? "The big problem is that I don't want it to seem like I'm the guy who got Larry fired," Brown pondered. "It's got to be their own decision up there. I couldn't take the heat if I had to come under a cloud like that."[5] Costello was caught in the middle of an intense power struggle. Now his friend was eyeing his job while he was still the head coach of the team. Though the team was powerful, he had few allies in his corner. The situation was taxing Costello, his wife, Barbara, and their four daughters. It came as no surprise that the friendship between Costello and Brown was permanently shattered as the soap opera dragged on.

More than enough time had passed for the Bucks faithful to make their voices heard. They saw the long, drawn-out affair grow uglier and they saw how Costello was getting a raw deal from ownership. They still supported their beloved coach. They decided to circulate a petition and got nearly 1,000 signatures. They wanted to see Costello retain his job after his contract expired that season. When the Bucks played their regular-season finale against the Bulls—a resounding 111–77 loss—Costello was showered with a deafening ovation by all 9,275 fans in attendance. Fans held signs saying, "We like Larry." He responded by waving and beaming that smile of his toward the crowd. Management knew exactly where they stood and after not having introduced Costello as the Bucks coach all season long, they made sure to introduce him before games going into their playoff run. "In light of what was happening, we figured this was a good time to do it again," said John Steinmiller, Bucks public relations director. "Many people didn't even notice that we hadn't been doing it, and if we hadn't done it this time, they would have thought it was deliberate."[6] Those displays of support carried into the Bucks' first-round series against the Pistons in a matchup that saw Milwaukee lose in the deciding Game 3. To see the fans rally behind him throughout a very trying experience and season led Costello to refer to it as the "most touching thing that has ever happened to me in sports."[7]

Fitzgerald was painted as the villain. Before he came along, hardly anything was mentioned about Costello's future in Milwaukee. There was hardly anything to mention. The Bucks had won 60 or more games in three straight seasons, won consecutive division titles and played for championships when they had a little luck on their side. It left Fitzgerald backed into a corner and he called a press conference at the Pfister Hotel once the Bucks opened their series with Detroit, and pledged his vote for Costello to remain as head coach. It was still not a vote that Fitzgerald could make alone. Costello—buoyed by all of those fervent Bucks fans— was not going to accept anything less than a multi-year deal. "I won't sign for one year. If I don't get more than one year, I'll have to start looking," Costello insisted. "I feel I deserve that much."[8] Costello's contract was up and it was to be voted on a month after the end of the season. As he waited to learn of his fate, Fitzgerald officially filed papers to take control of Milwaukee Professional Sports and Services, Inc. The changing of the guard was on the horizon.

When the Bucks board members arrived at the Milwaukee Athletic Club on May 18, they were immediately asked by members of the press to take a group photo. They all didn't agree to that, but it only took five minutes for them to agree that they'd keep Costello in Milwaukee as head coach. The two sides agreed to a two-year deal and Costello earned a pay raise in the process. When the Bucks made the announcement that Costello was sticking around, only Alverson appeared alongside him. Costello was thrilled. He had won the fight. He was stubborn and tenacious as a player and he was stubborn and tenacious as a coach. As it turns out, he was stubborn and tenacious as a negotiator, too. The wrinkles in Costello's face started to grow longer, little by little, and so did the bags under his eyes. He was always a fighter, but now the punches started to land a little harder. It took a toll on him in many ways. The same was true of the Bucks board. The shareholders had divided into groups and were sparring against one another. And no longer were those spats behind closed doors.

The summer passed and the Bucks prepared for the 1976–77 season, Costello's ninth year at the helm. He had a new assistant coach alongside him. Don Nelson originally tried to make it as the first player-turned-NBA referee after retiring that offseason, but quickly found that it wasn't for him. When he and Embry were having beers one night, Embry asked whether he wanted to be an assistant coach for the Bucks. The two went back to their days with the Celtics, and Embry felt Nelson could help bridge the gap between Costello and the young Bucks players. Nelson took the proposition to his family and put it up to a vote. It was unanimous. He jumped on board in Milwaukee and was Costello's new right-hand man. But Fitzgerald had more aces up his sleeve. In fact, lots of them. He sought to buy the rest of the shares within the team to fully take over. He weeded out those who didn't buy into his vision and was in the process of installing a new board of directors. Those who had gone against the grain were put on notice and heard the bell tolling in the distance. Fitzgerald didn't assume all shares of stock, but 71 percent of shares eventually did the trick. The Bucks started off that season by losing their first five games—just as they had the previous season. Off the court, the machine started to whir once again. Alverson resigned not long after Fitzgerald assumed full control and Fitzgerald subsequently stepped in as team president. The Bucks stopped the bleeding at 0–5 and won two straight games to kick off November—only to lose the next nine of their 10 games.

Embry saw the writing on the wall. Not just for Costello, but for himself. The two parties were constantly under fire by Fitzgerald's faction and he knew it wouldn't end. It wasn't doing anyone any good—not Embry, not Costello and not the players. After a 115–106 loss to the SuperSonics on November 21, the Bucks' sixth straight defeat, Embry approached Costello. He knew it was time for a change, but he wanted to give Costello the very thing that no one else had given him over the last two years. Embry wanted to give Costello a chance to leave with dignity. Costello resigned as head coach of the Milwaukee Bucks the very next night. He finished with a 410–264 record, and those 410 victories put him in the elite club of five coaches who had won that many games or more in the NBA at the time. Wearing a mustard-yellow shirt and a Mr. Rogers–style cardigan, Costello spoke to the press about his decision. He was clearly dealing with the fact that he was leaving the job and the place he had called home for nine years. "In the best interest of the Milwaukee Bucks, their organization, the fans, everyone concerned, including myself and my family, I've resigned as coach of the Milwaukee Bucks," Costello announced. "It was initiated by me because I thought that was the best for everyone concerned."[9]

In his speech, Costello referred to the team as "our Bucks." He wished for his replacement, Nelson, to be given the patience he wasn't afforded in rebuilding the Bucks. As he stood there at the podium, Costello dissected why things had changed so fast: "I think we won so many games so fast once we got Kareem that we were spoiled. We didn't build a team then. We just got Kareem. When we lost Kareem, we had to build a team. It takes time."[10] He thanked the Milwaukee press for treating him fairly and thanked the Bucks fans who had gone to bat for him when he needed it most. Costello had fallen on his sword. There were no more fights to be fought. Embry was Costello's biggest ally and he unexpectedly announced that he'd resign along with him, though at a later date.

There weren't many players who came to Costello's defense after his resignation. Not Dandridge, who'd leave the Bucks during free agency the following offseason. When McGlocklin had his no. 14 jersey retired by the Bucks on December 10, 1976—the same night that he and Doucette announced the creation of the MACC (Midwest Athletes Against Childhood Cancer) Fund—there was no shortage of players and coaches at the halftime ceremony. Teammates like Robertson and some of his former coaches joined McGlocklin and his family on the floor. The one exception was Costello, who attended the game on press row. He wasn't on the floor as McGlocklin was being celebrated for an 11-year NBA career and he left as the ceremony was underway to have some drinks. "I was very surprised he didn't invite me. I was his coach for eight years. We ran a lot of plays for him so he could shoot. I was sort of hurt a little bit. But I can accept it."[11] McGlocklin was apologetic about Costello taking offense to not being on the court with him during this landmark moment. But he was clear as to why he never thought to have Costello alongside him, his teammates and his family. "Larry was just a coach I played for. I never considered him a friend," explained McGlocklin. "He wasn't someone I was close to. I wanted the people I cared for and was close to. He wasn't one of those."[12]

Still, Costello wanted to give back to the Bucks fans one last time and it didn't take too much imagination to know how he would show his gratitude. He rented out the Milwaukee Arena on December 11, 1976, and held a free coaching clinic for fans 14 years or older. Close to 200 people came into the Arena to see Costello do what he did best as he donned gym shoes, white pants and a green Bucks T-shirt. The clinic ran for two and a half hours and participants worked on fundamentals. Costello rented the Arena for a $1,000 fee and Nelson donated his time and showcased his trademark jumper. When it came toward the end, Costello reiterated his thanks to those Bucks fans in attendance and the city of Milwaukee. He said he wanted them to support Nelson and knew how hard a job he'd have going forward. Most of all, Costello wanted one thing. "I hope you continue to support the Bucks. They deserve your support," he told those in attendance.[13]

Epilogue

In all of his years of basketball, Costello was a perfectionist. He did the work. He did his job and he expected the same of his players. All of the attention on how much players were making before they had even entered the NBA mystified Costello. He was all business and saw everything unrelated to the game of basketball as excess. In Costello, Milwaukeeans saw themselves: someone who put his head down and did the work that was asked of him. It's no surprise that they rallied around him in his time of greatest need. They recognized all he had done to build up the Bucks from the moment the team entered the NBA. When he saw that they appreciated all that he had done for the team and what they accomplished together, his chiseled exterior cracked. The smile poked through.

All Costello wanted was recognition of what he had done to establish the Bucks—a franchise that still stands today more than half a century later. He was given two of the greatest players to have ever played in the NBA. For that reason, his efforts and work have been discounted in the years since. Their greatness overshadowed just how hard Costello worked to help get the machine up and running, even if his star players didn't always see eye to eye with what he was preaching. He coached every player the same and didn't cater to any one player's needs over another, which is as it was during those days. Costello got one more shot in the NBA when he coached the Bulls during the 1978–79 season. He only lasted 56 games. It was clear by the time he left Chicago that the NBA was no longer looking for Costello types. He coached the Milwaukee Does in the Women's Basketball League the following year before financial problems folded the club at the end of the season. He returned to his Upstate New York roots to finish out his coaching years at Utica College throughout the 1980s. He never could stand being away from basketball and always chased that perfect game. He wasn't perfect, but Costello could find solace knowing that he had achieved perfection, albeit for one season. He left his mark on the NBA when he was inducted into the Naismith Memorial Basketball Hall of Fame posthumously in 2022. But his legacy is felt nowhere greater than in Milwaukee, a place he called home and helped bring up an expansion club that won a championship faster than any NBA team has done before or since. Little did he know, he coached the perfect team.

Chapter Notes

Chapter 1

1. Howard Bryant, *The Last Hero: A Life of Henry Aaron* (New York: Pantheon, 2010), 306.
2. Patrick W. Steele, *Home of the Braves: The Battle for Baseball in Milwaukee* (Madison: University of Wisconsin Press, 2018), 189.
3. Marv Fishman with Tracy Dodds, *Bucking the Odds: The Birth of the Milwaukee Bucks* (Chicago: Raintree, 1978), 6–7.
4. Oliver Kuechle, "Nothing Must Happen to Hurt Packers," *Milwaukee Journal*, June 27, 1965.
5. "Detroit Has Not Contacted Packers about Ron Kramer, Says Lombardi," Appleton (WI) *Post-Crescent*, July 11, 1965.
6. Fishman and Dodds, *Bucking the Odds*, 16.
7. Ibid., 20.

Chapter 3

1. "Milwaukee Good Sports City, Says NBA Head," *Milwaukee Sentinel*, July 27, 1965.
2. Lloyd Larson, "Pro Cagers Admit They Want Milwaukee," *Milwaukee Sentinel*, Sept. 16, 1951.
3. Gilbert Rogin, "You're Looking at Success," *Sports Illustrated*, Oct. 24, 1960.
4. Ibid.
5. Bob Wolf, "Kerner Boosts NBA Club Here," *Milwaukee Journal*, Oct. 11, 1967.
6. Ibid.
7. Bob Wolf, "Boss' Deadline Is Met by Bucks," *Milwaukee Journal*, May 2, 1971.
8. Lou Chapman, "Bulls' Owner Says: City Should Try for NBA 5 Now," *Milwaukee Sentinel*, Sept. 23, 1967.
9. Marvin Fishman with Tracy Dodds, *Bucking the Odds: The Birth of the Milwaukee Bucks* (Chicago: Raintree, 1978), 26.
10. Lou Chapman, "City Applies for NBA Franchise," *Milwaukee Sentinel*, Dec. 16, 1967.
11. "NBA Bid Monday Planned by Kohl," *Milwaukee Journal*, Dec. 16, 1967.
12. Fishman and Dodds, *Bucking the Odds*, 38.
13. "Pro Cage Franchise in Milwaukee—'If,'" *Milwaukee Journal*, Apr. 2, 1967.
14. Bob Wolf, "Bulls Victors at Gate and on Court; Trounce Knicks, 109–96, Before 5,048," *Milwaukee Journal*, Nov. 24, 1967.
15. "Everybody's Happy about NBA Team," *Milwaukee Journal*, Jan. 22, 1968.
16. Ibid.
17. Terry Bledsoe, "Milwaukee Granted Pro Basketball Team," *Milwaukee Journal*, Jan. 22, 1968.
18. Ronald Anzia, "Stock Offered in NBA Club," *Milwaukee Sentinel*, Apr. 16, 1968.
19. Ronald Anzia, "NBA Stock Appeal Up; Offer Expanded," *Milwaukee Sentinel*, Apr. 20, 1968.
20. Fishman and Dodds, *Bucking the Odds*, 57.
21. Bob Wolf, "Alcindor Could Wind Up in Milwaukee, Depending on How Well New Club Does," *Milwaukee Journal*, Jan. 24, 1968.

Chapter 4

1. Lou Chapman, "Milwaukee Back in Majors: Offer Fans 'Share' in New NBA Team," *Milwaukee Sentinel*. Jan. 23, 1968.
2. Marvin Fishman with Tracy Dodds, *Bucking The Odds: The Birth of*

the *Milwaukee Bucks* (Chicago: Raintree, 1978), 71.

3. Mike Christopoulos, "'MU' Fr. McAuley Insists: Won't Release Al," *Milwaukee Sentinel*, Mar. 6, 1968.

4. Oliver Kuechle, "McGuire Case an Unfortunate Incident," *Milwaukee Journal*, Mar. 13, 1968.

5. Tom Kertscher, *Cracked Sidewalks and French Pastry: The Wit and Wisdom of Al McGuire* (Madison: University of Wisconsin Press, 2002), 132.

6. Fishman and Dodds, *Bucking the Odds*, 75–76.

7. Bob Wolf, "Good Old Fashioned Pro, Costello Thinks Modern," *Milwaukee Journal*, Apr. 4, 1968.

8. Lou Chapman, "Bucks—That's the Name of City's New Pro Five," *Milwaukee Sentinel*, May 22, 1968.

9. Ibid.

Chapter 5

1. "Smith Ordinary Name; Rookie Isn't," *Milwaukee Journal*, May 12, 1968.

2. Wayne Embry and Mary Schmitt Boyer, *The Inside Game: Race, Power, and Politics in the NBA* (Akron: University of Akron Press, 2004), 166–167.

3. Lou Chapman, "Embry Holds Key to Hope of Bucks," *Milwaukee Sentinel*, Sept. 17, 1968.

4. Bob Wolf, "Bucks Open Camp; Players Integrated," *Milwaukee Journal*, Sept. 17, 1968.

5. Embry and Schmitt Boyer, *The Inside Game*, 170.

6. Ibid., 171.

Chapter 6

1. Terry Bledsoe, "Alcindor Could Wind Up in Milwaukee, Depending on How Well New Club Does," *Milwaukee Journal*, Jan. 24, 1968.

2. "Reassurance Offered Fans," *Milwaukee Journal*, Feb. 16, 1968.

3. Terry Pluto, *Loose Balls: The Short, Wild Life of the American Basketball Association* (New York: Simon & Schuster, 2007), 191. Originally published in 1991.

4. "Bucks Front Office Praised," *Milwaukee Journal*, Oct. 17, 1968.

5. Bob Wolf, "Bucks Drub Detroit to Gain 1st Victory," *Milwaukee Journal*, Nov. 1, 1968.

6. "Bucks 4th in NBA Crowds," *Milwaukee Journal*, Nov. 12, 1968.

7. Roger Kahn, "The Perfect Toy," *Esquire*, December 1970.

8. Bob Wolf, "Electric Eye Provided Large Charge for Bucks," *Milwaukee Journal*, Nov. 24, 1978.

9. Lou Chapman, "Lady Luck Could Get Lew Here," *Milwaukee Sentinel*, Jan. 14, 1969.

10. Ibid.

11. Pat Putnam, "Now He Gets to Shoot," *Sports Illustrated*, Feb. 24, 1969.

12. Ibid.

13. Ibid.

14. Ibid.

15. "Mikan Insists ABA Plans Solid Draft War," *Milwaukee Sentinel*, Feb. 6, 1969.

16. Bob Wolf, "Lew Here? Not Just Yet," *Milwaukee Journal*, Feb. 19, 1969.

17. Bob Wolf, "Bucks Risk Streak Against San Diego," *Milwaukee Journal*, Feb. 25, 1969.

18. Bob Wolf, "Bucks Lose to Warriors, but Set an Attendance High," *Milwaukee Journal*, Mar. 11, 1969.

Chapter 7

1. Marvin Fishman and Tracy Dodds, *Bucking the Odds: The Birth of the Milwaukee Bucks* (Chicago: Raintree, 1978), 109.

2. Robert Lipsyte, "Sports of *The Times*: Flipping," *New York Times*, Mar. 20, 1969.

3. "Bucks Win Flip of a Coin—And a Chance at Alcindor," *Milwaukee Journal*, Mar. 20, 1969.

4. Bob Wolf, "Phoenix Players Say Flipping Coin in Draft Unfair, Slur to Integrity," *Milwaukee Journal*, Mar. 20, 1969.

5. Terry Bledsoe, "An Alcindor Interview, Sort Of…," *Milwaukee Journal*, Mar. 20, 1969.

6. Lew Alcindor, "A Year of Turmoil and Decision," *Sports Illustrated*, November 1969.

7. Kareem Abdul-Jabbar and Peter Knobler, *Giant Steps: The Autobiography of Kareem Abdul-Jabbar* (New York: Bantam, 1983), 15.

8. Abdul-Jabbar and Knobler, *Giant Steps*, 42.

9. Dave Begel, "Pavalon Semi-Recluse Now," *Milwaukee Journal*, Jan. 18, 1976.
10. Abdul-Jabbar and Knobler, *Giant Steps*, 192–193.
11. Ibid., 193–194.
12. Lou Chapman, "Alcindor Agrees to Sign with Bucks," *Milwaukee Sentinel*, Mar. 29, 1969.
13. Bob Wolf, "Lew Cool to New ABA Bid," *Milwaukee Journal*, Mar. 30, 1969.
14. Bob Wolf, "Alcindor Officially Affixes 'Ferdinand Lewis' to Pact," *Milwaukee Journal*, Apr. 3, 1969.

Chapter 8

1. Lou Chapman, "Alcindor 'Hits' NCAA," *Milwaukee Sentinel*, Apr. 15, 1969.
2. Ibid.
3. Ibid.
4. Lou Chapman, "Alcindor 'Adds' an Inch," *Milwaukee Sentinel*, June 20, 1969.
5. Bob Wolf, "10,482 Watch Alcindor Score 35 in Bucks Debut," *Milwaukee Journal*, June 23, 1969.
6. "Goodby to the Old Balance of Power," *Sports Illustrated*, Oct. 27, 1969.
7. Lew Alcindor, "A Year of Turmoil and Decision," *Sports Illustrated*, Nov. 10, 1969.
8. Ibid.
9. Ira Berkow, "When Some Wondered if Lew Had It," *New York Times*, Apr. 22, 1989.
10. Evans Kirkby, "A Short Visit with Lew Alcindor," *Milwaukee Journal*, Nov. 9, 1969.
11. Terry Bledsoe, "Lew Finds Fast Pace Confined to Basketball," *Milwaukee Journal*, Dec. 26, 1969.
12. Bob Wolf, "Bucks Learn Knack of Knocking Knicks," *Milwaukee Journal*, Jan. 3, 1970.
13. Bob Wolf, "Front Office Job 'Fulfills Every Dream' of Erickson," *Milwaukee Journal*, Apr. 4, 1968.
14. Bob Wolf, "Irate Pavalon Throws Jabs at Officials, Businessmen," *Milwaukee Journal*, June 21, 1968.
15. Lou Chapman, "Bucks Plan 2nd Sport," *Milwaukee Sentinel*, June 13, 1968.
16. Brad Weinstock, "Coach Still Mystery Man," *News (Kenosha, WI)*, Feb. 16, 1968.
17. Bob Wolf, "Bucks Want Arena Jam Relieved within 5 Years," *Milwaukee Journal*, Jan. 6, 1970.
18. "Plastic Canopy Urged for Bucks," *Milwaukee Sentinel*, Jan. 8, 1970.
19. "Study Set on Shift of Events to Let Bucks Use Arena," *Milwaukee Sentinel*, Jan. 16, 1970.
20. Lou Chapman, "Star Appearance Bores Alcindor," *Milwaukee Sentinel*, Jan. 20, 1970.
21. Bob Wolf, "Twyman Awed by Bucks Potential," *Milwaukee Journal*, Feb. 10, 1970.
22. Terry Bledsoe, "Playoff Victory Is Worth Bucks to Bucks; Pavalon Gives $1,000 to Each Team Member," *Milwaukee Journal*, Apr. 4, 1970.
23. Terry Bledsoe, "Knicks' Edge Shakier Now," *Milwaukee Journal*, Apr. 19, 1970.
24. Terry Bledsoe, "Bucks Finish on Sour Note," *Milwaukee Journal*, Apr. 21, 1970.
25. Ibid.
26. Kareem Abdul-Jabbar and Peter Knobler, *Giant Steps* (New York: Bantam, 1983), 208.

Chapter 9

1. Oscar Robertson, *The Big O: My Life, My Times, My Game* (Lincoln: University of Nebraska Press, 2003), 137.
2. Ibid., 229.
3. Ibid., 232.
4. Ibid., 233.
5. Bob Wolf, "Unhappy Big O to Meet Bucks Here Today," *Milwaukee Journal*, Mar. 1, 1970.
6. Robertson, *The Big O*, 242.
7. Ibid., 243.
8. Wayne Embry and Mary Schmitt Boyer, *The Inside Game: Race, Power, and Politics in the NBA* (Akron: University of Akron Press, 2004), 188.
9. Terry Bledsoe, "Oscar Sees No Problems, Pavalon Sees Great Things," *Milwaukee Journal*, May 2, 1970.
10. Terry Bledsoe, "Big O and Big $ Strike Happy Balance with Bucks," *Milwaukee Journal*, Apr. 26, 1970.
11. Robertson, *The Big O*, 249.
12. Sam Goldaper, "N.B.A. and A.B.A. Agree to Merge, Subject to Approval of Congress," *New York Times*, June 19, 1970.
13. Bob Wolf, "Oscar Reflects on Game," *Milwaukee Journal*, July 22, 1970.

Chapter 10

1. Bob Wolf, "Oscar Reflects on Game," *Milwaukee Journal*, July 22, 1970.
2. Kareem Abdul-Jabbar and Peter Knobler, *Giant Steps* (New York: Bantam, 1983), 212.
3. Oscar Robertson, *The Big O: My Life, My Times, My Game* (Lincoln: University of Nebraska Press, 2003), 253.
4. Ibid., 255.
5. Ibid., 259.
6. Jack Olsen, "We've Got to Spread a Little Anarchy," *Sports Illustrated*, Apr. 19, 1971.
7. Richard Vonier, "Letters to Lew," *Milwaukee Journal*, May 16, 1971.
8. Ibid.
9. Chuck Johnson, "Lew Walks Alone, Pursued by Vapid Questions," *Milwaukee Journal*, Feb. 8, 1971.
10. Bob Wolf, "Lew Waves Olive Branch, Praises Milwaukee's Fans," *Milwaukee Journal*, Feb. 16, 1971.
11. Bob Wolf, "19th Straight No Problem as Bucks Break Record," *Milwaukee Journal*, Mar. 6, 1971.
12. Rel Bochat, "Bucks Win Record 19th," *Milwaukee Sentinel*, Mar. 6, 1971.
13. Bob Wolf, "Knicks Are Test for Bucks," *Milwaukee Journal*, Mar. 12, 1971.
14. Robertson, *The Big O*, 262–263.
15. Rel Bochat, "Warriors No 'Match' for Bucks?" *Milwaukee Sentinel*, Mar. 23, 1971.
16. Bob Wolf, "Ellis Shoots: Series Returns to Madison," *Milwaukee Journal*, Apr. 2, 1971.
17. Rel Bochat, "Bucks Eliminate Warriors," *Milwaukee Sentinel*, Apr. 5, 1971.
18. Rel Bochat, "Costello's Grim, the Party's Over," *Milwaukee Sentinel*, Apr. 16, 1971.
19. Bob Wolf, "Smith Leads Bucks: He's Shocked Too," *Milwaukee Journal*, Apr. 19, 1971.
20. Ibid.
21. Robertson, *The Big O*, 266.
22. Ibid., 267.
23. Bob Wolf, "Bucks Too Strong, Alcindor Maintains," *Milwaukee Journal*, Apr. 25, 1971.
24. Bob Wolf, "Bucks No Longer Deny Their Goal: Clean Sweep," *Milwaukee Journal*, Apr. 26, 1971.
25. Dale Hoffman, "Bucks Coolin' It with 3–0 Lead," *Milwaukee Sentinel*, Apr. 29, 1971.
26. Chuck Johnson, "Lew's Wedding Bells Go 'Clunk,'" *Milwaukee Journal*, Apr. 29, 1971.
27. Bob Wolf, "Big O + Big A Do = Title," *Milwaukee Journal*, May 1, 1971.
28. "Bucks Cup Bubbleth Over," *Milwaukee Journal*, May 1, 1971.
29. Ibid.
30. Robertson, *The Big O*, 274.
31. Rel Bochat, "Costello Says: Togetherness Buck Secret," *Milwaukee Sentinel*, May 3, 1971.
32. Bob Wolf, "Boss' Deadline Is Met by Bucks," *Milwaukee Journal*, May 2, 1971.
33. Seymour R. Smith, "Milwaukee Loves Those Bucks," *Baltimore Sun*, May 1, 1971.
34. John W. Kole, "Call Me Kareem,' Says Lew," *Milwaukee Journal*, June 4, 1971.

Chapter 11

1. "Players Plan Star Tilt," *Milwaukee Sentinel*, May 12, 1971.
2. "Maier Says Bucks Belong Downtown," *Milwaukee Journal*, May 14, 1971.
3. "Bucks Aren't Paying Fair, Charges Unhappy Dandridge," *Milwaukee Journal*, July 3, 1971.
4. "G'By, Dick and Sue," *Milwaukee Journal*, Oct. 17, 1971.
5. Bob Wolf, "Jabbar's Goal: Repeat '71 Fans," *Milwaukee Journal*, Sept. 19, 1971.
6. Kareem Abdul-Jabbar and Peter Knobler, *Giant Steps* (New York: Bantam, 1983), 240.
7. "Players at Odds over Merger Bill," *Milwaukee Sentinel*, Sept. 23, 1971.
8. Oscar Robertson, *The Big O: My Life, My Times, My Game* (Lincoln: University of Nebraska Press, 2003), 280.
9. "The Best Team—Ever," *Sports Illustrated*, Nov. 15, 1971.
10. Chuck Johnson, "Jabbar's Picture Evoked Much Reaction," *Milwaukee Journal*, Dec. 3, 1971.
11. "Photo Criticized by Patterson," *Milwaukee Journal*, Dec. 4, 1971.
12. "Mayor Incensed by Pictures," *Milwaukee Journal*, Dec. 3, 1971.
13. Rel Bochat, "Bucks Trade Greg Smith," *Milwaukee Sentinel*, Dec. 10, 1971.

14. Abdul-Jabbar and Knobler, *Giant Steps*, 254.
15. Bob Wolf, "Knicks Find Way to Rally, Win—Again," *Milwaukee Journal*, Jan. 5, 1972.
16. Bob Wolf, "Bucks Force Lakers to Start Over Again," *Milwaukee Journal*, Jan. 10, 1972.
17. Rel Bochat, "Bucks Win, But It's Different Now," *Milwaukee Sentinel*, Feb. 28, 1972.
18. Bob Wolf, "Patterson Says Move Doesn't Mean One for Bucks," *Milwaukee Journal*, Feb. 16, 1972.

Chapter 12

1. Wayne Embry and Mary Schmitt Boyer, *The Inside Game: Race, Power, and Politics in the NBA* (Akron: University of Akron Press, 2004), 187.
2. Roger Kahn, "The Perfect Toy," *Esquire*, December 1970.
3. Marvin Fishman and Tracy Dodds, *Bucking the Odds: The Birth of the Milwaukee Bucks* (Chicago: Raintree, 1978), 91.
4. Embry and Schmitt Boyer, *The Inside Game*, 193.
5. Ibid., 194.
6. Bob Wolf, "'No Big Deal' as Bucks Win Division," *Milwaukee Journal*, Mar. 15, 1972.
7. Bob Wolf, "Bucks Humiliate Lakers," *Milwaukee Journal*, Apr. 10, 1972.
8. Bob Wolf, "Dandridge: Bucks Now Starting to Roll," *Milwaukee Journal*, Apr. 12, 1972.
9. Rel Bochat, "Ref Gives Lakers Helping Hand," *Milwaukee Sentinel*, Apr. 13, 1972.
10. Bob Wolf, "Costello Believes Victory Already Overdue for Bucks," *Milwaukee Journal*, Apr. 18, 1972.
11. Bob Wolf, "Prediction, Bucks Are Off," *Milwaukee Journal*, Apr. 19, 1972.
12. Rel Bochat, "Bucks Shy on Hunger, Emotions?" *Milwaukee Sentinel*, Apr. 24, 1972.
13. Bob Wolf, "Kareem's Image as Best Suffered in Bucks Defeat," *Milwaukee Journal*, Apr. 24, 1972.
14. Bob Wolf, "Patterson Has Single Regret: Bucks' Failure to Keep Title," *Milwaukee Journal*, Apr. 30, 1972.
15. Bob Wolf, "Pay Justified, Says Kareem," *Milwaukee Journal*, May 2, 1972.
16. Kareem Abdul-Jabbar and Peter Knobler, *Giant Steps* (New York: Bantam, 1983), 257.
17. Ibid., 258.
18. Ibid., 260.
19. Tom Flaherty, "Bucks Sign Jabbar to a New Pact," *Milwaukee Journal*, Aug. 18, 1972.
20. Ibid.
21. Bob Wolf, "Kareem Is Hoping for Some Help," *Milwaukee Journal*, Sept. 15, 1972.

Chapter 13

1. Wayne Embry and Mary Schmitt Boyer, *The Inside Game: Race, Power, and Politics in the NBA* (Akron: University of Akron Press, 2004), 200.
2. Rel Bochat, "Erving Still Ours—Bucks' Embry," *Milwaukee Sentinel*, Apr. 12, 1972.
3. Bob Wolf, "Erving Decision Assailed by Bucks," *Milwaukee Journal*, Sept. 13, 1972.
4. Bob Wolf, "Hawks to Fight Decision Giving Erving to Bucks," *Milwaukee Journal*, Sept. 21, 1972.
5. Ibid.
6. Bob Wolf, "Kareem Is Hoping for Some More Help," *Milwaukee Journal*, Sept. 15, 1972.
7. Bob Wolf, "What's Oscar's Longevity?" *Milwaukee Journal*, Sept. 17, 1972.
8. Bill Dwyre, "Bucks' President Sprang from Anonymity," *Milwaukee Journal*, Sept. 24, 1972.
9. Embry and Schmitt Boyer, *The Inside Game*, 219.
10. Bob Wolf, "Costello: Bucks Need Jolt," *Milwaukee Journal*, Nov. 22, 1972.
11. Kareem Abdul-Jabbar and Peter Knobler, *Giant Steps* (New York: Bantam, 1983), 263.
12. Peter Carry, "Center in a Storm," *Sports Illustrated*, Feb. 19, 1973.
13. Terry Bledsoe, "Danger Adds to Strain of Jabbar's Life on Tightrope," *Milwaukee Journal*, Feb. 25, 1973.
14. Ibid.
15. "We're Digging Out after 13 Inch Snow," *Milwaukee Journal*, Apr. 10, 1973.
16. Rel Bochat, "Big O to Play, Hopes

for Change," *Milwaukee Sentinel*, Apr. 16, 1973.
17. "Trade Might Prove Best—Dandridge," *Milwaukee Sentinel*, Apr. 18, 1973.
18. Embry and Schmitt Boyer, *The Inside Game*, 207.
19. Abdul-Jabbar and Knobler, *Giant Steps*, 265–266.
20. Ibid., 266.
21. "City Hails New Pact for Bucks," *Milwaukee Journal*, June 13, 1973.
22. Ibid.

Chapter 14

1. Peter Carry, "Milwaukee Has New Gusto, and Detroit Is in Gear," *Sports Illustrated*, Oct. 15, 1973.
2. Bob Wolf, "Costello: Quiet Power behind Bucks," *Milwaukee Journal*, Nov. 15, 1973.
3. Oscar Robertson, *The Big O: My Life, My Times, My Game* (Lincoln: University of Nebraska Press, 2003), 289.
4. Bob Wolf, "Allen Would Help, Figures He Can't," *Milwaukee Journal*, Mar. 21, 1974.
5. Bob Wolf, "Big Night for the Big O Is a Big Success," *Milwaukee Journal*, Mar. 27, 1974.
6. Ibid.
7. Bud Lea, "Bucks Sail Troubled Waters," *Milwaukee Sentinel*, May 9, 1974.
8. Kareem Abdul-Jabbar and Peter Knobler, *Giant Steps* (New York: Bantam, 1983), 268.
9. Mike Gonring, "Kareem's Miracle Shot Rescues Bucks," *Milwaukee Journal*, May 11, 1974.
10. Abdul-Jabbar and Knobler, *Giant Steps*, 269.
11. Bill Dwyre, "Crowd Just Couldn't Do It for Bucks," *Milwaukee Journal*, May 13, 1974.
12. Ibid.

Chapter 15

1. Oscar Robertson, *The Big O: My Life, My Times, My Game* (Lincoln: University of Nebraska Press, 2003), 305.
2. Ibid., 311.

Chapter 16

1. Wayne Embry and Mary Schmitt Boyer, *The Inside Game: Race, Power, and Politics in the NBA* (Akron: University of Akron Press, 2004), 233.
2. Ibid., 234.
3. Sam Goldaper, "N.B.A. Opens Play Thursday with 5 Big Names Gone, 2 Big Men Arriving," *New York Times*, Oct. 13, 1974.
4. Bob Wolf, "Bucks Need .716 Pace," *Milwaukee Journal*, Nov. 21, 1974.
5. Michael H. Drew, "Kareem Scores Again, as Local DJ," *Milwaukee Journal*, Dec. 8, 1974.
6. Bob Wolf, "Signing Off: Kareem Quits Radio Show," *Milwaukee Journal*, Dec. 11, 1974.
7. Bud Lea, "ABA May Make Pitch to Land Abdul-Jabbar," *Milwaukee Sentinel*, Feb. 10, 1975.
8. "Jabbar to Leave?" *Milwaukee Journal*, Mar. 14, 1975.
9. Bill Dwyre, "Namedropping for Fun, Profit," *Milwaukee Journal*, Mar. 14, 1975.
10. Bob Wolf, "Kareem Admits It's True," *Milwaukee Journal*, Mar. 15, 1975.
11. Sam Goldaper, "Bucks See No Need Now to Make Deal for Unhappy Abdul-Jabbar," *New York Times*, Mar. 18, 1975.
12. Embry and Schmitt Boyer, *The Inside Game*, 237.
13. Sam Goldaper, "N.B.A. Playoffs Worrying TV," *New York Times*, Feb. 25, 1975.
14. Bob Wolf, "Kareem's Quick Exit Symbolic of Bucks?" *Milwaukee Journal*, Apr. 7, 1975.
15. Bob Wolf, "Alverson Offers No Ready Answers," *Milwaukee Journal*, Apr. 18, 1975.
16. Embry and Schmitt Boyer, *The Inside Game*, 239.
17. Ibid., 242.
18. Ibid., 243.
19. Kareem Abdul-Jabbar and Peter Knobler, *Giant Steps* (New York: Bantam, 1983), 270–271.
20. Leslie Johnson Clevert, "Bucks' Fans Sulk over Kareem," *Milwaukee Journal*, July 14, 1975.
21. Frank Clines, "A Big Roar for Kareem," *Milwaukee Journal*. Dec. 12, 1988. Bob Wolf, "Alverson Offers No

Ready Answers," *Milwaukee Journal*, Apr. 18, 1975.
22. Bob Wolf, "Alverson Offers No Ready Answers," *Milwaukee Journal*, Apr. 18, 1975.
23. Dale Hoffman, "Bucks Will Retire No. 33 at Ceremonies Next Fall," *Milwaukee Sentinel*, Dec. 12, 1988.
24. Kareem Abdul-Jabbar and Mignon McCarthy, *Kareem* (New York: Random House, 1990), 113–114.

Epilogue

1. Jim Cohen, "New Bucks, Same Coach?" *Milwaukee Journal*, June 17, 1975.
2. Ray Kenney, "Bucks Takeover in Works," *Milwaukee Sentinel*, Jan. 3, 1976.
3. Ibid.
4. Wayne Embry and Mary Schmitt Boyer, *The Inside Game: Race, Power, and Politics in the NBA* (Akron: University of Akron Press, 2004), 250.
5. Dave Begel, "Brown Views Bucks' Job Cautiously?" *Milwaukee Journal*, Apr. 13, 1976.
6. Bob Wolf, "Fans Show Costello Where They Stand," *Milwaukee Journal*, Apr. 12, 1976.
7. Bill Dwyre, "Bucks Fans Stand Up," *Milwaukee Journal*, Apr. 18, 1976.
8. Bob Wolf, "Costello: No 1 Year Pact," *Milwaukee Journal*, Apr. 19, 1976.
9. Jim Cohen, "Costello Quits, Coup Complete," *Milwaukee Journal*, Nov. 23, 1976.
10. Ibid.
11. Charley McKenna, "Costello Can't Just Leave the Game," *Milwaukee Sentinel*, Dec. 15, 1976.
12. Bill Dwyre, "Latest Bucks Fuss No Major Event," *Milwaukee Journal*, Dec. 19, 1976.
13. "Costello Thanks Bucks Fans with Free Clinic," *Green Bay Press-Gazette*, Dec. 12, 1976.

Bibliography

Books

Abdul-Jabbar, Kareem, and Peter Knobler. *Giant Steps: The Autobiography of Kareem Abdul-Jabbar*. New York: Bantam, 1983.
Abdul-Jabbar, Kareem, and Mignon McCarthy. *Kareem*. New York: Random House, 1990.
Bryant, Howard. *The Last Hero: A Life of Henry Aaron*. New York: Pantheon Books, 2010.
Embry, Wayne, and Mary Schmitt Boyer. *The Inside Game: Race, Power, and Politics in the NBA*. Akron: University of Akron Press, 2004.
Fishman, Marv, with Tracy Dodds. *Bucking the Odds: The Birth of the Milwaukee Bucks*. Chicago: Raintree, 1978.
Kertscher, Tom. *Cracked Sidewalks and French Pastry: The Wit and Wisdom of Al McGuire*. Madison: University of Wisconsin Press, 2002.
Robertson, Oscar. *The Big O: My Life, My Times, My Game*. Lincoln: University of Nebraska Press, 2003.
Steele, Patrick W. *Home of the Braves: The Battle for Baseball in Milwaukee*. Madison: University of Wisconsin Press, 2018.

Periodicals

Appleton (WI) *Post-Crescent*
Baltimore Sun
Esquire
Green Bay Press-Gazette
Kenosha News
Milwaukee Journal
Milwaukee Sentinel
New York Times
Sports Illustrated

Website

Basketball-Reference.com

Bucks' Annual Reference Guides

Official Press and Media Guides, 1968–1975

Index

Numbers in ***bold italics*** indicate pages with illustrations

Aaron, Henry 9
Abdul-Jabbar, Habiba 99, 130
Abdul-Jabbar, Kareem 1–3, 57, ***59***, 100, 103–105, 107–108, 110–111, 113, 115–118, 121–125, 127–129, 131–141, 145–164, 168
Adderley, Cannonball 150
Africa 84, 99–100
Alabama 34, 109
Albert, Marv 151
Alcindor, Lew 1, 35–36, 38–42, 46- 51, 53–61, 63–68, 74–76, 78–80, 82–89, 91–100, 159
Algeria 99
Ali, Muhammad 56, 125
Allah 57, 117
Allen, Lucius 59, 79, 122, 131, 133, 136, 149
Alverson, Bill 117–118, 122, 142, 146, 152, 154–156, 163, 166–167
American Association 5
American Basketball Association 1, 20, 22, 30, 36, 38–41, 47–50, 52–53, 70, 73, 76, 102–103, 119–122, 127, 129, 142–146, 151, 156, 158–159, 165
American Broadcasting Company 17, 55, 80, ***96***, 106, 159
American Football League 10–12, 20–21
Antetokounmpo, Giannis 1
Arabic 116, 129
Armstrong, Neil 53
Atlanta, Georgia 5, 7–9, 12, 49, 120
Atlanta Hawks 37, 107, 120–121, 150, 155
Auerbach, Arnold "Red" 18–19
The Autobiography of Malcolm X 56

"Baeza, Braulio" 54
Baltimore Bullets 20, 37, 42, 66, 72, 73, 80, 89–97
Baltimore Civic Center 94
Barbee, Lloyd 15–16
Barry, Rick 119, 127

Bartholomay, William 7, 8
Basketball Association of America 39
Belmont Abbey College 25
Beloit College 27
Benny the Bull 135
Beverly Hills, California 50
Bing, Dave 133
Birmingham, Alabama 56
Black Commandos 16, 28
Black Journal 115
Black Muslims 100, 124
Bledsoe, Terry 46–47, 125
Bloch, Richard 45
Boozer, Bob 71, 79–80, 89, 97, 103
Borchert Field 5
Boston, Massachusetts 7–9, 18, 85
Boston Celtics 19–20, 22, 31, ***33***, 37, 64, 66, 69, 72, 74, 103, 135–141, 148, 158, 160, 167
Boston College 71
Boston Garden 22, 137
Boston Red Sox 8
Bowling Green, Kentucky 31
Bowling Green State University 26
Bradley Center 160–161
Bridgeman, Junior 155–157, 163
Brookfield, Wisconsin 146–148
Brooklyn Dodgers 51
Brown, Arthur J. 49
Brown, Hubie 121, 133, 142, 165
Brown, John W. 151
Brown, J.W. 70, 72- 74
Brown vs. the Board of Education 14, 34
Buffalo, New York 148
Buffalo Braves 86
Built for This: The Milwaukee Bucks' Historic Run to the 2021 NBA Title 1

Cantaloupe Island 150
Career Academy 40, 99, 117
Carlos, Juan 99

182　Index

Carroll College 79
Carter, Fred 91–*92*
Chamberlain, Wilt 35, 47, 54, 65–66, 88–89, *106*–107, 112, 135
Chappell, Len 30, *43*
Charlotte, Tennessee 69
Chicago, Illinois 5, 7, 9, 20, 21, 23, 39–40, 109, 122, 124, 156, 169
Chicago Blackhawks 117
Chicago Bulls 20, 22, 36, 38, 80, 86, 88, 112, 117, 123, 132–133, 135, 150, 154, 165, 169
Chicago Stadium 117, 135
Chicago White Sox 63
Churchill, Winston 45
Cincinnati, Ohio 30, 40, 69, 73–74, 134, 143
Cincinnati Royals 30, 54, 64, 69–74, 76, 136, 143
City Stadium 11
Civil War 9
Cleveland Cavaliers 84, 141
Clevert, Leslie Johnson 157
Cobo Arena 86
Coca-Cola Company 8, 29
Colangelo, Jerry 46
College of William & Mary 121
Coltrane, John 150
Continental Football League 12–13
Cooke, Jack Kent 156
Cosell, Howard 24
Costello, Larry 1, 26–32, 34, 37–38, 41, *43*, 50, 52–54, 59, 61, 63–68, *75*, 79–84, 86–88, 90–91, 93, 97, 98–100, 102, 105–108, 112–113, 115, 121–123, 125, 131–140, 145, 149–154, 158, 163–169
Cousy, Bob 69, 70- 72, 74
Cowens, Dave 138, 140
Crawford, Freddie 67
Crowe, Ray 134
Cummings, Terry 160
Cunningham, Billy 66
Cunningham, Dick 38, *43*, 103
Cypress College 129

Dandridge, Bob 52–53, 63–64, 74, 80, 93–95, 102, 105, 112, 127–128, 131–133, 136, 138–139, 141, 149, 151, 153, 158, 164, 168
Dane County Coliseum 65
Dartmouth College 25
Davenport, Iowa 17
Davis, Mickey 137–138, 141
Davis, Miles 150
DeBusschere, Dave 103
Denver, Colorado 155–156, 158
Denver Nuggets 144, 158

Denver Rockets 122
Detroit Pistons 37, 41–42, 45, 55, 80, 86, 107, *126*, 132–135, 150, 166
Donohue, Jack 48
Doucette, Eddie 37–38, *43*, 53, 139, 150, 159, 168
Drake University 47
Duke University 121

The Ed Sullivan Show 47
Ellis, Joe 87
Embry, Terri 34
Embry, Wayne 2, 31–34, 37–38, 42–*43*, 71, 74, 109–111, 119–123, 125, 128, 131, 133, 135–136, 142, 146–147, 149, 151–156, 163–165, 167–168
Erickson, John 27, 29–32, 45–46, 48, 52, 54, 61–62
Erving, Julius 101, 119–122, 129, 158
Europe 84

Fader, Mirin 1
Finkel, Henry 138–139
Fiserv Forum 3, 162
Fishman, Marvin 2, 7, 9–13, 20–27, 29, 34–36, 38–39, 42–45, 95, 98, 101, 117, 148, 162
Fitzgerald, Jim 158, 160, 164–167
Fleisher, Larry 70–71
Foss, Joe 10
Frazier, Walt 155
From Coin Toss to Championship: 1971— The Year of the Milwaukee Bucks 2

Garber, Arnie *43*
General Mitchell International Airport 27, *43*, 93, 97, 122
Georgia 9
Giannis: The Improbable Rise of an NBA Champion 1
Giant Steps 161
Gilbert, Sam 48–49, 146
Glendale, Wisconsin 76–77
Golden 1 Center 143
Golden State Warriors 104, 111–112, 127, 134
Goodrich, Gail 46, 156
Gottlieb, Eddie 17
Green Bay, Wisconsin 11–12, 62
Green Bay Packers 4, 10–12, 23, 29, 62, 107
Grey, Dennis 53
Grobschmidt, Eugene 12
Groppi, James 15, 28, 110

Hairston, Happy 113
Hancock, Herbie 150
Hannum, Alex 25, 122

Index

Harlem, New York 35, 48, 56, 115
Harlem Globetrotters 18
Harley-Davidson 160
Harris, Eddie 150
Harvard University 22, 116–117
Havlicek, John 138, 140
Hawaii 79
Hayes, Elvin 39
Haywood, Spencer 35
Heinsohn, Tommy 70–71, 140
Honolulu, Hawaii 79
Houston Rockets 103, 105, 108, 129
Hruska, Roman 103
Humphrey, Hubert 34

Indiana Pacers 73, 144
Indianapolis, Indiana 40, 69
Iowa 84
Irish, Ned 67
Islam 56, 57, 68, 99–100, 103, 116, 125, 161

Jackson, Mahalia 54
Janesville, Wisconsin 164
Johnson, Chuck 84–85, 104
Johnson, Gus 72, 90
Johnson, Lyndon B. 28, 34
Johnson, Marques 160
Jones, Wali 123–124
Joseph A. Schlitz Brewing Company 44

Kansas City-Omaha Kings 72, *75*, 133–134, 143
Kennedy, John F. 34, 46, 55
Kennedy, Robert F. 46
Kennedy, Walter J. 17, 19, 21–23, 36, 38, 39, 41, 45, 55, 62, 76, 120–121, 123
Kentucky 97
Kentucky Colonels 30, 142, 151, 165
Kerner, Ben 17–19, 23, 43, 61
Kerr, Johnny "Red" 46
Khaalis, Hamaas Abdul 57, 99–100, 115, 117, 124–125, 129–130
King, Martin Luther, Jr. 16, 28, 34
Klein, Dick 20–22, 44
Kohl, Herb 21–23, 26, 160
Kutsher's Hotel and Country Club 54, 75

Lambeau Field 11
Lanier, Bob 132
LaSalle Corporation 7, 8
Lathan, Stan 115
Lee, Clyde 104
Lombardi, Vince 10–11, 13, 25, 132
Long Island, New York 119
Los Angeles, California 31, 38, 85, 146–147, 151–153, 157, 161
Los Angeles Lakers 31, 37, 38, 64, 73, 79,
  86, 88–89, **106**–108, 111–115, 127, 135, 149, 152, 155–161
Louisville, Kentucky 46
Love, Bob 30
Lucas, Jerry 71
Lucey, Patrick 134

MACC Fund 168
Madison, Wisconsin 4, 36, 61–62, 65, 87, 127
Madison Square Garden 59–60, 67, 74, 82, 89
Maier, Henry 16, 23, 28, 44, 97, 102, 104, 130, 134
Major League Baseball 2, 5, 7, 9, 23, 24, 63, 71
Malaysia 129
Malcolm X 56, 124
Mali 99
Maravich, Pete 69, 80
Marin, Jack 94
Marquette University 9, 22, 25–26
McAuley, Raymond 26
McGlocklin, Jon 3, 30, 38, 42–**43**, 67, 76, 80, 89, 92–95, 97, 107, 112, 115, **126**, 128, 136–139, 141, 153, 160, 168
McGuire, Al 25–27
McLemore, McCoy 84
Mequon, Wisconsin 103
Metropolitan Milwaukee Association of Commerce 42
Mexico City, Mexico 51, 56–57, 88
Meyers, Dave 155–157, 163
Miami Dolphins 12
Mikan, George 20, 35, 39, 41, 49–50
Miller, Fred 17
Miller Brewing Corporation 8, 17
Milton College 32, 54
Milwaukee Arena 17–19, 21–22, 29, 36, 42–43, 53, 59–62, 84, 87, 89–90, 93, 107–108, 115, 127, 130, 136–137, 140, 148, 154, 158–160, 168
Milwaukee Auditorium 43
Milwaukee Braves 2, 5, 7–9, 11, 14, 17–20, 22–24, 42, 51, 57, 98, 102, 107, 157
Milwaukee Brewers 3–4, 63
Milwaukee Brewers (minor league) 5, 7
Milwaukee Brewers Baseball Club, Inc. 22–23, 61
Milwaukee Common Council 15, 28, 62
Milwaukee County 12, 61, 97
Milwaukee County Courthouse 12
Milwaukee County Historical Society *33, 59, 95*
Milwaukee County Stadium 7–12, 18, 61–63, 102
Milwaukee Does 169

Index

Milwaukee Hawks 17–19, 24, 43, 61
Milwaukee Journal 10, 21, 46, 58, 84–85, 103–104, 122, 125, 143, 149, 157
"Milwaukee Miracle" 7, 18
Milwaukee Police Department 15–16
Milwaukee Professional Sports and Services, Inc. 24, 164, 166
Milwaukee Public Library *43, 55, 92, 126*
Milwaukee Public Schools 15, 109
Milwaukee School of Television Services, Inc. 40
Milwaukee Sentinel 21, 61, 98, 164
Milwaukee United Schools Integration Committee 15
Minneapolis, Minnesota 5, 38
Minneapolis Lakers 17
Minnesota 84
Mitchell Park Domes 63
Moline, Illinois 17
Moncrief, Sidney 160
Monroe, Earl 90, 94
Motta, Dick 135
Musberger, Brent 143–144
Muslim 57–58, 99–100, 115, 125, 129, 141, 147

NAACP Youth Council 15, 28
Naismith Memorial Basketball Hall of Fame 169
Nater, Swen 129
Nation of Islam 124
National Basketball League 39
National Basketball Players Association 1, 70, 76, 120, 144
National Broadcasting Company 10
National Collegiate Athletic Association 52
National Football League 4, 10–12, 20, 71
National Hockey League 71, 117, 122
National League 7–9
NBA on CBS 143, 153, 158
NCAA Tournament 25–26
Neaher, Edward 121
Nebraska 103
Neimann, Rich *43*
Nelson, Don 148, 160, 166–168
New Orleans Jazz 142
New York City, New York 23–25, 38, 45, 48–50, 57–58, 66, 68, 79, 97, 146–147, 151–153, 157, 159
New York Jets 12
New York Knicks 20, 25, 37–38, 47, 60, 64, 66–68, 73, 81–85, 86, 89–91, 106–107, 149, 151, 155
New York Nets 48–49, 52, 119, 144, 145–146, 151
New York Times 148

New York Yankees 8, 19, 51
Newell, Pete 155–156
Niagara University 27, 121, 165
Nicholas Senn High School 39
Nigeria 99–100, 134
1968 Olympic Games 47, 48, 56, 57, 88, 99
Nissalke, Tom 32, 90, 102
Nixon, Richard 34, 88, 161
Norfolk State University 52, 64
North Division High School 9

Oak Creek, Wisconsin 34
Oshkosh, Wisconsin 4, 17

Paschke, Jim 3–5
Patterson, Ray 48, 62, 93, 104–105, 108–109, 111, 115
Paulk, Charlie 28, 74
Pavalon, Wesley 2, 21, 23–24, 26–29, 35–36, 39–41, 43, 45, 46, 48, 50, 55, 58, 61, 66, 74–76, 88, 95, 98–99, 109–110, 117, 127, 146, 148, 162, 164
Perini, Lou 8
Perry, Curtis 105, 141–142
Pettit, Bob 19
Pettit, Jane Bradley 160
Pettit, Lloyd 160
Pfister Hotel 28, 51, *75*, 166
Philadelphia, Pennsylvania 48, 65–66, 123
Philadelphia 76ers 26, 37, 65–67, 83, 85–86, 111, 160
Philadelphia Warriors 17, 27
Phillips, Vel 15–16, 28
Phoenix Suns 23, 31, 45, 47, 50, 73, 80, 153
Pollard, George 160
Portland, Oregon 64
Portland Trail Blazers 111, 123, 150
Powell, James 56
Power Memorial Academy 35, 47–48, 159
Pressey, Paul 160
Price, Jim 149, 151
Purdue University 47
Putnam, Bill 120–121

Quran 57, 116, 129

Ramsay, Jack 25–26
Reed, Willis 63, 65–67, 78, 83, 86, 155
Robertson, Oscar 1, 3, 54, 63, 69–82, 84, 86–87, 89–91, 93–103, *106*, 108–115, 121, *126*–128, 131–134, 136–139, 141–145, 147–148, 158–159, 168
Robinson, Flynn 38, 41–*43*, 63, 67, 74
Robinson, Jackie 110
Rochester, Minnesota 4
Rock Island, Illinois 17

Rodgers, Guy 30–31, *43*, 60
Rothenberg, Alan 156
Rowe, Curtis *126*
Russell, Bill *33*, 35, 56, 66, 135

Sacramento Kings 143
St. Louis, Missouri 19–20, 40, 61
St. Louis Hawks 19–20, 61
San Antonio Spurs 144, 168
San Diego, California 84
San Diego Rockets 30, 79, 85
San Francisco Warriors 42, 85, 87–89, 102
Sanders, Carl 9
Saudi Arabia 100
Schabowski, Rick 2
Schayes, Dolph 25, 44
Schroon Lake, New York 119
Seattle Coliseum 59
Seattle Pilots 63
Seattle SuperSonics 59, 64, 79, 86, 123, 167
Selig, Allan H. "Bud" 22–24, 63
Selma, Alabama 15, 34
Senegal 99
Seymour, Paul 25
Shapiro, Ralph 48–49
Sharman, Bill 135
Sheboygan, Wisconsin 4, 17, 24
Skibinski, Gerald B. 62–63
Smith, Adrian 71
Smith, Don *43*, 79
Smith, Dwight 31
Smith, Elmore 155–157, 163
Smith, Greg 30–31, 38, *43*, 74, 80, 89, 93, 95, 97, 105
Smith, Tommie 99
Sokol, Manny 113
Somali Republic 99
The Spectrum 65
Sports Illustrated 40, 54, 56–57, 83, 104, 125
State Fair Park 11–12, 102, 130
Steinmiller, John 132, 166
Stokes, Maurice 54
Strom, Earl 135
Sunni Muslim 100, 124

Tanzania 99
Tedwell, G. Ernest 120
Thailand 129
Thurmond, Nate 54, 87, 111, 127
Trebilcox, R.D. 29
Tri-Cities Blackhawks 17

Tunisia 100
Twyman, Jack 54, 64, 70–71, *96*

United States of America 9, 28
U.S. Army 56
U.S. Congress 76
U.S. State Department 99
University of Alabama 34
University of California–Los Angeles 35, 46–48, 52–54, 56, 115, 129, 146, 149, 159
University of Cincinnati 69
University of Massachusetts 119
University of South Carolina 156
University of Wisconsin 4, 9, 27, 62
University of Wisconsin–Milwaukee 134
Unseld, Wes, Sr. 39, 90
Utica College 169
UW Field House 65, 87, 127

Vietnam War 56
Virginia 52
Virginia Squires 119–121, 129

Wallace, George 34, 109
Walther, David L. 28
Walton, Bill 129
Warner, Cornell 131, 136, 141–142
Washington, D.C. 28, 99–100, 117, 123, 125, 130, 146–147
Waukesha, Wisconsin 79
Wesley, Walt 157
West, Jerry 65, 72, 88, 112–*114*, 135
West Bend, Wisconsin 99, 146
West Indies 100
Western Kentucky University 30–31
White, Jo Jo 138
Whitefish Bay, Wisconsin 29
Williams, Ron "Fritz" 131, 136
Williams, Sam *43*
Winters, Brian 155–157, 163
Wirtz, Arthur 117
Wisconsin 4, 9, 13, 29, 40, 62, 146
Wisconsin Avenue 8, 18, 97–98, 127
Wisconsin Club 93
WITI 3
WNUW-FM 150
Women's Basketball League 169
Wooden, John 35, 47, 159
World War II 4–5, 7, 9, 14
Wright Junior College 39
WTMJ-AM 11, 37

Yoruba 100